"This is a compelling story, one that deserves being far better known than it is. . . . This book is very well written. It is clear, well organized, and rises here and there to a quiet grandeur. . . . It is much more than a labor of love, for his love is backed by solid industry and intellectual craft."

—DAVID HAMILTON, AUTHOR OF *Deep River: A Memoir of a Missouri Farm*

"*Looking After Minidoka* is an innovative and engaging excursion into buried history—global and personal. A compelling family narrative, peppered with fragments of memory, history, and poetry, this heartfelt memoir underscores the power of the American Dream, as well as how easily fear and intolerance can corrupt it."

—DEAN BAKOPOULOS, AUTHOR OF *My American Unhappiness*

"By his skillful blending of history and memoir, Nakadate lifts the veil on a story too often shrouded in shadow, revealing beneath a portrait of a Japanese American family in search of the differences between home and homeland."

—B. J. HOLLARS, AUTHOR OF *Sightings: Stories*

"Neil Nakadate's clear-eyed, carefully researched but nonetheless passionate book is rich with the closely observed details of internment camp life. *Looking After Minidoka,* written with wisdom, understanding, and a writer's eye for the stories worth telling, is not only an important contribution to the literature of internment but also an important story about the promise and peril of America."

—LAUREN KESSLER, AUTHOR OF *Stubborn Twig: Three Generations in the Life of a Japanese American Family*

"Neil Nakadate's *Looking after Minidoka: An American Memoir* is a beautifully crafted, powerfully moving American narrative. . . . Nakadate's memoir gives poignant life to chapters of American history that are still being written today by all who dream to be, as Nakadate's mother's transcribed name of 'Meriko' says it, 'a child of America.'"

—RAMÓN SALDÍVAR, EDITOR OF *The Imaginary and Its Worlds: American Studies after the Transnational Turn*

"The story of our country is the story of a family is the story of a man, Neil Nakadate, whose richly researched and deeply felt memoir will move your head and your heart."

—BENJAMIN PERCY, AUTHOR OF *Red Moon*

break away books

ALSO FROM THE AUTHOR

Understanding Jane Smiley

A Rhetoric of Doing: Essays on Written Discourse in Honor of
James L. Kinneavy (edited with Stephen Witte and Roger Cherry)

Writing in the Liberal Arts Tradition: A Rhetoric With Readings
(with James L. Kinneavy and William J. McCleary)

Robert Penn Warren: Critical Perspectives (editor)

Looking After MINIDOKA

NEIL NAKADATE

INDIANA UNIVERSITY PRESS

Bloomington & Indianapolis

This book is a publication of

Indiana University Press
Office of Scholarly Publishing
Herman B Wells Library 350
1320 East 10th Street
Bloomington, Indiana 47405 USA

iupress.indiana.edu

Telephone orders 800-842-6796
Fax orders 812-855-7931

⊖ The paper used in this publication meets
the minimum requirements of the American
National Standard for Information
Sciences—Permanence of Paper for Printed
Library Materials, ANSI Z39.48-1992.

Manufactured in the United States of America

Cataloging information is available
from the Library of Congress.

ISBN 978-0-253-01102-2 (paper)
ISBN 978-0-253-01111-4 (ebook)

1 2 3 4 5 18 17 16 15 14 13

Could a greater miracle take place than for us to look through each other's eyes for an instant?

HENRY DAVID THOREAU, *Walden* (1854)

CONTENTS

PREFACE · MY NICKEL

"Hello."

"Hello? Is this Neil, uh . . . Naka . . . ?"

"Yes—this is Neil. . . ."

"Well, hi. My name is A_____, and I live just over here in Boone, and I saw your letter in the paper and wanted to talk with you about it."

He was calling from ten miles away, so there was something neighborly in it, but also reason to give me pause. Long distance. The *Des Moines Register* had recently published a letter to the editor I had written, urging support of legislation working its way slowly through the U.S. Congress. Invoking the First Amendment of the Constitution, Japanese Americans were petitioning for redress—recognition and compensation from the government for the violation of their rights due to their mass removal and incarceration during World War II.

During the preceding week I had already received several unsigned pieces of mail, apparently (if not explicitly) in response to my letter, containing both hand-written and printed material to the effect that if I rethought my approach to prayer or politics, or both, I might be a better and happier person. I had just put away the supper dishes when the phone rang.

"Well, I just don't agree with your letter," my caller told me. "I'm against apologizing to the Japanese, and I'm against paying them anything. After all, there was a war going on, and the Japs were our enemy. Why should we apologize?"

I winced at his use of "Jap," aware that this could become a testy conversation. "Well," I said, "it's important to remember that these weren't Japanese, but Japanese *Americans*. A third of them were legal immigrants, including my grandparents, and two thirds were their children, born in the U.S., American citizens, like my mother and father. The people the government locked up in camps weren't 'the enemy,' they were 110,000 people whose ancestry happened to be Japanese."

"But they bombed Pearl Harbor!"

"Well, not really—I think we both know that. The war was started by the Japanese military—but the Japanese in America had nothing to do with Pearl Harbor. They were as angry about it as you were. Believe me, they wished it hadn't happened."

I resisted mentioning how embarrassing it had been in 1941 that the government had ignored diplomatic warning signs and intelligence alerts in the weeks and even hours before the attack on Hawaii. I resisted mentioning how tempting it always is in a situation like that to divert questions and designate an "other" who can get the scrutiny and take the blame.

"But it did happen, and they did it. And out there on the West Coast, in a military zone . . . they could have done even more harm."

"Well, Pearl Harbor happened," I repeated, "but not because of the Japanese Americans. There was never even a documented case of spying or sabotage on their part. Pearl Harbor was terrible, but the wrong people were punished. Innocent people."

"But they were the enemy. Our enemy. I was in the army and fought against them. I was a POW over there, in the Philippines. They tortured us. They killed my buddies, they . . ." They. "The Japanese."

I did not ask if he was a survivor of the Bataan Death March, but it was clear that his pain came from a very dark place. My father couldn't describe the darkest moments of his army experience, either, wouldn't describe them, especially the Battle of the Bulge. When pressed, he would only say it was "tough . . . really tough." Isolated fragments had worked their way out over the years, but no narrative line, no hint of perspective.

"I'm sorry that happened to you . . . it *shouldn't* have happened to you. My father would agree with that—he was with the 17th Airborne in Europe. . . ." I was about to say that my uncle, too, had served in the Pacific Theater, with the Military Intelligence Service, when my caller added, "How can I describe it? They . . . they were the enemy."

His personal horror warranted an explanation—a cause, a reason, a name. But I could only repeat that Japanese Americans were not "the enemy." "The *Japanese* badly mistreated you, but the Japanese *Americans* didn't—"

"That's what my son-in-law says," he blurted. "He teaches history in high school and has told me the same thing you're telling me—but I can't accept that, I can't—"

"He's right, of course," I said, grateful for the help. "It wasn't right to punish an immigrant group and their children for something done by the country they came from." And I added, "I'd guess from your last name that your background is German, so you probably know that many German Americans were attacked during World War I and that German immigrants were told they couldn't even use the German language . . . right here, in Iowa."

"He said that, too, but I can't—"

So there we were, a veteran and a child of a veteran of the same war, separated by only ten miles but also by radically different experiences and perspectives. A victim himself, he needed to tell a stranger what he had suffered. I needed to explain three generations of pain and confusion brought on by the imprisonment of an innocent civilian population. My need had emerged in a letter to the editor, his in a phone call to someone he'd never met.

Neither of us knew then that H.R. 442 and S. 1007, the redress legislation generated during the administration of Jimmy Carter, would finally be passed by Congress and signed into law by Ronald Reagan. We could not know that the terms of the legislation would finally be carried out under George H. W. Bush. But we both understood that the damage done in the name of war is permanent. And despite the distance between us it was important enough to continue, even though the phone charges were adding up. "As long as we're having a conversation," he said, "and since it's my nickel, do you think we can keep talking?"

So we went on for a good hour, dusk slipping into evening, not long enough for either of us, really, but perhaps enough for the time being. And he caused me to believe that I might try to do a better job of telling the story as it was lived by my family, people he never had the chance to know. And for that, and for his service to our country, I thank him.

ACKNOWLEDGMENTS

This book has benefited from the contributions of many others, and I express my appreciation here.

For their generosity to a stranger in search of his past I thank Lynn Davis and Thelma Stone, of Eden, Idaho.

For remembered details and ongoing perspectives on our family's stories I thank my brother Jim. I also owe a debt of gratitude to the following, whose memories reinforced my own and at times extended their reach: Carolyn Bicknell Black, James Lee, Phyllis McNair, Sandy Macnab, Keith Nakayama, Michi Robbs, Gary Severson, and Ambrose Shields.

For their ongoing encouragement of my work I thank these friends, colleagues, and former colleagues at Iowa State University: Dean Bakopoulos, Barbara Blakely, Rebecca Burnett, Susan Carlson, Barbara Ching, Dan Douglas, Marty Graham, Frank Haggard, Michael Mendelson, Steve Pett, Lee Poague, Connie Post, Dale Ross, Loring Silet, and Jane Smiley. In particular I wish to thank Barbara Blakely for her thoughtful reading of the full manuscript.

For conscientious and exacting counsel regarding the Japanese language, I thank Ann Nakadate Kotas and Frederick Kotas. Any idiosyncrasies or stubborn errors in translation or usage are mine alone.

For their assistance with technical questions having to do with the preparation of the manuscript, I thank Sheryl Kamps and Brent Moore.

Some of the background research for this book took me to key repositories, where I received the generous assistance of the following: the research staff in the library of the Oregon Historical Society, Portland; the reference staff in the Literature and History Room at the Multnomah County Library, Portland; the staff at the Oregon Nikkei Legacy Center, Portland. In addition I received generous and timely help from staff at the online archives of Densho: The Japanese American Legacy Project, in Seattle (http://www.densho.org/).

Finally, I wish to thank the staff of the Indiana University Press for making possible this telling of the story of "Minidoka." I thank Linda Oblack for shepherding the project and Sarah Jacobi and Angela Burton for shepherding an author who was occasionally bemused by the publication process. I thank Peter Froehlich for his counsel regarding permissions. And I am grateful to Emma Young for copyediting with insight and grace.

NOTE ON TERMINOLOGY AND LANGUAGE

To classify by name the ten major facilities into which Japanese Americans were placed after their mass removal from the West Coast in 1942 has proven problematic, in part because the terminology has shifted over time. "Internment camps" has long been used in much of the discourse on the subject—historical, legal, and otherwise—although "internment" more precisely refers to the imprisonment of specified "enemy aliens" and prisoners of war. (During World War II the U.S. government actually operated several smaller-scale Department of Justice "internment camps" that functioned in that manner.) Some scholars and writers advocate "incarceration camps," and Roger Daniels argues eloquently for that term in "Words Do Matter: A Note on Inappropriate Terminology and the Incarceration of the Japanese Americans." Some prefer the term "concentration camps" to categorize the major camps, although that term is also widely and differently associated with the extermination or death camps of the Holocaust. In this book I favor the use of "incarceration" but at times refer to "internment," depending upon the context. Of course, any of the more recently advocated terms is preferable to "relocation centers," the U.S. government's euphemistic label in 1942.

JAPANESE AMERICANS

Issei (*ee-say*): The first or immigrant generation of Japanese Americans, born in Japan and until 1952 prohibited by law from becoming citizens of the United States. Most Issei immigrated to the U.S. between 1890 and 1924.

Nisei (*nee-say*): The second generation, American citizens by birth. Most were born between 1910 and 1940.

Kibei (*kee-bay*): Nisei who received much of their education in Japan and then returned to the United States.

Sansei (*sahn-say*): The third generation, children of the Nisei. Most were born between 1930 and 1960, approximately 6,000 of them in the camps.

Yonsei (*yohn-say*): The fourth generation.

Japanese is based on a fixed set of syllables (a syllabary), some of which are individual letters. Examples: *gi, ma, ni, te, to, tsu, san, kyo, i, u, o.* Hence: *to-kyo, kyo-to, o-sa-ka, ya-ma-to, tsu-na-mi.* The characters as traditionally written are referred to as *kanji.*

Pronunciation: Consonants are usually pronounced as in English (but with *g* always "hard"); vowels are "pure" and distinctly pronounced (there are no diphthongs), approximately as in Italian. There are no silent letters. Syllables are not stressed or accented, and differences in meaning are achieved through variations in pitch.

Commonly used suffixes include those that indicate basic relationships, such as affiliation or status. Examples: -jin (person, people), -ken (prefecture), -mura (village), -san (indicates respect), and -chan (indicates informality or intimacy).

Looking After
MINIDOKA

NAKADATE

MARUMOTO

Moriji Ashizawa
b. 1892, Yamanashi-ken, Japan
d. 1939, Portland, Ore.

Bun'ichi Nakadate
b. 1877, Yamanashi-ken, Japan
d. 1965, Yamanashi-ken

Minejiro Marumoto
b. 1880, Wakayama-ken, Japan
d. 1963, Portland, Ore.

Hatsune Imoto
b. 1890, Wakayama-ken, Japan
d. 1966, Portland, Ore.

Katsumi
b. 1914, Portland
d. 2007, Portland

Meriko (Mary)
b. 1915, Portland, Ore.
d. 2000, Beaverton, Ore.

Fumie
b. 1913, Portland
d. 1999, Portland

Jiro Sakano
b. 1903, Sapporo
d. 1993, Calif.

Yoshiro (George)
b. 1918, Portland
d. 2009, Portland

Montana Suyama
b. 1919, Great Falls, Mont.
d. 2005, Portland

Toru
b. 1915, Portland, Ore.
d. 2006, Tokyo

Tomiko Nishida
b. 1918, Kumamoto-ken, Japan
d. 2008, Tokyo

Neil
b. 1943

James
b. 1946
East Chicago, Ind.

Jean K.
b. 1949

Mary Ann
b. 1951

Grace Michiyo
b. 1937

Phyllis Yurie
b. 1939
Portland

Phillip
b. 1946

Georgia
b. 1950
Portland

Kerry
b. 1953

Katsumi, b. 1945,
d. 1987, Tokyo

Emi, b. 1951, Tokyo

∽ Introduction

This is a Japanese story, a story of origins and imagination, and ambition and hope. And insiders and outsiders, trauma and silent tears. It is a story of what it can mean in America to be from somewhere else.

This is, even more, an American story, so it is about promises made and promises broken, audacity and courage, stubbornness, serendipity, and luck. There is war in this story, and love, and ignorance, and education. There are pathos and bravery and grief.

This is a story of trolleys and trains, of Studebakers and Fords, of expensive telegrams and five-cent phone calls. This is the story of three generations of a Japanese American family, from immigration through the twentieth century.

There is still a "Minidoka" on the map, in southern Idaho, a tiny community in a county with the same Native American name. But that is not my Minidoka, as I discovered over 30 years ago, when I first tried to find it. My Minidoka is four miles north and one mile west of Eden, Idaho (pop. 405 in 2010). You go north on Idaho Street out of town, then west a mile or so on Hunt Road. There are some helpful historical markers in strategic locations now, telling you how to get there after you have left Interstate 80N. That's good, because the site of the "Minidoka War Relocation Center" can be tricky to find, especially if a person is ambivalent about being successful. Life cannot flourish out there without plenty of water, and irrigation has long been the lifeblood of the region—sagebrush country, the wind-scoured high-desert West, where winter demands heavy clothing and the summers might tempt you to forgo the protection of sunglasses to get the full effect.

Between 1942 and 1945 "Minidoka" was the incarceration facility (widely referred to as an "internment camp") situated near the barely-existent Hunt, Idaho—a facility that was officially and euphemistically referred to by the

Minidoka, Idaho, 2001.

U.S. government as a "relocation center"—where my mother's family was imprisoned because of where they were from and how they looked. They had been forced from their home in Portland, Oregon, first to live in quarters that had once sheltered animals, and then to be sent into desert exile.

Minidoka is not a pleasant memory for my family or for the 9,390 other Japanese Americans who lived there, or for over 100,000 Japanese Americans who were displaced and then imprisoned in other camps. But it has become important to me to search for and give substance to the memory, and in doing so I have watched an invisible and almost forgotten life—my ancestors, my Japanese family, and our shared American experience, before and after Minidoka—emerge from documents and letters, from photographs and memory and text.

This book explores the territory between memoir and history. It is a Japanese American story, though not *the* Japanese American story, since no individual or family can ever be more than a variation on a theme. This is the story I found—a gathering of smaller stories that constitute a larger one—when I went looking after Minidoka.

1 ∞ *Issei*

Japan and the United States face each other, but across the broadest ocean of them all. Once such a body of water was almost like the space between us and the moon.

—EDWIN O. REISCHAUER, *The United States and Japan* (1950)

AFTER THE SHOGUNS

The Japan from which my grandparents came to the United States was post-feudal and eager to be part of the "modern world." By the end of the nineteenth century, an economy and culture of farms and fishing villages was being supplanted by an economy based on manufacturing and commerce. Japan was in flux, and trying to catch up with "America." Japan wanted factories and trains.

As a viable social force the samurai had been in decline since the seventeenth century, even as the intrigues and epic clashes of the shoguns came to dominate the culture. An ethos of loyalty, obedience, and honorable conduct persisted, but samurai prestige and power were drawn into the service of great political and military alliances—and centralized authority was flowing to Edo (now Tokyo) and Osaka. By the early eighteenth century the samurai had devolved into a class of idlers and bureaucrats, and by the mid-1700s they were being stylized and memorialized in the kabuki theater. The last of the shoguns stepped down in 1868, and the samurai themselves were formally disbanded a decade later.

By the end of the nineteenth century Japan had been paying attention to Europe (which is to say, the West) for several centuries. Following an accidental landing in Nagasaki in 1542, Portuguese merchants and Jesuit missionaries (the leading edge of colonialism) had brought their religion and the prospect of trade to Kyushu. They brought tobacco and bread, and the Japanese adopted them (the Japanese word for bread is the same as the Portuguese, *pan*). About the time Shakespeare was writing *King Lear*, English and Dutch "commercial agents" displaced the Portuguese and Spanish, and Protestantism replaced Catholicism as the version of Christianity to be either embraced or resisted. But in 1614 Christianity was banned and the missionaries expelled as subversive interlopers (which they were, in effect if not by intention) and alien barbarians, and Japan officially re-isolated itself from foreign travel and trade. Even so, the tenacious Dutch held on, and when they reestablished a major presence in Nagasaki in 1641 European ideas, learning, and trade goods entered Japan once more. Through Europeans the Japanese became familiar with firearms, and used them in clashes with each other.

In July 1853 Commodore Matthew Perry sailed uninvited into Edo Bay to briefly but forcefully introduce Japan to the United States, and he returned the following February, pointing the cannons of his *kurofune* (black ships) at archaically assembled ranks of Japanese soldiers with swords and spears. This opened up a dialogue on coal and whales, through which Perry insisted on offering Japan the opportunity to establish trade relations with America. For the next five decades the United States would gesture at empire building in Asia, and this was the start. Perry's successful mission highlighted the obsolescence of the shoguns and accelerated the denouement of Tokugawa Japan.

The Japan into which my grandparents were born, under the Meiji Restoration (1868–1912), embraced precepts that had informed samurai culture, including loyalty, obedience, and self-control. Meiji Japan continued to demonstrate the importance of group affiliations—traceable at least as far back as the fourth century A D, when the Yamato clan asserted its hegemony over other clans and consolidated power in Kyoto. It also declared its autonomy from Chinese hegemony and asserted its own identity. My grandparents' Japan was imbued with a Shinto spirituality of purity, filial piety, duty, loyalty, and obligation that linked ancestors to descendants and human existence to the natural world. Given all of this, individual achievement had meaning in the context of group affiliations and the greater good, whether of family, *ken* (native prefecture), school, team, company, or nation. Meiji culture was also layered and textured with the Buddhist precepts of stoicism, patience, self-denial, and devotion to learning—learning in the search for spiritual enlightenment, learning reflected in scholarly occupations and artistic patronage. And learning was aggressively promoted by the creation of a ministry of education in 1871 and by Emperor Meiji's 1890 Rescript on Education. If Japan were to play a major role in the modern world, it would have to continue to learn and grow. Formal education was seen as fundamental to national identity and long-term success—and this decreed commitment to formal education would continue to find expression through future generations, even in America.

Late in the nineteenth century, Japan was still socially and administratively hierarchical, but the tradesmen and merchants who had been marginalized and disdained under the samurai and shoguns had risen in status and significance along with the cities they animated—Edo, Osaka, and Kyoto, ambitious commercial as well as political and cultural entities, and numerous reinvigorated port cities such as Nagasaki and Yokohama. Four decades after Commodore Perry's visit, Japan was eager to take a major economic, political, and military role in the world: it had made an ambitious statement in the Sino-Japanese War and was on the verge of a successful war with Russia. Japan was focused on what it could learn from the West, and particularly fascinated with the United States, five thousand miles away.

Meanwhile, the United States was doing its own empire building—not only in the Caribbean, with Cuba and Santo Domingo, but across the Pacific, with the Hawaiian Islands, Midway Islands, Wake Island, and the Philippines, among other acquisitions. American missionaries were among those killed during the Boxer Rebellion, and other Americans were trapped in the 55-day Siege of Peking in 1900, which was eventually lifted by an international force that included U.S. Marines. Rough Rider Teddy Roosevelt was waiting, somewhat impatiently, in the wings. On the verge of the twentieth century the United States and Japan were positioning themselves for major roles, destined to enlarge their acquaintance on a recurring basis.

STUMPTOWN

In the early days Portland, Oregon, was a settlement full of stumps. Much later it would be known for its bridges and gardens, but in 1900 there were only two bridges and there was not enough city to celebrate with a festival of roses. You knew the place by where the cedars and firs had been. Cutting, digging, or pulling out the stumps was difficult and took time, so when the prime real estate along the Willamette River was first cleared, people often built and worked around them.

Still, turn-of-the-century Portland had 90,426 people, and at 70 miles from the Pacific Ocean was already an established deep-water port, linked to the Columbia River by the Willamette, linked by road and rail to the wheat fields of the Willamette Valley. Oregon fortunes were to be made in agriculture, timber, shipping, fishing, canning, mining, and commerce, and Portland intended to be indispensable. By 1900 it had attracted foreign consuls from Europe and from Mexico and Peru (though none quite yet from Japan). In the preceding decade, the population had almost doubled. "Stumptown" had ambitions.

There was a need for workers of every kind, from teamsters and butchers to dressmakers and clerks, and especially for cheap manual labor. Three decades after the end of slavery, immigrant labor and "slave wages" were fundamental to the building of America. In 1865, while the Union Pacific Railroad was recruiting Irish workers to construct the Transcontinental Railroad, the Central Pacific was recruiting Chinese. And in Portland in the early 1890s, a decade after passage of the Chinese Exclusion Act, Shintaro Takaki and S. Ban Company began recruiting and contracting Japanese labor whose sweat was less objectionable from a political and diplomatic perspective—and especially needed on railroad crews and in logging camps. Like the Chinese before them the Japanese were lured by the promise of jobs and visions of prosperity, by the aura of America. Like the Irish before them, like the Italians, Bohemians, and Poles, these Japanese were lured to America by the agents of industries intent on procuring a cheap and docile workforce. Meanwhile, traveling salesmen from S. Ban, M. Furuya, and other mercantile enterprises would make sure that both the earlier and the more recently arrived "orientals" had food and clothing.

In 1900, Minejiro Marumoto, my mother's father, was among the naïve, ambitious, and uninformed newcomers—and pathetically untutored in American ways. He was the youngest of three sons from a village in Wakayama-*ken* (prefecture), on the Pacific Ocean. He was probably recruited by Takaki, who focused on Okayama and Wakayama prefectures, and he eventually worked on a railroad crew, in a lumber camp, and on an eastern Oregon farm.

Bun'ichi Nakadate, my father's father, the oldest of five surviving sons, was from Toyotomi, a farming village in the middle of Honshu, near Kofu and Mount Fuji, a region then at the heart of Japanese sericulture, the silk-worm industry. More importantly, he came to the United States in 1903 on the strength of a prior acquaintance with a Yamanashi kinsman or *ken-jin*, Masajiro Furuya, who sold dry goods and recruited laborers—and promised him a job.

Of course my grandfathers were joined in their Oregon ambitions by many other recent immigrants, whose origins and identities were marked by their various old-country affinities, their religious denominations, and the foreign language newspapers they started. These immigrants were also identified by the mutual aid organizations that declared them to be authentic, worthy, and determined to stick around—the C. Columbo Aid Society, Der Danske Forening, the First Hebrew Benevolent Association, the German Ladies' Aid Society, the Scandinavian Society, and more. All of these appeared in the *City Directory* for 1899–1900, alongside the Waverly Golf Club and the Young Men's Republican Club, among others (no mention yet of an organization for the Japanese)—and alongside individuals whose listed occupation was "scavenger."

Minejiro Marumoto and Bun'ichi Nakadate were unknown to each other in Japan and about as likely to meet as a Welshman and a Scot—short of booking passage to America and starting their new lives in Stumptown, a few blocks apart. But there was certainly a passing moment, sometime in the first decade of the century, in which one of Furuya's salesmen (perhaps even Bun'ichi Nakadate) made a sale—some rice, some tiny dried fish, or a notebook to write his diary in—to Minejiro Marumoto, contract laborer, one of 2,500 other Japanese in Oregon at the time.

GODFATHER

Among the earlier Japanese immigrants to arrive on the U.S. mainland, Masajiro Furuya left Japan for Seattle in 1890 at the age of 27. If the United States was to set the pace for the new century, he wanted to be part of it. By training he was both a teacher and a soldier, by instinct and opportunity a captain of commerce, and in this way, a pioneer. He was an ambitious visionary—and more important to my family than any Carnegie or Ford.

He might have briefly misled others when he started out by apprenticing to a tailor, but he never underestimated himself, never misunderstood his own mission and agenda. Before long he set up his own business, and in short order the Furuya tailor shop engendered a grocery store, a labor recruitment agency, and then an import/export house that eventually contained a branch of the Japanese Commercial Bank. Furuya's business model was simple: recruit young, single men (wives and families created needs and problems, not profits) who, as traveling salesmen, would pursue a clientele of Japanese laborers to canneries, mining operations, lumber camps, and railroad construction and repair sites. And then promote into supervisory positions those who had proven themselves on the road. The model was also tight: he could control paychecks and monitor employee behavior by requiring that his salesmen room (and sometimes also board) in company-owned or rented houses. And entrust their savings to his bank.

So Masajiro Furuya both served and exploited his countrymen's hopes and needs. He was a shrewd opportunist who recognized that whatever their economic condition, the Asian immigrants would always value a powerful countryman, a safe place to deposit their money, and something familiar from home: *soba, shoyu,* and sandals; *sake, daikon,* and rice; *tofu, mochi,* and fish cakes; *kimonos,* reading material, art work, and amusements. Furuya's Model T trucks struck out from the cities and always managed to find customers—"oriental" strangers in a strange land who took on tedious and risk-laden tasks, who learned they could not always trust a *hakujin* (Caucasian or white person), and who could tolerate only so much meat-and-potatoes cooking. With other branches in Kobe, Yokohama, and Yokosuka, the M. Furuya Co. expanded from Seattle to Tacoma, Portland, and Vancouver, B.C., its commercial empire growing with the Pacific Northwest itself. Competing in Portland with Teikoku, S. Ban, and others, Furuya supplied first the Chinese, then the Japanese with the comforting foods and sundries of a life they had left behind. His Oregon territory extended as far as Weiser, Boise, and Shoshone in southwestern Idaho. And Masajiro Furuya's power and status grew accordingly, within and beyond the Japanese American community. He became something of a godfather figure to his employees as well as his adrift-in-America clientele.

Old Man Furuya expected hard work and undivided loyalty. He imposed a dark and rigid dress code ("Furuya suits" they came to be called, without affection) and insisted on conformity of deportment—that is, fit-into-the-community behavior. He held a short meeting every morning to lay down the rules, offer inspirational words, and ensure promptness. His employees stood in a circle for announcements and instructions and, one by one, read verses from scripture. (These meetings may have originated in similar events mandated for every school in Japan under the Meiji Restoration.) Furuya required his personnel to attend the local churches, in order to strengthen community relations within the culture of their commercial lives—and, not incidentally, to reinforce their learning of English. Masajiro Furuya was an autocrat, a martinet, a no-nonsense boss, who mirrored in his own domain the legendary management control of Marshall Field and Henry Ford. Years before Calvin Coolidge is supposed to have coined the phrase, Furuya clearly believed that the business of America is business.

Apparently he had no male heirs, although any significant estate they might have inherited was lost due to some questionable investments and then the Great Depression, and the residue disappeared between 1942 and 1945. But that is not to say there were no beneficiaries of Furuya's Japanese American enterprise. Shortly after the turn of the century, and in a mutually beneficial move based on their shared origins in Yamanashi-ken, Masajiro Furuya promised Bun'ichi Nakadate a better-than-average start in America, and thus became the godfather of us all.

FURUYA MAN

I once wondered why my father's father, the oldest of ten children, including five sons, left Toyotomi-*mura* (village) and Yamanashi-ken in the first place. After all, in the Japan of the late nineteenth century Bun'ichi Nakadate was in the family catbird seat. His given name was a constant reminder of his position and status, since *ichi* is Japanese for "one" or "number one." He could have stayed in place and built a secure life based on inherited advantage, favored by gender and culture. So I once imagined his having to leave home under duress, having gotten himself into a jam that made it necessary to skip town—a legal hassle, an indiscretion, an insult or altercation of some kind, something risky or even disreputable—intending to return eventually.

But the skipping-town scenario is too melodramatic, the 40 years he stayed in the U.S. (a lifetime, after all) a bit long for just waiting for the fog to lift. It seems (my Uncle Toru told me) that Grandpa Nakadate was driven by ambition and an adventuresome impulse. "He was looking for something different, seeking new pastures" by leaving the agrarian nineteenth century behind. In this sense he was typical of many turn-of-the-century immigrants, although he had a bit more education than most, including some coursework at a business school. (Three of his younger brothers also left home eventually, for Kofu and Tokyo; my grandfather's leap of faith into an American business venture may well have encouraged those moves, too.)

And family obligation was not the least of it. Both my uncle and my father reported that Bun'ichi Nakadate decided he could best discharge his filial responsibilities by making money in America and sending it home. As the oldest son of a large family he had certain privileges and prerogatives, but also the near-term obligation to improve family fortunes and the eventual responsibility of caring for his parents. His ambitions, then, were also undeniably economic, and accordingly he made sure that his new pastures included a guaranteed job—as it turned out, driving a Model T panel truck and selling Furuya goods on the Oregon circuit.

It was a modest place to start, but a good way to come to understand America and modern business. And in making this hire, as in other matters, Old Man Furuya was an accurate judge of character and potential. Bun'ichi Nakadate was ambitious and strong-willed, he could tolerate risk, and he was willing to work his way into more responsibility and less travel. What he hadn't learned in business school in Japan about how to complete a transaction without getting sold a bill of goods, how to make money and how to put it back to work, he learned in America from a master. And what soon developed into a white-collar job as clerk-cum-business manager of Furuya Company's Portland store at 51–53 N. Fourth Street gave him some job security and a reliable income. Like many immigrants from both Europe and Asia, my grandfather arrived in the U.S. thinking of himself as a sojourner and ending up an all but permanent resident. (That he eventually died in Yamanashi owed as much to politics and fate as to planning.) When

I met him as a boy my grandfather was a 69-year-old steel rod of galvanized opinions who had seen it all and backed away from nothing.

In the early years, his remittances from the United States helped capitalize what I only knew of as "an electric company" whose fortunes rose with the expanding Japanese economy and with his brothers' skill at negotiating the elaborate network of relationships that characterized Japanese commercial enterprise. By the time second son Kiyoshige fell victim to some contaminated raw oysters, he and brother Yoshizo had guided the family business well enough to make it a major regional contractor—and Nakadate Denki (Electric) even found ways to inch its way forward during the Depression.

When my father was still a boy he, too, began to work part-time for M. Furuya Co., initiated into the workforce as a stock-boy. At 14 he was sent to the flagship store for the summer, in order to avoid accusations of favoritism while fetching kegs of soy sauce and hauling huge sacks of rice upstairs. When he asked if he could try driving one of the delivery trucks he was reminded that he was just the right size to crawl underneath the engine and reach up to change the oil. In Seattle he also overheard irreverent employees refer in private to Masajiro Furuya as "Big Boy," and he never forgot the tense morning employee meetings or those occasions when the voice of God from the office upstairs—"*Na-ka-da-te!*"—summoned him for a lecture on his shortcomings.

In his nineties, Dad had hanging above his bedroom door a carefully preserved, multicolored cloth banner that celebrated the far-flung holdings of M. Furuya Co., represented as a tree with several sturdy branches. "S. Ban was pretty good," my father told me decades later, "but Furuya was better." Loyal to the end, and like his father before him, he understood both the entrepreneurial achievement of Masajiro Furuya and the relevance of M. Furuya Co. to our family's American fortunes.

CENTRAL PACIFIC

Huntington sleeps in a house six feet long.
Huntington dreams of railroads he built and owned.
Huntington dreams of ten thousand men saying: Yes, sir.

—CARL SANDBERG, "SOUTHERN PACIFIC"

Collis P. Huntington (1821–1900) may have ended up in a six-foot box, but he led a privileged life. He was a financier and promoter, and some called him a robber baron. In 1890 he was president of the Southern Pacific and Central Pacific railroads.

Minejiro Marumoto, my mother's father, came to the United States at the age of 19 from the coastal village of Ukui, near Minato, in Wakayama-ken. He was sensitive, earnest, even-tempered, willing to please. He was apparently not desperate, but as the youngest of three sons he was not in line to inherit property. And in a Japan that was converting from a farming to an industrial economy, he was part of a nationwide labor surplus. He was certainly attracted to Oregon by word-of-mouth tales of American success drawn from letters sent back to Japan by a small group of Wakayama immigrants who were among the first Japanese to establish themselves in Portland. He was attracted by descriptions of western Oregon's mountain greenness and rocky coastline—after all, on the same Pacific Ocean. But he was naïve to the motives of the labor recruiter and his encouraging hype.

As it turned out, Minejiro Marumoto was one of millions who, while getting a toehold in America, helped make other people rich—and said "Yes, sir" many times over. His life in America was evidence that for decades after the Civil War the United States remained addicted to the cheapest possible labor for its least enviable work. With the end of Reconstruction in 1877, the South found its solution in sharecropping and Jim Crow laws, poll taxes and literacy requirements, harassment and lynching. And elsewhere in the country, during the decades of headlong immigration from Europe and rapid expansion toward the west, the country's economic ambitions were sustained by a system of contract labor. Foreign contract labor. Asians were welcome to join the party as long as they knew their place and stayed in it.

Minejiro Marumoto arrived in Seattle on the *Tose Maru* on February 2, 1900, a contract laborer—but listed on the manifest as a farmer, since farming was more generally respected as an occupation. And until 1906, Minejiro Marumoto worked as a contract laborer, repairing and replacing rails for first the Union Pacific and then the Southern Pacific, helping to build the early infrastructure of the Pacific Northwest. He was aware of following in the footsteps of Chinese who had been recruited earlier by the Central Pacific and who, once the railroad was completed, were declared to be "invaders" and blamed for high unemployment. He was aware that further immigration from China had been barred by the 1882 Chinese Exclusion Act, since that had made him, in turn, a desirable commodity. And he was happy to overlook the possibility that the United States might eventually decide that Japanese were a "yellow peril" in their own right. He might have caught the irony that Japanese countrymen such as S. Ban were among those making a fortune at his expense. Labor recruiters never said how much of a man's wages might be withheld to pay for their job-finding services, or for "insurance," or "translation fees," or other items hidden in contract language no immigrant could understand. Nor did anyone explain that American employers would have him do jobs that "Americans" wouldn't take, under living conditions they wouldn't abide, for wages they deemed inadequate. Grandpa later maintained that what he actually took home was not much more than five cents an hour.

Of course, such low wages all but guaranteed that he would be unable to accumulate wealth, and the exclusion of Asian workers from trade and labor unions made it unlikely that this would ever change. After a while, it became clear to him that his life might improve incrementally from year to year, but his story would be one of survival, not "transformation." And, short of financial success, Minejiro Marumoto had little incentive to return to Japan. He was one of the tens of thousands who built America from the ground up. He was one of the tens of thousands who have been misplaced by the history books—lost in the rounded-off statistics of immigration, in the incomplete and sketchy "records" of harassment "incidents" and racist assaults and killings, in spotty and inconsistent data on accident, disease, and death. Even when there was a chance to enter these workers into the record, they were often ignored, dismissed, or simply ordered to step aside— undocumented: Chinese section hands, field workers, miners, cooks, and houseboys; Japanese railroad crewmen, cannery workers, and loggers; Irish laborers and domestics, Jewish textile workers, Mexican field hands, Lithuanian meat packers. . . .

This is why, in the famous celebratory photograph taken at Promontory, Utah in May 1869 to document the completion of the Transcontinental Railroad, we see no Asian faces, though we know that there would have been no railroad without Chinese labor. They are present in their absence, missing persons standing somewhere outside the frame. Leland Stanford is there, of course, to tap ceremoniously on the golden spike (he is reported to have

M. Furuya delivery truck and driver, 1912.

needed help, the actual tools of railroad-building being unfamiliar to his hands). After he became Governor of California and before he and his wife founded the university that one day would be my alma mater, he succeeded Collis Huntington as a president of the Central Pacific.

MONTANA

Auntie Tana, who married my Uncle George Marumoto in 1942, was born Montana Suyama in 1919, in Great Falls, and named for the state in which her family's fortunes and misfortunes were to play out in the early decades of the century. By the usual measures, the misfortunes prevailed. For the Suyamas, as for many Asian immigrants, Montana offered hard labor under a hard blue sky. (Like my Marumoto grandfather, Ichiro Suyama was at the mercy of the employer who held his contract, so he was in no position to enjoy what poet Richard Hugo later called "the last best place.") He worked for the railroad, and the Suyamas were far from the consolations and homeland comforts provided by the commercial lifeline of an M. Furuya or S. Ban.

Aboard the Amtrak *Cascade: Portland to Seattle, via Vancouver, Kelso-Longview, Centralia, Olympia-Lacey, Tacoma (March 1999)*

Tie, spike, and rail you laid this track,
Grandpa, in the immigrant obscurity
of a nickel-an-hour Japanese "extra gang,"
a young man living out recruiters' lies in
endless railroad labor. Now it's mile-a-minute

on a train loaded down with urban-khaki tourists
and cell-phone commuters, our right of way
marked by cable spools, graffiti scrawls, treadless
tires, sawmill scrap, cordwood-laden
gravel cars, filmy plastic snagged on bushes,
abandoned shopping carts. Track repairmen
in shiny hardhats drive bright yellow machines,

and wave. Beyond in shadow I see the not-yet-
Great Northwest you found—rhododendron, cedar,
blackberry, fern, and moss, muddy footing, bigotry,
stoop labor—and a Wakayama village boy,
laying rail back when horse-power really meant
horses, and man-power meant exhaustion.

Rousted at dawn into a dark mist, the drab
seepage of Oregon winter, you ate strange food
and asked tired muscles to recall their pain,
to work more than one honest shift
for every college class I would sit through
under palms and Spanish tile—and for the half
dozen I missed in those ignorant years of learning,
when the California morning came too soon.

He had actually tried Europe first, but didn't like it much, so refocused his ambitions on North America. Ichiro Suyama took a look at Alaska, "just to see what it was all about" (as Tana recalled him saying), but didn't stay. Traveling south he saw the detritus of failed ambitions strewn alongside the Alaskan roads—furniture and personal effects abandoned by the desperate and failing. In the United States his first taste of success was "owning" a railroad extra gang made up of other immigrant Japanese, which meant that Suyama was contracted to assemble, train, and supervise a maintenance crew that would work its way across the northern tier of states, scratched by sagebrush, sedge, and switchgrass, constantly skirting outcroppings and negotiating soapweed gullies. Their long days of repairing track only kept them from starving to death and falling into statistical oblivion. The bluebells and sunflowers were all but irrelevant to their attention. At some point Ichiro also began to be called "Harry."

But once they got the lay of the land Harry Suyama's crew, like others up and down the line, began to run off in search of less dangerous and more promising ways to survive America. This was one of the reasons, Auntie Tana reported decades later, that "oriental" restaurants "sprang up in towns all across Montana and North Dakota." To reconstruct his extra gang, Harry then added immigrant Filipinos, whose presence led to inter-ethnic frictions and periodic knife fights. Frustrated and disenchanted, Harry, too, abandoned railroad work, bought some dairy cattle, and started a farm at Havre that eventually grew to 30 milk cows and a lot of labor.

Tana's father had come from a family that owned a large sanitarium in Japan. Her mother Tami was the daughter of a physician in the Japanese emperor's compound in Tokyo, so she had had a comfortable start in life. But in Montana her fear of being switched and kicked made milking a misery, even with the help of five children—Mary, George, Tana, Frank, and Betty—who tried to protect her from tails and hooves. Tami Suyama's anxiety prevailed until Harry gave up dairying for truck farming—25 acres of blue-ribbon carrots, cabbage, rutabagas, and tomatoes in only a four-month growing season. People in Havre missed the Suyama milk, but Tana's mother didn't miss the cows. She missed Japan, and as Tana put it, "always wanted to go home." Harry, meanwhile, continued to "cuss out" Teddy Roosevelt. As president, Roosevelt had promised Harry and other Spanish-American War veterans that they would become American citizens, but then reneged. And that betrayal coupled with alien land laws meant that Harry could never own the property on which he was investing sweat and years. So much for the American Dream.

When their mother died of a stroke, Tana was 18; Mary was 21, George 19, Frank 16, and Betty 13. Their father's death of stomach cancer eleven months later left the children dependent only on each other and their collective resources. Two weeks later a man representing the property owner showed up, announced that they didn't live there anymore, and started tearing down the house. They tried to save what furniture, silverware, and dishes they could carry. And they began to scatter. Tana became a cook and housekeeper in Seattle, and Betty worked as a maid while attending high school. George would soon try to look out for his family's future in America by leaving Montana for the army. Mary and Frank would find their way to Chicago.

Immigrant life was hard all around, but it is worth remembering that in a time before farm machinery and home appliances mitigated the difficulties of making a home and raising a family, immigrant life was particularly hard on women. "She played with the princesses in Japan," Tana later said of her mother, "but she came to a hard, hard life in Montana." For years, no one thought to explain the source of Auntie Tana's name (as Japanese-sounding as it was), but I eventually learned that the family story behind it was so quintessentially Japanese American in its tenacity, frustrations, and faith as to be both a paradigm and a summary.

"MONGOLIANS" AND "MONGRELS": CIVICS LESSON, PART 1

Many of the problems faced by immigrants to the United States are not inherent, but created. Many of the promises made to immigrants were never meant to be kept. And in the American West, the cultural prejudices and political forces that blamed Chinese immigrants for everything from unemployment and low wages to racial "mongrelization" gave rise to a network of legal restrictions and social behavior that then made it difficult for the Japanese to establish themselves, let alone flourish. Or fully participate in "America" as citizens of the United States, with voices and votes. Often equated with the Chinese as "Mongolians" and "cheap coolie labor" that had outstayed its exploitable potential, the Japanese were deemed "unassimilable" and demonized as part of the "Yellow Peril." U.S. immigration and naturalization policy were manipulated for social and economic reasons and for the benefit of those who had already arrived.

The prejudicial attitudes were sustained by labor leaders, journalists, and politicians, and were to follow Japanese Americans well into the twentieth century. California was often where the rhetoric and legislation were first tried out before spreading throughout the West, and from there to Washington, D.C. It's an interesting civics lesson, my father might have said. You could look it up:

1790 Federal law limits citizenship to "free white persons."

1852 California imposes a Foreign Miner's Tax.

1859 Chinese are excluded from public schools in San Francisco.

1862 Congress authorizes the naturalization of aliens who have been honorably discharged from military service.
Federal law restricts naturalized citizenship to free whites and peopleof African descent.

1875 Congress stipulates that naturalization law applies only to "free white persons, and to aliens of African nativity and to persons of African descent."
The Page Act, aimed at contract laborers and "immoral Chinese women," prohibits entry into the U.S. of "undesirable" immigrants, but specifically people from Asia.

1880 California Civil Code prohibits marriage between whites and "negros," "mulattos," or "Mongolians."

1882 The Chinese Exclusion Act is passed, legitimizing race and nationality as criteria for immigration.

1888 The Scott Act renders void the re-entry certificates of Chinese workers.

1892 Chinese Exclusion is extended under the Geary Act, with special resident identification papers now required.
The "Barbary Plague" leads to a quarantine of Chinese in San Francisco.

1904 Chinese Exclusion is extended indefinitely.

1905 The Asiatic Exclusion League is organized in San Francisco. The San Francisco Chronicle begins 18 months of anti-Japanese articles.

1906 The California legislature urges a limit on Japanese immigration

The San Francisco School Board segregates 93 Japanese children, of whom 25 are American-born citizens.

1907   Theodore Roosevelt's Gentlemen's Agreement leads to restrictions on Japanese emigration.

1908   The Asiatic Exclusion League of San Francisco includes 231 organizations.

In Washington State, Buntaro Kumagai, an army veteran, is ruled ineligible for naturalization, based on the 1875 law.

1909   Anti-Japanese legislation is introduced in the California legislature.

1911   The Japanese Association of Oregon (*Nihonjinkai*) is founded.

1913   California passes an Alien Land Law, prohibiting "aliens ineligible to citizenship" from owning land or other property—to be followed soon by similar laws in Arizona, Oregon, Washington, Idaho, Montana, Minnesota, and other states.

The Hearst newspapers publish a series of anti-Japanese articles.

1917   The U.S. designates a "barred zone," from which immigration is restricted.

An alien land bill is introduced in the Oregon legislature.

1919   A second alien land bill is introduced in the Oregon legislature.

1920   California's Alien Land Law is revised to prohibit leasing to aliens and to prohibit "aliens ineligible for citizenship" from serving as guardians of property for their minor citizen children.

1921   With the Emergency Quota Act the federal government establishes a three percent quota system for immigration, based on country of origin and the 1910 census.

A third alien property bill is introduced in the Oregon legislature.

1922   In *Takao Ozawa v. United States* the Supreme Court determines that naturalized citizenship is open only to "free white persons" and people of African descent—Japanese are ineligible.

The Cable Act is passed, dictating loss of citizenship by any female citizen who marries "an alien ineligible to citizenship."

Oregon enacts its alien land law.

This sad timeline offers several instructive insights: (1) American responses to a particular immigrant group are often tied to attitudes established in response to immigrant groups that preceded them; (2) immigration politics grow out of local and regional controversy, and are often tied to concerns over property; (3) historically, discriminatory federal and state statutes and local regulations have been piggybacked and overlapped so as to obscure their true targets and their true intentions; and (4) the statistical "minority" status of mid- and late twentieth century Asian Americans was a direct result of prejudicial legislation—based on race, ethnicity, and country of origin—enacted decades earlier.

If Bun'ichi Nakadate had known in advance that U.S. law would keep him from becoming a citizen and that Oregon law would eventually prohibit him from owning or leasing land, he would have recognized the insult but might not have been dissuaded from coming. His intention was see what "America" was all about and to fulfill his obligation to his family by succeeding in business there. But in 1940, when he took his late wife's ashes to Japan, he certainly saw the irony of having achieved a version of the American Dream in an America that had never let him buy a house to live in, never let him vote.

If Minejiro Marumoto had had the same information (never mind not being able to anticipate his incarceration at "Minidoka") he might have decided to take his chances with the pecking order in Japan rather than live as a "guest worker" for life. By 1942, could it have come to him as a total surprise when his family was evicted from the Oregonian Hotel, "evacuated" from Oregon itself, and incarcerated behind barbed wire in Idaho? And with what longstanding pain did he ponder the disingenuous assertion that such an un-American phenomenon as "Minidoka" could only have been the spontaneous result of "wartime hysteria" on the part of the American people, their president and other elected leaders, and their courts?

And once the United States and Japan were engaged in war, did my grandfathers recall their earlier, better days in Portland, when they could still imagine the future and when both of them were duly registered for the World War I draft, in case they were needed to serve "their" country?

NIHONMACHI

Japantown. In San Francisco it evolved around Post and Geary, south of Lafayette Park. In Los Angeles it spread out from E. Third Street and S. San Pedro. In Seattle it was several blocks east of Second Avenue and between

S. King Street and Washington. In Portland it was north of Burnside, south of Union Station, and west of the Willamette River, at the start of what became known as the Alphabet District. Like many other immigrants on both coasts, the majority of the Portland Japanese first settled near where they arrived by ship or train, as if they had used every bit of stamina, patience, and money just to make it that far. And while many white Portlanders did not particularly care where in the expanding city the Asian population lived, many others assumed that the Chinese and Japanese would not mind sharing the same neighborhood.

The Alphabet District was first subdivided by Captain John Heard Couch, but only labeled alphabetically in 1866. Later, in the Great Renaming of 1891, the cobblestone streets were given names from earlier Oregon history that later immigrants came to know on an intimate basis—from Ankeny, Burnside, Couch, Davis, and Everett through Flanders, Glisan, Hoyt, Ingram, and on all the way to Upshur, Vaughn, and Wilson. The names of the Alphabet District memorialized the Northern European Americans who had preceded the immigrants from Asia. Some of the names (*kooch, gleeson*) were tricky to pronounce, and some of the names contained the letter "L," difficult for a Japanese to say—as was the case, of course, with "Portland," and "Willamette." But all of it was consistent with the American fervor for city planning that spread from Boston to San Francisco as the country left the nineteenth century behind. From the Park Blocks to named districts to the unifying grid itself, Portland would be a coherent municipality of ordered spaces in which everything would be appropriately sited. Early Portland was reflexively European, and its downtown architecture was at once imitative, trendy, and eclectic. The buildings in which most of the Japanese immigrants lived and worked—so far from the thatched-roof *minka* and *shoji* screens of their native land—were Richardsonian Romanesque and Renaissance revival, with neo-Gothic and Italianate features in the ironwork and windows.

Many of the Chinese had moved north from California once railroad work got harder to find and they became the focus of harassment and violence when they tried to enter other forms of employment. Of course, for a cost-cutting employer one Asian was as good as another, so Chinese workers were simply replaced by the not-yet-excluded Japanese, many of whom entered the U.S. through the ports of San Francisco and Seattle. When the Japanese drifted into Portland they found themselves starting out in the Alphabet District, and learning to get along with, among others, the already-resident Chinese—even though many Japanese believed from the outset that they were a cut above their neighbors. Recalling his Nihonmachi boyhood, my Uncle George claimed that the Chinese children envied the somewhat nicer clothing of their Japanese peers, and that, with reference to the outcome of the recent Sino-Japanese War, the Nisei boys would taunt, "*Nippon katta, Shina maketame*"—"Japan won, China lost"—while the two groups walked to the same public school on opposite sides of Davis Street. The adults got along when they had to; it was a dance of Asian American pragmatism and empathy that would last until 1942.

Masajiro Furuya established his Portland store in Nihonmachi in 1897, and a few years later my Nakadate grandfather began to work there once he had proven his worth as a salesman and learned the Furuya way in Seattle. By 1900—when my Marumoto grandfather arrived in the U.S.—there were six Portland businesses that sold "Chinese and Japanese Goods." They served a population of residents and transients that included not only Chinese and Japanese, but an occasional Italian, Greek, or African American, and anchored a culturally diverse community of laundries, barbershops, dentists, pool halls and gambling parlors, midwiferies, bathhouses, boarding houses, tailors, restaurants, retail enterprises, prostitutes, and the Japanese Methodist Episcopal Mission Church. In 1903 a Buddhist temple was founded. Most of these businesses and all of the housing was stacked and layered in two- and three-storied, steep-stairway, narrow-hallway buildings, in the warren-like spaces typical of immigrant housing across America.

Restricted from becoming citizens and participating in political life, the immigrant Japanese—they called themselves *Issei*, or first generation—nurtured business connections and created networks of social, service, and ancestral organizations that affirmed prefectural kinship and cultural roots. Soon after, they created language schools so the next generation, the *Nisei*, would understand Japanese language and culture. The rest of Portland, the rest of America lay beyond, but for everyday necessities there was no need to leave the neighborhood, or to speak English. Meanwhile, the immigrants were quite aware that inappropriate conduct would betray the Japanese government's assurances to the United States and reflect badly on their homeland—and that bad behavior might jeopardize their resident alien status.

At the end of the twentieth century my father, then well into his eighties, would get his hair cut on the third Wednesday of every month at Ben's Barber Shop on W. Burnside Street. Technically, it wasn't Ben Soejima's place anymore, but now belonged to Clifford, an African American who took Wednesdays off and let Ben cut hair so he could stay busy in retirement and keep up his connections. Around them extensive renovation was taking place, a new face being put on the old neighborhood, but in their eyes W. Burnside was still the essence of Nihonmachi, where their Japanese American lives began.

GENTLEMEN'S AGREEMENT

Why did the President's pants fall down? Roosabeltu!

—OLD JAPANESE AMERICAN JOKE

Neither Minejiro Marumoto nor Bun'ichi Nakadate was interested in marrying outside of Japanese culture, so they were probably not concerned with Oregon's 1867 anti-miscegenation statute, which made it unlawful for a white person to marry any "Negro, Chinese, or any person having one-quarter or more Negro, Chinese or Kanaka [Hawaiian] blood, or any person having more than one-half Indian blood." But Japanese immigration, shaped as it was by the interests of labor contractors and various employers, had created a bachelor society, much like that of the early cohorts of Chinese. The early Japanese community was overwhelmingly composed of single males—96 percent, according to the 1900 U.S. census—who now had to wonder what a Japanese man looking at the prospect of long-term residence in the U.S. might hope to do with the rest of his life.

One answer lay in the so-called Gentlemen's Agreement of 1907–1908, a series of diplomatic notes in which educational issues, immigration politics, and U.S. foreign policy were interwoven. This on-the-fly negotiation exemplifies the truism that the lives of America's immigrant minorities are directly affected—sometimes in unanticipated or irrational ways—by shifts in global affairs and diplomatic relations between their country of origin and the United States. It was also a reminder that in both Japan and the United States the lives of women were legislated by male decision-makers with their own interests in mind.

In this instance, the gentlemen involved were Theodore Roosevelt and Elihu Root, his Secretary of State, various Japanese diplomats—and the San Francisco school board, which in October 1906 had ordered 93 Japanese pupils to attend segregated schools with their Chinese counterparts. Racist anti-immigration lobbies and politicians—intent on marginalizing Asian immigrants if they could not get them expelled outright—had brought about the policy. But given that Japanese immigrants had been benefiting since 1882 from agitation and legislation against Chinese immigration, and given that the Japanese government considered the Chinese to be culturally and politically inferior, the imposition of this particular racist school policy to solve a California problem created an international flap. The Japanese government, proud of its recent victory in the Russo-Japanese War and its ongoing role in creating a Japanese empire, wanted its emigrants to America treated with equity and respect—and allowed to pursue their education. The Roosevelt administration needed to placate the California lobby, nurture good will and productive relations with Japan, and at the same time act pragmatically.

The result of several months of wrangling by these various groups of men was that the school segregation policy was rescinded, established resident aliens would henceforth be allowed to return to the U.S. after visiting Japan, the Japanese government would cease issuing passports to mere laborers, and the U.S. government would honor Japanese passports issued to "parents, wives, and children of laborers already resident" in the country. All of this amounted to only a temporary fix for Roosevelt and the United States, if only because the "anti-Asiatic" lobby was not finished with its work. And the Empire of Japan would continue to be sensitive concerning its image in the world. More to the point of my family history was this: after the Gentlemen's Agreement the Japanese immigrant male/female ratio shifted to 7 to 1 by 1910, and the 1920 census showed it to be slightly less than 2 to 1. Two of the female immigrants from this period were my grandmothers. One of them was a conventional picture bride, and one apparently was not.

After the Gentlemen's Agreement Minejiro Marumoto and Bun'ichi Na-kadate wasted no time, employing both tradition and innovation in their eagerness to get married and to get their wives to the United States.

Tradition came into play in the form of arranged marriages, agreed to between two families whose offspring were separated by 3,000 miles of ocean but who were deemed compatible and whose marriage was considered timely. This was the case with the Marumotos. Innovation came into play in the use of photography, which provided a means for the couple to make each other's acquaintance through the exchange of pictures—never mind that some men sent their future brides photos that were a decade or more out of date. A second, "American" ceremony might also be performed once the wife reached American soil, but for practical purposes courtship was a long-distance affair and proxy participation in Japanese marriage rites was enough to make matters legal. Besides, cultural conviction said that the extension of a man's family line was of paramount concern and that love—or something like it—would follow marriage, not precede it. The process was efficient and workable, if not infallible. As earlier, Minejiro Marumoto identified himself in the paperwork as a farmer, since farmers (and their families) sat a notch or two higher on the immigration scale than laborers, who were not generally to be admitted to the U.S. under the agreement.

After a passage of 16 days and after having been "medically examined and passed" on February 28, 1913, Hatsune (Imoto) Marumoto was admitted to the United States at Seattle, under her married name, on March 1, the date that has also always been given for her marriage. She had been born in the village of Miwasaki in Wakayama-ken, between two brothers, and was almost 23 when she departed from the port of Yokohama. She was a typical picture bride, though it might be good to recognize that with her sixth-grade education and youthful hope of making her life matter in an unknown place, she was as much a pioneer as any woman leaving Saint Louis for the Oregon Country a half century earlier. I see her walking down the gangplank of the *S. S. Yokohama Maru* toward my grandfather, a small, nondescript Japanese woman only a shade over five feet tall even wearing *geta*, dressed in her best kimono and otherwise as presentable as possible after a decidedly unglamorous passage. I see her with tightly tied bundles of worldly goods so meager as to make a twenty-first century traveler blush. I see her approaching a husband ten years older than she, a man whose 13 years in America had proven anything but lucky. Who, after railroad work and menial service jobs, not to mention a futile pass at farming, had yet to find an occupation open to him that would provide even a modicum of security, let alone success. She is, of course, oblivious to these important details of her reality. I see her determined smile, hiding fears and doubts, as she enters her uncertain American future. Many years later she tried to teach me how to make sushi, but I was too blinded by my hurry-up, baseball-obsessed youth to recognize the gift she was offering, the colors and textures and fragrances of a heritage, the deft beauty of her wrinkled hands. On that same visit to Portland I, who had not thought once about what it meant that I had been born in the United States to citizens of the United States or that I had grown up speaking and reading English, helped her study for her citizenship examination in American history and government. "One nation indivisible," she recited, in an Issei English that embarrassed me then, "with liberty and justice for all." In ignorance of what it really meant to her after four decades of being an alien-other, I helped my grandmother finally become "naturalized." She and I, together with Grandpa, memorized the succession of presidents from Washington to Eisenhower, with the two Roosevelts properly inserted in between.

∽

Moriji Ashizawa was the fourth child and younger daughter of a regional official in Yamanashi-ken. She was born on January 1, 1892, into a prosperous family of office holders and professionals, and had been brought up in an architectural marvel of a house. Its woodwork was elegant, its *tatami*-matted rooms ample, and its landscaping tasteful and tended, making the Ashizawa place a public statement. In photographs from that time, Moriji is a proud creature of that house and family, securely beautiful, and defiant—a picture bride, indeed. My Uncle Toru once said that, given his mother's status and temperament, he could not figure out (and of course never asked directly) how his father ever persuaded her to marry him. Toru's sense of it, though, was that she was attracted to Bun'ichi Nakadate's initiative in coming to the U.S., his willingness to take a risk. And that she always had a mind of her own. And that her older sister Naoji may already have established herself as the female decision-maker of the family.

The Ashizawa-Nakadate marriage was apparently arranged and then formalized during a 1912 trip to Japan by my grandfather, so Grandma Nakadate was not a picture bride in the usual sense, even though her coming to America was also made possible by the Gentlemen's Agreement. Unlike many of his manual laborer contemporaries, Bun'ichi Nakadate had the means to take care of this business in person, so he did not have to bet his future strictly on the judgment of relatives. ("Never let somebody sell you a bill of goods," was the generic wisdom my father later passed on to me.) It is also worth considering that, having heard of "picture husband" deceptions by means of decade-old photographs, my future grandmother, too, wanted to see what she was in for. Moriji Nakadate accompanied her new husband to Seattle on the *Inaba Maru*, in June 1912, when she was 20 and he was 34.

By training she was a teacher, having attended normal school, and as an educated woman she embodied the charge of the 1872 Imperial Rescript, which linked education with the moral code of an emerging nation. She arrived in America having already taught in Japan, and she soon started what may have been the first Japanese language school in Portland. She would recall for her sons the day when she, among a group of school children filing through the street, encountered a military procession led by General Nogi Maresuke, a celebrated hero of the Russo-Japanese War. The general stopped his column and bowed, she said, and waited for the children to pass, deferring to those in pursuit of learning. So Moriji Nakadate's uncompromising ambitions for her sons included higher education. She never became a naturalized citizen, she never converted to Christianity, and she did not live to see my father graduate from medical school or Toru receive his business degree. She never saw a Sansei grandchild go off to college. But her influence transcended a hard life that ended in kidney failure when she was 47. Her American grandchildren all earned graduate degrees, and all ended up teaching. When I announced that I had completed my doctorate and was about to start an academic career, my father—who had expected me to follow him into medicine and was deeply disappointed when I gave up on lab courses to write papers on Shakespeare and Faulkner—glanced up and

Moriji and Bun'ichi Nakadate, 1912.

Minejiro and Hatsune Marumoto, 1913.

said, almost as if he had been waiting for the chance, "Grandma Nakadate was a teacher, you know."

⁌

Hatsune Marumoto. Moriji Nakadate. My grandmothers. Like their husbands, they were unlikely ever to have met in Japan, but at one point lived a few blocks from each other in America. From strikingly different backgrounds and with much different prospects and expectations, they left a country in which a woman's primary role was to help extend her husband's lineage for a country where women could not yet vote and Japanese immigrants were "aliens ineligible to citizenship." They came to the United States to help complete the marginalized lives of Japanese men and gave birth to American children.

WEST SIDE, EAST SIDE

Having abandoned railroad labor, Minejiro Marumoto had tried various types of ad-hoc employment, farming included, and had barely gotten by. Even if he had found success in farming he would have encountered the increasing hostility of white farmers and others who did not like seeing "Orientals" on the land as lessees, let alone owners. So he and his picture bride turned away from rural itinerancy for the relative stability of urban life. And from their arrival in Portland until 1942, the Marumotos were a fairly typical West Side family, working hard in the face of the prevailing prejudices and making do at the vulnerable edge of American life. Any improvement in living quarters was accomplished one neighborhood move, one apartment at a time. A brief residency on East Couch was merely an interlude in what was fundamentally a West Side, Nihomachi story. The Marumotos lived a tenacious, hopeful, and unexceptional existence among others who shared their history and their language, their needs and limitations. They ventured into other neighborhoods because of work or shopping or recreation, and to see how the rest of the city lived. Economic progress meant incremental gains, a new tool or household item here, a new coat or pair of shoes there, a savings account. And of course, children.

Fumie, my aunt, was born in Portland in December 1913, in the Quimby Hotel at NW Third and Burnside, and to the end of her days could recite a litany of impermanence, a succession of little boxes within boxes, the one-and two-room domestic spaces of "resident alien" life: the Quimby, where all three Marumoto children were born; then the Graystone, on N. Albina; the Teikoku, on NW Third between Couch and Davis; the Overland at Second and Couch, where their rented space expanded to two rooms because their mother made beds while their father cleaned rooms at the University Club; and eventually the Oregonian Hotel, in 1928. Yoshiro, my Uncle George, was born in March 1918 (there was passing mention of a stillborn brother a year or so earlier) and would grow up exploring the streets and testing the limits of Nihonmachi. Meriko, my mother, was the middle child. The official record for the city says that a midwife named Kariya Riki attended at her birth on October 16, 1915, that her parents were from Japan, that her father was a farmer, and that her "race or color" was "brown."

As with many other immigrants who might once have entertained thoughts of returning to their homeland, once Minejiro and Hatsune Marumoto had children the meaning of their lives became clearer and the living of them more demanding. Over a decade would pass before they would be able to move up a step by investing their small savings and a lot of two-job sweat in the chance to "operate" the Oregonian Hotel at NW Third and Couch. And there would be the Great Depression. But while they were still in the same neighborhood of cramped domestic spaces, they were finally able to expand beyond a single room by washing linens, cleaning bathrooms, and troubleshooting plumbing. Their friends helped them make a claim to their lives and labor by referring to the Oregonian as the "Marumoto Hotel." Yet whatever their ambiguous status as aliens "not eligible to American citizenship" but also unlikely ever to return to Japan, they saw far different prospects for their American-born children. As was true for Japanese families up and down the West Coast, the arrival of the second generation, the Nisei, American citizens by birth, permanently changed the focus of their story.

ᗷ

The Nakadate family, in contrast to the Marumotos, clearly benefited from the aggressive, hard-nosed, and (by some accounts) ruthless entrepreneurial ambition of our unofficial godfather, Masajiro Furuya. That, and my grandfather's ability to learn very quickly under Furuya's mentorship that business is business. My father's family also benefited from the relative laxity of restrictions on where in the city the newly-arrived were allowed to live, despite de facto pressures to stay clustered (if not segregated) in Nihonmachi-Chinatown. (This attitude toward the presence of "orientals" was to shift; in 1913 California led the way by passing an alien land law that kept "aliens ineligible to citizenship" from owning land and even limited their leases to three years.)

In Portland at that time, residential restrictions had more to do with individual attitudes and habits of mind than with formal codes, making it unlike many other West Coast cities and cities elsewhere in the country. Against the usual odds, a few persuasive civic leaders resisted the more aggressive forces of segregation and exclusion, if only because compromising the city's workforce was counterproductive to economic growth. So the Portland Japanese congregated in Japantown for economic, social, and cultural reasons more than pure political necessity. While some Issei farmers encountered resistance and hostility in rural Oregon communities, others found it possible to establish themselves in northeast Portland. Similarly, merchants, clerks, and restaurant owners could envision a life beyond Ankeny, Burnside, Couch, and Davis, could make more than occasional visits beyond Glisan and Hoyt. There was expansion to the east side of the Willamette River; there were other apartments, houses, and schools. Bun'ichi and Moriji Nakadate—he an eldest son, she a proud Ashizawa—believed in their capacity and their right to live where their ambitions and resources could take them.

And so, although my father was born when his family was listed at 415 NW Davis and his first playground was the North Park Blocks, he was to spend only a short time there. His arrival, on February 3, 1914—the same year that "M Furuya Co., 51–53 4th St. North" appeared for the first time in the Portland *City Directory*—was reported to the family in Japan and duly recorded in the registry in Toyotomi-mura. He was, technically, a citizen of both countries, with the right to go "home" to Japan in the future. (He too was delivered by a midwife, but unlike my "brown" mother, he was listed in the American registry as "yellow.") In 1919, when my father was five and his brother Toru two, their father, having been promoted from salesman to clerk, moved the family across the Burnside Bridge. They were not alone in doing this, joining their friends the Azumanos, the Nogumas, and others, and their housing there was both modestly better and a symbolic step away from the putative limits of Nihonmachi. They moved first to a rented house on Union Avenue, then to a house at NE Union and Couch that was either owned or leased by Furuya, and finally to 1033 NE Hancock, where my father would grow up. Many decades later, I asked my mother's lifelong friend Kiyo Nakayama if she had been acquainted with my father and his family when she was young. Fetching a distant memory with a twinkle and a laugh, she said, "Oh, yes, but we thought they were high-toned people, thought he was kinda stuck up—you know, *East* Side boy!"

Some might refer to these modest shifts in housing and this movement across the city as early evidence of upward mobility, a movement toward the middle class. I see them as a claim and a statement on having an American life.

2 ⁀ Nisei

Each human being must live within his time, with and for
his people, and within the boundaries of his country.

—LANGSTON HUGHES, "DRAFT IDEAS" (1964), *Collected Works*, VOL. 9

AMERICANS, OF JAPANESE ANCESTRY

My father was—in an intuitive, assertive, and surprisingly uncomplicated
way—an American boy. When introduced for the first time he would simply say, "I was born here. My mom and pop were born in Japan." This was
important for him to clarify, and depending on the situation it was a de-
scription, an explanation, an argument, or a dare. He was neither oblivious
nor unconflicted about being both Japanese and American, but he believed
deeply in "America," knew that he wanted live an American story. And in a
society that would repeatedly ask a Nisei boy both to explain himself and
prove he belonged there he was determined to claim his story for himself.

By contrast, my mother was a Nisei girl, born five years before the United
States would ratify women's suffrage, to parents raised in an oppressively
patriarchal culture. Nisei women were doubly "sheltered"—some might say
circumscribed—first by Japanese tradition and then by American discour-
agement of personal success and public or professional lives for women. A
full-time job might be an early, temporary opportunity for a woman to avoid
idle hands and to help her parents and siblings, but a career was hardly to
be imagined. A "working woman" was often the sad creature who had lost
or couldn't find a husband, or the "damaged" woman who emerged from a
failed marriage. Higher education was the stuff of dreams. Nisei men might
be encouraged, even groomed to go to college, and they might be allowed

Katsumi Nakadate, c. 1925.

to venture from the West Coast, but Nisei women belonged close to home. Stretching before Meriko Marumoto was a girlhood made up of lessons in the arts of domesticity, then courtship, marriage, and a family. Beauty and intelligence (she and her sister had both) could make the dance more interesting than otherwise, but in the end a Nisei woman was supposed to be a wife and mother—a "homemaker."

Of course, my parents' aspirations and restrictions were shared by a generation of Americans. But as Nisei, my parents shared with the first American-born generations of many other immigrant groups a difficult, pivotal role: even as children they found themselves translating America for their non-citizen, non-English-speaking parents, and translating their parents for other people. Sometimes the translation was literal and simple, moving deftly from one language to the other in speaking to teachers or sales clerks. Sometimes it was an attempt to translate a concept or behavior that had no counterpart in the other language or culture. Occasionally it even involved matters of law. The Nisei and their parents were growing to understand America at the same time. (Eventually the Nisei would also find themselves bridging the gap between their old-country parents and their "all-American" children, the Sansei.)

Yet it was no easy matter for the Nisei to help their parents with so many adjustments. The Issei were classified as "resident aliens" and had no political identity even when they had status for economic or cultural reasons. And every difference in values and expectations between the Issei and the country where their children had been born created dissonances that eventually had to be acknowledged and negotiated. To complicate matters even more, by the 1920s Japan was already a far cry from the country my grandfathers had left at the end of the nineteenth century: Japan had experienced military success, had learned quickly from the West and was industrializing apace, and (like the United States) made no secret of its ambitions for economic and political influence in Asia.

In this sense my mother's experience was more poignant and revealing than my father's; her female version of being Nisei certainly made clear the crucial roles played by social class and gender even when, in the eyes of outsiders, "race" was the critical issue. Her parents had been raised in a homogeneous, heredity-conscious culture grounded in conformity and ruled by an emperor who was considered a deity. The Japanese ethos in which they had grown to adulthood was essentially Buddhist with Shinto underpinnings, and they read and spoke a language exotic in America, non-European, incomprehensible. Her father had started out by working ten-hour days for an America that wanted only his sweat, certainly not his membership in a labor union, and never his vote; he could never return to Japan as an American success story. Her mother had accepted a one-way ticket to Oregon in exchange for a commitment to a man in a photograph and a country she had never seen.

Meriko grew up bilingual and amid two cultures, and before long became (as she put it) "just Mary." In everyday terms this meant *sukiyaki* and *gohan* (rice) at home and ice cream sundaes at the corner fountain. In cultural terms this meant *Hina Matsuri* with its "Girls' Day" dolls on March 3, the floating lantern-lit *Obon* festival in August, and the Fourth of July sandwiched in between. Like her older sister, Mary wore richly embroidered kimonos on special occasions, but was also intrigued by the flash and celebrity of Rudolph Valentino and Jean Harlow, the phenomenon of Al Jolson (not only an actor in a "talking" movie, but a Jew mimicking a black man), the screen stardom of Dick Powell and Loretta Young. (The theater balcony, she recalled, was supposedly to be avoided, but the Nisei referred to it as "seventh heaven.") She was a member of the Japanese American Methodist Church. In more practical terms, being bicultural meant that while her Issei parents had voice and authority within the family and immigrant community, she and her brother and sister would also learn from non-Japanese public school teachers and be mentored by non-Japanese counselors and coaches. In school they would come to understand (for example) that a Nisei girl had more legal status in the United States than her mother and father, and very different American prospects. In such nontraditional intra-family paradoxes lay irony, confusion, and difficult choices, differences and contradictions that the future would only amplify.

Perhaps nothing exemplified Nisei identity and its dual affinities as much as my mother's formal education—or, more properly, educations. The Marumoto children attended Atkinson Grammar School, but their early learning was in preschool at *Katei Gakuen,* the neighborhood Japanese language school. My Uncle George, who as a student paid less attention to syntax and calligraphy than to sports, would later find his boyhood study of Japanese useful to the U.S. Army, while my mother and Aunt Fumie would continue to read and speak Japanese as long as their parents were alive. But it was on my mother, one of the few Nisei who attended Japanese school through senior year in high school, that this education in language and culture eventually made its most enduring mark.

KATEI GAKUEN

The Meiji Restoration in 1868 had brought universal education to Japan, declaring it central to being Japanese, and a commitment to school-based language learning in America was no doubt an outgrowth of that belief in a new context. Most of the Issei had received from four to six years of elementary education in a local school, but they knew that would not be enough for their American children. And they believed it would take more than public education to make their children's learning complete. As soon as there were children to teach, Japanese language schools started up in communities up and down the Coast—to fulfill many of the same needs as Yiddish schools in New York and New Jersey, Lithuanian schools in Ohio and Pennsylvania, German schools in Wisconsin, Dutch and Danish schools in Iowa, and of course Chinese schools in Portland and other West Coast cities.

But like other organizations started by immigrant groups to sustain cultural ties to native countries, the *nihongogakko* (Japanese school) attracted criticism from xenophobes and anti-immigrant groups for supposedly retarding assimilation. "If you really want to be American," the Nisei children would be asked disingenuously (it was more taunt than invitation), "why don't you just learn English, and forget about Japanese?" Of course the Nisei needed an American education, with its three R's and lessons in history and civics. But to use English only, to speak "only American" and blend into a dominantly Northern European American way of life would be to erase one's culture and ethnic identity. The Nisei could no more abandon Japanese than they could abandon their parents, or become white.

To read and write the language of their parents and to understand and embrace the customs of the country of their parents' birth was a crucial way for the Nisei to honor fathers and mothers who would always be Japanese once they were prohibited from becoming Americans. And for more than a few families there may also have been some hedging of bets: the Nisei were American citizens, but because the Issei were ineligible for citizenship and the family's long-term status and stability in America were problematic, who could know for sure that the Nisei would never need to know Japanese? Meanwhile, they would benefit from learning formal Japanese, rather than regional dialects and the socially compromised language of the working classes. For Issei parents working two or more jobs, the *nihongogakko* also provided several hours of child-care each week.

Katei Gakuen—roughly translated, "home academy or institute"—was one of several Japanese language schools in Portland between approximately 1900 and 1942. These schools would start out in homes or churches, but then expand and relocate to other buildings, perhaps taking over an entire floor. They were staffed by ministers and other community members with advanced academic experience. Moriji Ashizawa Nakadate, my father's mother, who had arrived in the United States with more education than most Japanese women and a teaching certificate earned in Japan, started her own school for a half dozen East Side students once her family moved across the river. But Katei Gakuen was the school attended by the children of Japantown, including my mother and her siblings. The public schools could teach the Nisei English and give them practical skills, and then for an hour after public school and on Saturday mornings Katei Gakuen would enable them to understand the culture most intimate to their lives. There such home-taught precepts as *enryo* (deference) and *giri* (duty) were reinforced—along with the power of *haji* (shame) to encourage self-discipline and honorable conduct, and if necessary, apology. The children checked in at home after afternoon dismissal from Atkinson and then walked up to NW 14th and Hoyt or (after a move) Fifth and Everett to language school.

The Japanese language schools were sometimes accused of being "un-American," or even subversive "indoctrination cells," though that was hardly their intent or their effect. Of course the Emperor Meiji's decree on education was familiar to the Japanese community, and in language school the children might recite its 250 words routinely, like the Pledge of Allegiance they recited every morning in public school. The Imperial Rescript begins by invoking "loyalty and filial piety" across generations and goes on to link "Our Empire" with marital harmony, "modesty and moderation," benevolence, and the pursuit of learning and cultivation of the arts in developing "intellectual faculties and perfect moral powers." All of this would serve to advance the common good—an admirable goal whether in Japan or the

U.S. But for the Nisei the emperor was largely an abstraction, and far, far away, and the Constitution that truly mattered to them was the one with the Bill of Rights that they learned about in public school. There were no report cards at Katei Gakuen, Uncle George was always happy to recall. But everyone knew that attendance was required, and in the emperor's stead the community kept an eye out. If a school-aged child were seen wandering the neighborhood during the hours designated for language school, his parents would not need a telephone to be informed that truancy had occurred.

While her younger brother and some of her classmates found such a focus on learning a burden and language school a distraction, my mother accepted it on faith, and that focus on learning helped define her life. What did she learn? To sing "Sakura," the Japanese national anthem, and other songs her parents had also learned in school. She learned respect for *sensei*, her teacher, and for education itself. She learned that filial piety was a cornerstone of culture. She learned when the Emperor's birthday was, and how to acknowledge it (*"Banzai! Banzai! Banzai!"*). Occasionally, the students put on a performance or play in Japanese; in one of them the central character was, strikingly enough, named Jean Valjean. But most of all she learned language, brushstroke by brushstroke of the *kanji,* syllable by carefully spoken syllable, phrase by subtle phrase. All in the context of Japanese culture. She came to understand the complex texture of *gimu* (duty or responsibility), the nuances of *gaman* (patience, endurance, perseverance), and of course *on* (obligation to remember those who have given to you).

So my mother's life as an American girl was infused and inspired by values set forth by Japanese tradition and culture—filial piety, domestic harmony, modesty and moderation, benevolence, and the pursuit of learning and the arts. These values merged with those instilled by the Japanese Methodist Church and reading from the Bible. Meriko/Mary's immersion in and commitment to language school as well as her public school education made her elegantly bilingual. Some experts would argue that such language proficiency contributed to the high level of academic achievement that she, my father, and other Nisei enjoyed—and eventually passed on to their children. In any case, while Saturday may have been a day of play for most children, at Katei Gakuen it was designated for *kakitori* (transcription and recitation practice), and that made it her day to shine. There were also times when the self-esteem Mary Marumoto acquired in Japanese language school served as her refuge from the traumas that public schooling sometimes served up—and from the ongoing dilemmas of Japanese American female life.

THE MARUMOTO SISTERS

In masks outrageous and austere
The years go by in single file;
But none has merited my fear,
And none has quite escaped my smile.

—ELINOR WYLIE, "LET NO CHARITABLE HOPE" (1932)

After a year in northeast Portland the Marumoto family returned in 1922 to the old neighborhood, where my mother, her older sister, and their younger brother all attended Atkinson School. Atkinson's enrollment was mostly "oriental," made up of Chinese and Japanese American children, with fewer than a dozen white students and (as Fumie recalled) at least one who was black. While enrollments in the Portland schools were not tied to race and ethnicity, they were (as elsewhere) clearly a function of family income and resulting housing patterns, which often were. But with familiar faces around them and Issei parents who encouraged education, the Marumoto children found a certain level of comfort, and learned. The teachers found most of the Nisei children likeable, respectful, and very well-behaved, and saw that some were very bright.

Fumie and Mary were not only smart, but also knowledge-hungry—Fumie, the older sister, with a mind of her own and a willingness to speak it, and Mary, the "always happy" middle child, situated without responsibility or expectation between an older sister and the only boy. They absorbed their school lessons and the promises of America as fast as the teachers could present them ("Miss Norberg in first grade," my mother recited a half century later, "Miss Sagorsky in second, Miss Macaulay in third. . . ."). In the obedient, self-conscious, and conflicted manner of many other children of immigrants, the Nisei began to construct the English-speaking public voices and personalities that would increasingly, inevitably separate them from their Japanese-literate, Japanese-citizen parents. Of course, when the children returned to the cramped apartments of Nihonmachi, they reported the progress of their American education in Japanese.

(Across town, Beverly Bunn, a contemporary, was living a very different childhood, later reflected in her stories about Henry, Ribsy, Beezus, and Ramona and the neighborhood of "Klikitat Street." Three decades later my mother, reading those books to my sisters, couldn't recognize Beverly Cleary's Portland as a place she knew.)

The differences between Japantown and much of the rest of Portland were manifest once Fumie and Mary left Atkinson School and their nurturing, culturally supportive neighborhood for Lincoln High. Lincoln, the only public high school south of the Willamette, drew not only the Nisei but also Jewish, Italian, and other non-Asian students from Holman School and Failing School, and upper-income white students from Shattuck and the Portland Heights, far on up Vista Avenue. Lincoln reflected the social, racial, and economic spectrum of Portland life, but the spectrum was also a pecking order of options and opportunities. For the Marumoto sisters, blossoming into two of the most attractive girls in the community, it was the best and worst of times. The attention they received from male eyes had to be deflected, even as it could not be ignored. In a society skewed by anti-miscegenation statutes, the Nisei boys constituted their pool of appropriate partners, and any other boys' notice was highly problematic. In addition, the sisters' opportunity to receive a high school education—distinguishing them even further from their parents—was vexed by the imposition of an "American" curriculum bent on erasing ethnic consciousness. Iambic pentameter, for example, was oddly rigid in contrast to the modulated rhythms of the Japanese they heard at home and in the classical *waka* poetry of the *uta-garuta* card game they played on New Year's Day.

"Americanization"—assimilation under a different name—was one of the premises of the public school curriculum, and the girls' teachers were the vehicles of this gospel, even though many in Portland (as across the country) believed that Asians could never be incorporated into American life. And for every faculty or staff member who befriended and mentored the Nisei ("Miss Downs was very nice to us," my mother and aunt recalled more than once), there was another whose disdain of their potential and hostility toward their academic ambitions were palpable. My mother's alienation from English literature was largely the result of a mean-spirited woman who ruined it for her, beginning with Shakespeare. (In any case my mother could always recall, "Out, out, damned spot," along with "*amo, amas, amat.*") And inevitably, her Lincoln High classmates included some who were more than a little class- and race-conscious, some whose parents had actually urged the passage of anti-Asian bills by the Oregon Legislature.

The positioning of Portland's ethnic minorities in the Rose Festival celebration was, then, symbolic, but not surprising. As a civic promotion the Rose Festival reflected the politics and ambitions of a city on the move and the values and attitudes of the time. The high-profile parade put civic pride, flowers, and pretty women on display. In the early years there was a Queen of Rosaria drawn from socialite royalty—daughters of the recently arrived need not apply—and by the 1930s the Rose Queen was chosen from among the city's high school seniors. But Portland's ethnic and cultural diversity (Japanese, Chinese, Italian, Serb . . .) was only obliquely acknowledged through the inclusion of an eclectic "International" float, on which each recognized ethnic group was represented by an attractive young woman in appropriate national-origin dress, including a Nisei girl. Occasionally there were additional floats sponsored by individual ethnic groups, and one year Fumie rode on the float sponsored by the Japanese Association. A few years later my mother was Benzaiten, the goddess of eloquence, art, and beauty, on a float that depicted the *Takara Bune* (Treasure Ship) carrying the *Shichi-fukujin* (Seven Lucky Gods of Japan). It was a nice view from a limited height. Some planners may have considered this approach to "inclusion" an elegant solution to an awkward problem, though today its separate-but-equal limitations seem obvious—and of course through it all ran a reality that affected American women of all backgrounds, that they were often rendered as passive figures, especially when they were honored by being put on public display. The Marumoto sisters were flattered to be selected and honored to represent their family and community, but also knew their "oriental" beauty was considered exotic and their individuality lost in a preoccupation with ethnicity and race.

There is a photograph of Fumie and my mother wearing kimonos at what appears to be an "oriental" theme party in the 1930s home of a well-to-do Portland couple. The hosts and guests are white, the men in dark suits and the women dressed in eclectic ensembles of Chinese, Japanese, and other

Mary (seated) and Fumie Marumoto, c. 1931.

Fumie (standing) and Mary Marumoto, c. 1935.

origins. The women seem at once awkwardly displayed and proud of their ability to improvise an oriental "look" for the occasion. Fumie and Mary Marumoto are smiling radiantly for the camera and appear happy to be sharing the evening. They certainly add some authentic local color. But they also exist in a cultural twilight zone of appropriated and misplaced "American geishas," and the situation seems both curious and grotesque given how they got there and what is soon to happen. Articulate in English and socially adept, the attractive sisters have become objects of admiration—yet as out of place as porcelain dolls in an auction barn. They will survive the moment, but the Marumoto sisters are going to need even more self-possession and not a little courage to negotiate the future.

FOREIGN SERVICE

Among others who took note of the Marumoto sisters was the Honorable Toyoichi Nakamura, posted to Portland as the Japanese consul from 1932 to 1938. The sisters had excelled in American public schools. They had also attended Japanese language school for twelve years, and (for example) had learned the subtle intricacies of the Japanese tea ceremony. Fumie had learned to play the *samisen*. They were fluent in both English and Japanese and had become personable, elegant embodiments and interpreters of both Japanese and American cultures. To be polite, tactful, deferential, and attentive to nuances in speech and behavior was second nature to them. And so, when Consul Nakamura and his wife hosted a tea to which they invited a number of young Nisei women, they were successful in finding the governess they needed for their son and daughter.

It was an honor, a unique opportunity, and an obligation on behalf of the community, and when the position was offered to her, Fumie accepted. She had an upstairs room in an imposing house on SW 16th Street, up in the Heights off Vista Avenue, with a panoramic view of the city. In caring for Toyoji and Sadako she was responsible for making sure they learned as much as possible from living in the United States—while not forgetting they were Japanese. (She also had the unusual status of working for the government of Japan.) Within a year, though, Fumie was engaged and soon after married, and at age 19 her younger sister was asked to take over. My mother's relationship with the Nakamuras was mutually appreciative, and when Consul

Nakamura announced that he was being reposted to China the family asked my mother to accompany them as governess. The domestic American life that she had been preparing for, the life of an interested but passive witness to public affairs that she had anticipated, had apparently prepared her to enter the world of international diplomacy.

But accompanying the Nakamuras seemed selfish—it would take her so far from her parents as to make it seem an abandonment. And in the 1930s it was not difficult to see that relations between China and Japan consisted less of diplomacy than conflict. What, then, would life be like in China for an American woman working for the Japanese government? (Indeed, what might have become of her if she had still been in either China or Japan when World War II began?) Mary Marumoto pondered the prospects of an international life, and turned them down. She was, finally, an American girl. (Many years later, after earning her college and graduate degrees in the United States, it was Sadako Nakamura—"little Sada," my mother called her—who entered the diplomatic corps in her father's footsteps, and under her married name eventually served as United Nations High Commissioner for Refugees.)

My mother's American reality was without adventure or melodrama, and at times disheartening. The Marumoto sisters and many of their peers had picked strawberries over several summers to earn money for college, but then lost everything when the stock market collapsed in 1929. The Depression dictated that the family had only enough money to help one child with additional schooling, and culture dictated that that would be the only son, a future breadwinner. A full higher education for the two girls was now out of the question. So the sisters attended Behnke-Walker Business College—to learn typing, shorthand, and basic accounting—and in 1936 Mary Marumoto became a bookkeeper for Farmer's Produce, tallying cucumbers, radishes, and tomatoes. It was, presumably, a holding pattern prior to married life, and in the meantime her family could use the extra income.

In the summer of 1938 my grandmother took daughter Mary to Japan, ostensibly to visit relatives, but actually because at age 23 (and counting) my mother's personality and good looks seemed to be doing little to keep her from becoming an old maid. Given the expense of that trip in the context of the family's modest means, we can see how important the moment was. In fact, Mrs. Matsura, a "family friend" in Wakayama, arranged a *miai* or "formal marriage meeting," in which a young man with a promising career in the Japanese Foreign Service was the other principal figure. It took my mother by surprise. But she managed to finesse the situation (diplomacy, diplomacy!) and later made clear to her mother her intention to choose a husband on her own. All of this might seem quaint and comic from a twenty-first century perspective, but for a Nisei woman in that time and place it was a self-defining act. An act of resistance to tradition and expectation that had to stop short of disrespect.

So my mother passed up her second chance to enter a life framed by foreign service. Apparently, two more suitors (one a dentist, she recalled, and the other "a good dancer") were also rejected right there in Portland. Otherwise, it was just a matter of counting celery and "cukes"—until some mutual friends introduced her to an East Side boy they thought might make her happy.

OF AMERICA

My Uncle George's boyhood memories were of playing and fishing in the sandy shadows of the Steel Bridge, roaming newly-paved streets garnished with "horse apples," and spending nickels on Tom Mix Westerns at the Burnside Theater. "Japanese movies," he told me, "were in a theater on the other side of the street." He heard neighborhood rumors about the "Shanghai tunnels" through which drunken or unconscious Stumptown bar patrons had been carried to the docks for involuntary "service" on sailing crews. He also shot a few bulbs out of streetlights with an air gun—although in the dynamic, polyglot, urban-transient society of Japantown/Chinatown in the 1920s George was guilty more of mischief than of misdemeanors as far as the authorities were concerned, and the authorities were distant. Even when the Portland police investigated the occasional neighborhood homicide, they found it hard to locate any witnesses willing to talk to them, in any language.

My father, living on the East Side, was equally unsupervised but much more self-conscious. He, too, walked his neighborhood and fished for carp in the river, and he grew up wending his way through the weeds and blackberry bushes of Sullivan's Gulch. But even with fewer Japanese around there were more than enough eyes, official and otherwise, to notice a footloose boy who, according to some, really belonged on the other side of the river.

Katsumi Nakadate was also the son of a status-conscious mother, and a reputation-conscious father who lived the micromanaged existence of a Furuya employee. They had ambitions for him—medicine, the law, or possibly the ministry—and made it clear that academic achievement and right conduct were essential. And then there were his own coalescing ambitions, not to be derailed by his being in the wrong place at the wrong time with the wrong friends. To make that even less likely, he kept busy taking harmonica, swimming, life-saving, and judo lessons, and pushing the envelope all the way. Once, when threatened by two neighborhood white boys who wanted to teach the "little Jap kid" a thing or two, he found himself in the ironic position of using his training in judo to convince them he had a right to be in America. At age 12 he joined the Boy Scouts, and a year later stopped attending his mother's Japanese language school. A few years later you could be saved from drowning by a 16-year-old boy who held a black belt in judo and had been invited to play "Humoresque" on the harmonica on a local radio show. The idea of being "of America"—democracy, equality, and all the rest—seemed so intuitively correct and sufficient to him that he hardly gave it a second thought. He was always aware of being Japanese, but the stars by which he steered were in the flag of the U.S.A.

It was not such a big leap, then, for the Boy Scouts to become the defining affiliation of my father's youth. Scouting was about patriotism, loyalty, skill-building, and individual achievement—and all but the last of those values were important in Japanese as well as American culture. The connection was implicit and the scouting affiliation a comfortable one—less a departure than an extension of a belief system. As if following Old Man Furuya's worship-in-the-community injunction—and in any case with his own parents' approval—my father started attending the otherwise "all-white" Centenary Wilbur Methodist Church on his own when he was only in kindergarten, and it was there that he later became the only Nisei scout in an otherwise white Troop 66. (This was to have remarkable repercussions in 1941.) Decades later he observed with a laugh, "I must have thought I was a hakujin!"

It was important to him that it was the Boy Scouts *of America,* just as it had been the *American* Red Cross for his swimming and life-saving lessons, given his conviction that he and "America" were truly inseparable. He believed his achievements in scouting were testament against the racial and cultural prejudices he encountered from time to time. He flourished under the tutelage of his scoutmaster, Van Watson, built enduring friendships and loyalties, and became an Eagle Scout in less than three years. In the process he came to believe that the essence of success was to be prepared and to be "trustworthy, loyal, helpful, friendly, courteous, kind, obedient, cheerful, thrifty, brave, clean, and reverent." He felt so strongly about this that a decade later, while in medical school in Portland, he became the founding scoutmaster of a new troop of Nisei boys—"So they would get to be scouts and know what it meant to be American." When a Methodist church wouldn't let them meet there because half of them were Buddhist and the others "mostly Shinto," my father searched around until he convinced the priest at a nearby Catholic church to give them a home.

For Grandma Nakadate in particular, it was never a matter of what my father "might" do or even what he "ought" to do, but what he *would*, in fact, accomplish. You *will* do this, she would say to him, you *will* do that. If there were men of ideas and men of action, then Moriji Ashizawa Nakadate's son would not be among those sitting around and thinking. The work itself, tangible on a day-to-day basis, would be the easy part—except that he was expected to do it well, very well, better than anybody else. There were no entitlements (the concept as alien to the family as *Wienerschnitzel* or kidney pie), only expectations, and there would be no complaints or excuses. Two decades after its initial publication, Elbert Hubbard's *A Message to Garcia* had become secular scripture for schoolboys across the country, and its story of Lieutenant Rowan's steadfast fulfillment of a seemingly impossible mission became a touchstone of my father's grab-it-by-the-horns philosophy—and an echoed refrain in my own boyhood ears.

Given all this, what possible "reasons" for not earning top grades in school could be taken as anything but pathetic "explanation" and excuse-making? The cornerstones of his life—and by extension his family's American success—would be education, sacrifice, hard work, and perseverance. (His Issei parents were far from alone in this, and this work ethic helped create the "model minority" image that has both enhanced and vexed Asian American life.) In elementary school he learned to write an elegant Palmer longhand, and in high school he took on the college prep curriculum. He took on American sports—baseball, basketball, tennis, and track; he was both a pitcher and a catcher, and in high school he ran 100 yards in ten seconds flat. The need for money for college and medical school meant stocking shelves for Furuya Company, then thinning and propping pear trees in orchards outside of Hood River, then working summers in an Alaskan cannery. It was all simply to be done. (Years later, as a parent, he sometimes employed the word "theoretically," but his point was never theoretical: "Theoretically, you should have started writing that paper a little sooner.") After growing up in the stiff shadow of M. Furuya, after studying Japanese under his own mother's demanding eye, after becoming the first Japanese American Eagle Scout in Oregon, after parsing Virgil and Plutarch at Washington High, Katsumi Nakadate could have told you that anything is doable, like emerging victorious from war: *Veni, vidi, vici.*

The game plan was simple: he would excel in high school, go on to excel at the University of Washington, excel in medical school, and then enter the practice of medicine, probably in Portland or Seattle. He thought of medicine as a kind of public service, a humanitarian calling, which he always referred to as "helping other people." Of course, he could not anticipate the Great Depression or a world war, and he underestimated the impact that racial prejudice might have on his career.

BASEBALL: OTHER FIELDS, OTHER DREAMS

The language was hard to pronounce, with idioms that made no sense. The food, from apple pie to hash, was strange. Almost everything about America was alien and new for the Issei—except for the national pastime.

Baseball had been brought to Japan in the 1870s, and immediately understood and embraced because its essence was so coincidentally, so inherently Japanese. Baseball was a blend of geometry and flow, predictability and improvisation, power and finesse, teamwork and self-sacrifice, and success as a result of patient effort. In baseball time was not the enemy of performance, and (as in judo) sheer size was not necessarily decisive. The core concepts lost nothing in translation. So, given the Japanese fascination with all things Western, from commerce to culture, *obesu-boru* was already known to the Issei when they came to the United States. When they and their children fully embraced the game it was less acculturation than re-acquaintance and consummation. (In 1914, the year my father was born, enthusiasm for baseball in Japan resulted in formation of the Tokyo Big Six University Baseball League.) And of course, even though the farthest western reaches of major league baseball were Saint Louis and Chicago, baseball itself was all-American, coast to coast. For Japanese Americans, and the Nisei especially, playing it was a way to demonstrate their ability to place themselves in the American picture. When they couldn't play, they watched the Hollywood Stars, San Francisco Seals, Portland Beavers, and Seattle Indians.

Throughout the 1920s and 1930s amateur and semipro baseball teams emerged in Japanese American communities, urban and rural, across the western states, and, where numbers warranted, entire leagues developed. The teams were sponsored by the players themselves, by local businesses and churches, and by communities at large. Like other local organizations, the Japanese American teams and leagues came into being in the face of exclusion from white-only athletic clubs (a phenomenon that my family could attest to well past mid-century). Team names were adopted out of ethnic pride and affirmation, often variations of such terms such as "Nippon," "Mikado," and "Fuji," and in return for community support the teams unified families, neighborhoods, and generations. Rendering the fictional world of "Yokohama, California," Toshio Mori said that a day at the ballpark was a perfect day, an intergenerational, cross-cultural celebration, and at such moments the score itself did not matter. Of course many of the biggest tournaments took place on the Fourth of July.

Beginning around 1914 and on into the 1930s teams from Seattle, San Jose, Fresno, Los Angeles, and other cities played exhibition games throughout the American West and even in Japan. My father played on one such baseball team while room-and-boarding on a farm outside of Salem as an undergraduate at Willamette University. In the spring and summer months he and other young men wrested weekend interludes from their work in broccoli, celery, and peas, and their "Salem Yamato" team borrowed one of the farm trucks for road trips as far away as Hood River.

In scope and impact, Japanese American baseball was in the shadow of a shadow—it did not approach the impact of the Negro leagues on either baseball or American culture at large. And mastery of the game notwithstanding, the Nisei could not simply Americanize their names as a strategy for "blending in," as could Ludwig Heinrich Gehrig and Guiseppe Paolo DiMaggio, among others. They may have been aware that a few African Americans had tried to play professionally by passing themselves off as "Spanish" or even "Indians." But in the America of their youth, the Nisei had as much chance of blending in and being accepted on equal terms as Detroit's Hank Greenberg had of not being recognized as Jewish. And even less chance of making it to the major leagues. In a dogmatically Christian, race-conscious society that feared, demeaned, and marginalized newcomers even as it supposedly welcomed them, many Nisei were relieved just to be thought of as "American Japanese" rather than "Japs" or "Nips," or generic "orientals" or "Asiatics"—or the "Yellow Peril." A handful of Nisei ended up leaving their native country to play baseball in Japan.

My grandparents' nonnegotiable focus on education and my father's economic circumstances eventually made playing sports a luxury he couldn't afford. That was the inescapable fact one spring when, squeezing in an intramural game in lieu of lunch, Katsumi Nakadate hit a softball so hard that it landed on the field where the Willamette varsity was practicing. Spec Keene, the coach, walked over with it and demanded to know who was responsible, and when my father answered, Keene responded with an invitation: "Anybody who can hit a ball that far should be over *there,* practicing with us." For a young man of a later generation such an offer might have included scholarship help, but this young man was working on a farm for room and board, and driven toward medical school by personal dreams and family obligation, which by then were very hard to tell apart. It was not an invitation he could accept.

Like their Mexican American and African American counterparts, my father, his brother Toru, and other Nisei could bask in the support their teams received from their communities, and the cohesion and ethnic pride the teams helped create. They could take satisfaction from the sport itself and comfort from the broader American promises the game implied. But that was it. (The boys from Salem Yamato went into farming, medicine, retail enterprise, banking—and one later became a professional wrestler.)

Had my Uncle George not been in uniform during the war, he would have found himself playing baseball with those incarcerated at Minidoka while cherishing memories of sneak-in afternoons at the Beavers' Vaughn Street ballpark. Had my father not escaped barbed wire by virtue of geography, luck, and military service, he, too, would have had to confirm his love for the national pastime in the midst of sagebrush and alkaline dust. By then Joe DiMaggio, the Italian American "Yankee Clipper" born the same year as my father on the same West Coast, had already begun to play out the dream they

Home and Away

"During the 1920's and 1930's, baseball flourished in every Japanese American settlement across the American West and Hawaii." Caption from exhibit, "Diamonds in the Rough: Japanese Americans in Baseball," 1997

They scrapped and hustled on the Coast
where they were born, but also took their game
far beyond Seattle, Portland, Stockton,
and San Pedro, some barnstorming to Japan, or east,
to Kansas, Oklahoma. Opposing clubs would marvel that
those little chaps could field and hit so well, surprised
their English wasn't half bad, either. Sometimes
they scheduled prison teams (who played all games "at home"),
not knowing that some bad calls after Pearl Harbor
would make them close their own careers behind
barbed wire, go the distance for Heart Mountain,
Poston, Topaz, Manzanar, and Minidoka.
                                                    Before the war
my father, working his way through college by hauling
produce into town on the way to morning classes,
was one of the boys from Lake Labish who tended lettuce,
peas, and broccoli until the weekend came around and
"Salem Yamato" would pile into a mud-crusted Chevy
and the celery truck with a mattress in the bed,
dreaming of being Yankees.

might have had. But it was not until 1947, after evacuation and incarceration had destroyed the communities that nurtured the Japanese American baseball teams, that Jackie Robinson would finally make major league baseball a place where Americans of color could begin to make their mark.

1924: CIVICS LESSON, PART 2

Let's be candid. The Johnson-Reed Act was ill-intended from the outset. Otherwise known as the Immigration Act of 1924, Johnson-Reed was racist legislation masquerading—badly—as democratic process. It was driven by "eugenicist" notions of "racial hygiene" and the presumed superiority of Northern European races—the kind of thinking that would lead to Nazi aggression and the Holocaust. It appealed to many who supported, if not "ethnic purity," then at least an ethnic status quo in the U.S. It appealed to many with a self-serving agenda that did not include having to compete with immigrant-founded businesses, or with "foreign" labor, much of which had been actively recruited and transported to America. Then (as later) immigrant labor was the kneejerk scapegoat for low wages and unemployment. Some proponents of Johnson-Reed asserted that they didn't like the way the Japanese were taking over truck farming, particularly in California. Some on the West Coast were even upset about "Jap" kids taking places on local sports teams that they felt their own children should have had.

Johnson-Reed was supported and fiercely lobbied by influential newspapers, many chambers of commerce, most labor unions, numerous civic organizations, and a cadre of regional nativist and hate groups. Crafted and sponsored in Congress by Representative Albert Johnson (R-Wash.) and Senator David Reed (R-Penn.) it passed into law by overwhelming margins. There were niceties in the details—some preference was given to new immigrants with agricultural expertise, never mind that the Japanese themselves were already known for that—and the law would be tweaked in the next few years. But the passage of the Immigration Act of 1924 marked great progress on "the immigration issue"—or did great damage, depending on your perspective.

One scarcely-disguised intent of the legislation was to manipulate and restrict immigration by establishing a "national origins quota system" that privileged a few countries but discriminated against many, particularly those that had contributed to the great wave of immigration from southern and eastern Europe that had begun in the 1890s. "Swarthy" (and typically non-Protestant) Italians, Poles, Hungarians, Lithuanians, and many more were the targets of the national quotas: new immigration for each given country was limited to two percent of the number who were *already living in the U.S. in 1890.* But 1890 was a full generation earlier, when the U.S. population was overwhelmingly white, with roots in northern and western Europe. Along with various state anti-miscegenation statutes and alien land laws, Johnson-Reed was a deliberate attempt to make sure that American minorities would always remain minorities—with obvious political, economic, and cultural implications. Johnson-Reed was intended to guarantee that the vast majority of legal immigration into the U.S. would always come from Northern Europe, with the British Isles and Germany leading the way.

The other goal of the Immigration Act of 1924 was to cut off completely the arrival of people who were particularly "undesirable" because they were supposedly "unassimilable" into American life—those from the so-called Asia-Pacific Triangle, including Japan, China, India, the Philippines, and the rest of South and Southeast Asia. But as in the case of the "two percent" masquerade (not to say Kabuki theater), Johnson-Reed avoided naming specific countries, this time by piggybacking on the Naturalization Act of 1790, which stipulated that only "free white persons" could become naturalized citizens. Asians and South Asians (among others, of course) had been called "brown" (as on the official record of my mother's birth) or "yellow" (my father), but never "white," and the 1924 immigration law simply barred further immigration of people ineligible for citizenship. The "barred zone" encompassed many countries and peoples, but the Japanese were a particular target. The already-arrived Japanese were legal immigrants—that is, legal "resident aliens"—but Johnson-Reed certainly made them feel unwanted. (When I was a boy and my mother tried to explain the barred zone to me, all I could grasp was that there was an unusual map with diagonal gridlines across some "foreign" countries. But we already lived in Indiana—so I couldn't see how that could have anything to do with her, or me.)

Many on the West Coast, in particular, had long wanted to get rid of the Japanese, and the manipulation of immigration policy was one of their tools. Eighteen years after the passage of Johnson-Reed, when the uprooting of Japanese Americans was authorized by executive order, the prejudiced and predatory didn't have to look very hard for inspiration or very far for support. Discrimination based on race and country of origin was already the law of the land.

1924   The Johnson-Reed Act or Immigration Act of 1924—also referred
        to as the "Oriental Exclusion Act"—becomes law. Further entry
        into the U.S. of "aliens ineligible to citizenship" is prohibited.
        Oregon election code requires voters to be able to read the
        Constitution in English.
1929   The Japanese American Citizens League (JACL) is founded,
        a human rights and civil rights organization for addressing
        discrimination issues and resisting anti-Japanese legislation.
1930   Oregon code declares intermarriage between races
        ("miscegenation") a felony.
1933   In his First Inaugural Address President Franklin Roosevelt
        declares, "the only thing we have to fear is fear itself."
1939   On June 4 the ship *St. Louis,* carrying Jews fleeing Nazi Germany,
        is denied entry into the United States—ostensibly in order to
        conform to restrictions under the 1924 Immigration Act.

WILLAMETTE AND WASEDA

Some of the Issei had disposable income, but their options were limited—if only because the Oregon Alien Land Law of 1923 said that "aliens ineligible for citizenship" were prohibited from purchasing land and housing. The welcome mat for Asians was unstable and the long-term economic viability of Japanese families unpredictable. A relative few Oregon Issei had managed to buy property prior to 1923, and some had purchased land with non-Japanese partners or in the names of their citizen children (a loophole that proved only temporary once the irrationalities of war came into play). Others determined that they could at least invest in family businesses—to the extent that this involved goods and services but not the buildings that contained them. After their early immigrant struggles the Marumotos followed that path by "leasing to operate" the Oregonian Hotel. The more successful Issei, such as the Nakadates, were able to send money to their families in Japan, demonstrating filial piety and satisfying other family obligations. (Much later in the century such remittances would still be associated with first-generation immigrants, such as those from Mexico and India, among other countries.) In the meantime, Japanese immigrants could invest in the future by paying close attention to their children's education.

Bun'ichi and Moriji Nakadate seemed fortunate in having two sons in my father and Toru, since that enabled them to survey the options and hedge their bets. My father and his brother were American citizens by birth, but were also claimed as citizens by Japan, and the ambiguity of their dual citizenship signaled two possible paths to success. Of course both brothers grew up working for Furuya Co.—as errand boys, stock boys, deliverymen—and there was nothing wrong with this in their father's mind. My father never forgot wrestling tubs of *miso* (seasoning paste) and carrying those 100-pound sacks of rice, and years later Toru would laugh when recalling that he had to deliver soy sauce to the Chinese restaurants and shops at 6 A M so no one would see that two traditionally hostile ethnic groups were actually doing business with each other. (In Asia the Japanese had recently invaded Manchuria—but in Portland Furuya's prices were quite competitive.) Yet the Ashizawas were a family of professionals and government officials, not of the commercial class, and Moriji Ashizawa Nakadate insisted that one of her sons would enter medicine or the law, not "commerce." With such unshakeable encouragement my father committed very early on to being a doctor. In America. But Bun'ichi Nakadate's success in Portland had also enabled him to fulfill his oldest-son obligations by helping his younger brothers capitalize Nakadate Denki, the electrical contracting company. So if Katsumi were going to be a doctor, Toru would be groomed to take a major role in the family business. In Japan. It proved a comfortable fit for the older brother and an awkward one for the younger.

My father prepared for college at Washington High, taking lots of math and science, and of course Latin. He was one of a sprinkling of minority students there and in that respect started a trail-breaking pattern that he seemed to take for granted and that my siblings and I ended up following in the pursuit of our own educations. He had his eye on Seattle and the University of Washington. Toru was sent to Benson Polytechnic, a few blocks away from home, with its vocational curriculum. More interested in baseball and football than electricity, he was also less impatient for the future. But then came 1929.

When the Furuya-affiliated bank went bust so did my father's savings, and he became one of thousands during the Depression for whom college suddenly became less a matter of where than of how. Having earned and saved the better part of the money he would need for college, he now had to do it all over again, under a modified plan. Family friends had spoken well of Willamette University, and other friends, the Otsukis, had a farm outside of Salem where my father could live and work while attending classes. The Monday after graduating from high school he enrolled as a pre-med major and moved to the Otsuki farm to work for room and board and 20 cents an hour. (The "Lake Labish" farm was itself part of a sweat equity phenomenon: by 1941 Japanese American truck farms on the Pacific Coast had developed to the point of producing well over 50 percent of many crops, including celery, cucumbers, and tomatoes—and in some areas almost monopolized those markets.)

So Katsumi Nakadate commuted to Salem in a farm truck, the tradeoff being that he had to deliver produce to various grocery stores before going to class. At the end of the day he would retrace his steps and collect money from the same businesses and return to the farm for supper. (One of those little grocery stores, he recalled many years later, was called "Fred Meyer.") On weekends he pitched in on the fieldwork and joined Salem Yamato for baseball tournaments. At Willamette my father, again one of only a scattering of Nisei students, worked his way through the lab-heavy pre-med curriculum and supported himself on campus during his third year by holding one job with the groundskeeping crew and another in the library. He trimmed shrubbery and cultivated rose bushes, and on Saturday mornings in the fall he would help put down the lines on the football field—though he never saw a game, since by kickoff time he was shelving or dusting books. (I once thought this was his exaggerated version of how hard life was "back then," but eventually concluded that I was reluctant to acknowledge the fact of his losses.) After three and a half years at Willamette he was admitted to the University of Oregon Medical School in Portland, still on the fast track and still convinced that he was living a quintessential and unambiguously American story. And he began to enjoy the company of Mary Marumoto, together with the tennis courts and rose gardens at Washington Park.

At about the time my father entered medical school and not long after high school graduation, Toru was happily making deliveries for Furuya Co. and

Born in the U.S.A.

Born and raised in the U.S.A.
my uncle went to college in Japan.
He was an easy-going but
obedient son
who left home to study "commerce"
(though his love was for words, not numbers),
play football with other Waseda students,
suffer under military training,
and awaken one day
to World War II and the embrace
of family obligation—a wife,
a child (a cousin of mine),
and the family business.

Unlucky man, indeed,
with two languages
and two homes.

"Gosh," he said to me
a lifetime later, "I missed it,"
and who wouldn't wonder
how it might have been. Sitting
in a Tokyo McDonald's
he spoke of July Fourth picnics,
Benson High, a Model T
he had driven in his youth,
and baseball. He mentioned a player
who had recently left Japan
for the major leagues. "That Nomo,"
Uncle Toru said,
pointing to the Asian edition
of an American magazine,
"going to the Dodgers and
starting a whole new life. He's
kind of a hero of mine."

otherwise enjoying life. But one day his mother asked to see his hands, which by then were full of scrapes and scratches from barrels and boxes. "This is not good," she declared, and within a few months they were on their way to Japan so that Toru could pursue a college degree—where the discipline of Japanese institutions would no doubt help him focus his intentions. He would first have to endure two years of intensive prep school to get his Japanese to the college level—but then college would be the prestigious Waseda University in Tokyo. He was to earn a degree in commerce, with which he had no affinity. But Toru was the second son, and was expected to fulfill his family obligation in this way. And this he tried to do.

Toru was one of hundreds of Nisei whose families sent them to Japan for some or all of their education, whether for strategic reasons or out of simple respect for cultural roots. They studied in Japanese, gave themselves up to an unfamiliar academic ethos, and received mandatory military training something on the order of ROTC in the United States. They played American football and shared their love of baseball with their "real" Japanese classmates. But family ambitions and undergraduate adventures aside, there was long-term impact on the lives of these "*Kibei*," who returned from their educational interludes as not-really Japanese and no longer "purely" American. And once World War II started, their military training in Japan became a real liability for some: in Japan they were vulnerable to the military draft, and in the U.S. they might be suspected of being potential spies. Who the Kibei "really" were and where they truly belonged were questions without simple answers, and individual responses to the conundrum ranged from bemused bewilderment to alienation and despair.

GRIEF

Moriji Ashizawa had married into the Nakadate family and arrived in America at the age of 21. A woman of learning, tolerance, and understanding, she founded a Japanese language school on Portland's East Side, and made clear to her sons that education was a family priority. Her life was not as physically strenuous as that of many Issei women, but it was difficult nonetheless, and there were times when she resented the way her domestic life played out. It was galling to her that her home in Portland was a "Furuya house," that

S

In the gray
and crackled snapshot,
eyes on shutterbug, ears up,
paws hooking the edge
of the modest porch,
a "German police dog,"
named for Mr. Sato, the friend
they got him from. S is
furred vigilance, sharing
as always that sunny space
with the smiling but life-heavy
middle-aged woman
whose steamer passage from Japan
was accounted for by photos, letters, and
future obligations. She has been
cooking for salesmen in her home,
is obliged to give them rooms and
endure their behavior because
her husband is office manager—
duties she is not happy with
at all. Her life will end
before her sons fulfill
a younger mother's dream
and she will be spared only
their father's anger
with America
and the agonies
of the coming war.

No one quite remembers
what became of him
between Grandma's death
and the family's departure
from the house on Hancock Street.
"His name was S," my father said,

handing me the photo—
"I loved that dog, because of how
he took care of Mom."

Moriji Nakadate and S, c. 1936.

she had to shelter and cook for ill-mannered young employees who shuffled in after sales trips or long days in the Portland store under their employer's heavy thumb. Her husband pinched pennies at home but invested heavily in the electric company in Japan, and her resentment of that couldn't be masked.

In Japan the Ashizawas believed that she was really the driving influence behind the Nakadate success in America, and apparently there came to be "a certain mutual coldness" between the families. Toru suffered the chill of it during his college days when his mother made a visit to Japan and there were some telling breaches in decorum, as when certain relatives did not greet her arrival and when she paid her respects at in-laws' homes without crossing the threshold. In Portland my grandmother's consolations were few—close conversations with her back-fence neighbor Eleanor Bither, the family dog named "S," and the achievements and promising futures of her sons. She died of acute kidney failure in February 1939, a week after her older son's 25th birthday and without seeing him graduate from medical school and follow in her brother's footsteps a few months later. Since Toru was in college in Japan, my father had to write it down: "Tough news, Kid—we lost Mom today. . . ." Separated by the Pacific Ocean, the brothers had to grieve without each other.

By 1940 Bun'ichi Nakadate was done with the United States. His extended family in Yamanashi had been provided for. His sons were grown and he was in the process of grooming Toru to take a prominent position in the electric company. Bun'ichi Nakadate had followed the sorry progress of American politics and law as they consistently erected barriers to the long-term success of immigrants from Japan, and his negative opinions on this topic were frequently expressed. He had recently retired from Furuya Company, which had finally disintegrated as a result of both problematic investments and the Great Depression. His brother Kiyoshige had passed away, leaving personal affairs to be looked after in Wakayama-ken. And his wife had died. So he returned to Japan with her ashes, in order to fulfill yet one more obligation before assuming an oldest son's place at the table—and exercising the prerogative of regularly examining the company books.

The point of no return for Uncle Toru was the spring of 1941, as reflected in a letter to my father. By then their mother had been dead two years, and Toru was no longer just a college student writing home to ask for a little extra spending money. "I visited Tokyo recently for the express purpose of talking to Dad about my citizenship and return to America," he wrote to older brother "Kats," and went on to describe his plight in the context of their father's disenchantment with the United States:

> Dad was against my return to the U.S. for reasons of his own, the reasons being that he wants one of his family near him in his old age and that there is no future for me in the U.S. (racial prejudice again). Although he admitted the U.S. was a better place to live in, he pointed out that we (Japanese-Nisei) would never be accepted on the same basis as that of a white person, be he Italian, German, or Jew. Here in Japan I'm just as good as anyone else, can go anywhere I please, and do just as I please, in short, I'm in my own country—racially speaking. . . . [But] after living in the U.S. I hate to give up the American way of life. After all, I'm just interested in "living" in the broadest sense of the word. I want to go back, but it wouldn't be right. I'm sure mother would understand my point, but . . . that is only wishful thinking. . . . Well, that's that—I'll have to accede to dad's wishes and do the best I can. I feel like a martyr, a sacrifice on the altar of filial piety. . . .

A plea and a surrender, all at once. My grandfather had been successful enough in Portland to be able to send money to Japan. But the marginalized status he had to endure while achieving this financial success in America had never allowed him to fully achieve an American life, and the patently racist Johnson-Reed Act in 1924 was yet another insult. So injury and anger caused Bun'ichi Nakadate to ignore the fundamental differences between his opportunities and those of his American citizen second son. My father seemed irrevocably American and well on his way to reaching his (and his mother's) goal of a medical career, so was left to his American dream. But Toru was being asked to give up his country. Seven months after the anguished letter, Toru's malaise of filial duty would be overtaken by the fog of war, and he would find himself irretrievably in the wrong place at the wrong time. Two years later he fell in love and got married, learning only then that under Japanese law his marriage could not be registered unless he declared himself a citizen only of Japan.

My father, ever the gung-ho American, always maintained that Grandpa Nakadate would have returned to Portland from his extended visit in

Yamanashi if it hadn't been for the war. But Toru, under heavy pressure to work in the company and make a life for himself in Japan—and in his own right a casualty of Grandpa's disenchantment—always understood that once Bun'ichi Nakadate had left the U.S. with his wife's remains, he would not be going back. When I saw Toru in Tokyo a half-century later he was still a cover-to-cover reader of *Time* magazine and still sprinkled his speech with "gosh" and "gee whiz"—an American at heart. He visited Portland a few times over the years but never came back.

WHY I AM A HOOSIER

A doctor with Japanese credentials occasionally appeared in Nihonmachi and set up shop, but medical professionals were far from commonplace or accessible. Japanese midwives, vital but ephemeral figures in the transitory immigrant community, oversaw the births of my parents and many others. Hence my father's intention was to earn his medical degree and practice medicine in Portland, and within it the Japanese community.

But despite being in the top quarter of his medical school class ("13th in a class of 56," he would remind me), he had to deal with the ongoing reality of anti-Asian prejudice. Despite casting a wide net on the West Coast he found it impossible to obtain the required internship that would lead to a residency and the completion of his formal training. It was not unheard of for a new Chinese or Japanese American doctor to be taken on by a hospital in Oregon, Washington, or California, but the hospital would no doubt have a sense of how many might be too many and whether some patients would balk at being treated by an "oriental" doctor. Katsumi Nakadate had been successful in scouting, sports, and academics, but to some he was still "the little Jap kid" who didn't belong in the neighborhood.

He suffered the same rejection that afflicted many other Nisei college graduates who were refused opportunities to move forward in their professions by government bodies, cultural institutions, colleges and law firms, and many in the business community. Minoru Yasui, a family friend, ended up going to Chicago in an effort to pursue his legal career. Journalist Bill Hosokawa, another friend, finally found a job with an English-language newspaper in Singapore. And it was common enough for Nisei with degrees in chemistry, biology, or agriculture to end their job searches back in the family business of growing or selling vegetables or flowers, or even working as gardeners. The cliché of the miracle-working Japanese gardener may well have emerged from the reality of college-educated botanists and agronomists who proved more than able to turn compost and make roses and rhododendrons bloom for their employers. My father recognized that he would have to leave Oregon if he were ever to serve it, and after a frustrating and ever-widening search he found himself at St. Catherine's Hospital in East Chicago, Indiana.

East Chicago was vibrantly industrial, bare-knuckles and working class. Across the street from Cook County, Illinois, East Chicago was crisscrossed by overhead cables and had two pairs of rails, the South Shore Line running right down the middle of town and on to the rest of greater Chicago. Hammond lay to the south and Gary to the east. Many families in East Chicago were only one generation away from central or southern Europe, and their Polish, Czech, Hungarian, Italian, and other origins were reflected in their accents and Sunday meals. There were immigrants from Mexico, and African Americans who had come up from the South in the Great Migration. It was a blue-collar, no-collar place, where many owed their livelihood and allegiance to steel, petroleum, and shipping. For them, the comfort and refuge of the Catholic, Methodist, and Baptist churches were complemented by jobs at Inland Steel, Standard Oil, and Indiana Harbor. And there was in-your-face high school football. Nobody in Indiana looked forward to meeting up with a team from the Calumet Region in the playoffs, but least of all a team from East Chicago, and not simply because the players' names were hard to pronounce. My fascination with language began when I first noticed the missing vowels and challenging syncopation of a memorable goulash of East Chicago names—from Arbeiter and Bartos to Treiber and Zandi, with Benchik, Gustaitis, Hrunek, and Karwasinski in between. My introduction to patriotism came when my mother told me that the statue in the park where she took me to play was that of a great general named Thaddeus (Tadeusz) Kosciuszko, who along with General Casimir Pulaski helped George Washington win the Revolutionary War. "Sometimes it seemed that everyone there had a long last name that ended in a vowel," my mother would observe with a smile many years later, "and maybe that's why we fit in."

My still-bachelor father became the junior partner of Dr. George Bicknell, whose family embraced him, and he found East Chicago a place to practice medicine without pretentions, helping patients who truly needed him. At St. Catherine's he joined a staff of interns that included "two Italian boys, two Jewish boys, and me," and it was there that my father took on, at others' urging, "an easier name for patients to pronounce"—James. Within a year St. Catherine's decided their "oriental" intern experiment was working out well, and asked if there were any more like my father "out there"—so the next year Julius Sue, a Chinese American medical school classmate (and by coincidence the Marumoto family's first-floor neighbor) also made the move from Oregon to Indiana. In the meantime, Mary Marumoto was 2,000 miles away. From a distance the young doctor began to focus his thoughts on marriage and a family of his own. Of course the war would soon change everything.

Among Dad's late-in-life convictions was that East Chicago turned out to be a good place for him and for our family. And years later, when I discovered that the graduate program that suited me best was at Indiana University I said to myself, well, what else is new? Even so, I see now that my father's forced absence from the place of his birth was a prelude to the sad diaspora brought on a few years later by removal and incarceration, the exile of all of the Japanese American families he had known as a boy in Portland, the destruction of the community that had nurtured him. In the meantime he was required to complete a medical residency, and he found one in Detroit, although "Eloise Hospital" turned out to be a capstone apprenticeship no status-conscious doctor would have sought: "Eloise" had been founded as the Wayne County Asylum and was part of a complex that included the former Wayne County Poor House.

FBI

Early on the morning of December 8, 1941, several hours before the United States formally declared it was at war with Japan, my father was awakened from the deep sleep of an overworked second-year resident by the administrative head of Eloise Hospital. "Doctor," he said, "there are a couple fellows from the FBI waiting to speak to you. I told them they could use my office...."

FBI AGENT: "Doctor, we need to interview you, and I assume you know why. . . ."

DR. NAKADATE: "Well, yes, I presume—"

FBI: "But let me just say right off that we already know a lot about you. We already know almost everything we need to. . . ."

DR. NAKADATE: "Oh . . . well—"

FBI: "You see, it turns out that one of the men here in our Detroit office has already told us about you and he says you're clean. Says he was a fellow Eagle Scout with you in Troop such-and-such in Portland, Oregon. Jim Kirby. So you don't have anything to worry about."

What were the odds? But once more my father had reason to appreciate his affiliation with the Boy Scouts of America, Troop 66, and Centenary Wilbur Methodist Church, his "all-American" associations. Between that day and his departure from Detroit he shared an occasional lunch with Jim Kirby and other agents—apparently never considering that those were also low-stress occasions for them to keep an eye on one of the few Japanese Americans in town. No telling who picked up the check.

But my father was more fortunate than most. In the hours and days immediately after the Pearl Harbor attack, FBI sweeps and the arrests of over 1,300 "suspicious individuals" disrupted Japanese communities up and down the West Coast and across the country. Suspicion of a "dangerous enemy alien" was often triggered by rumor, innuendo, ignorance, and misunderstanding—not by concrete evidence or specific acts committed. Longstanding connections with Japanese businesses or the Japanese government made a person suspect, even when those connections had to do with promoting trade or cultural understanding. Being an officer in the local *Nihonjinkai* or Japanese Association made one suspect. Being a Buddhist or Shinto priest or heading an arts organization made a person suspect. Teaching or writing the Japanese language (*haiku*, for example) made a person suspect, as did editing a Japanese-language newspaper. Having been heard speaking in public on politics or international relations made one suspicious. Or perhaps just being Japanese was enough to indicate that a person might well commit an act of espionage or sabotage. The U.S. government never felt it necessary to be specific about who was making an accusation, or to say just what it was that got a person arrested and sent away overnight to a remote Department of Justice prison. (Missoula, Montana; Santa Fe, New Mexico; and Crystal City, Texas were among the otherwise obscure locations that took on new meaning for some Japanese American families.)

So while my father had dodged the FBI bullet he was still under strict travel restrictions. He couldn't go anywhere near the West Coast and now had to worry about what might become of the belongings he had stored in Portland—clothing, camping gear, sports equipment, and baseball cards included—since he couldn't retrieve them anytime soon. (In fact they were never recovered.) And of course that also meant that any plans he and Mary Marumoto might have made would have to be put on hold.

The truth was that the government had for some time considered Japanese Americans a potentially disloyal lot and had had them under surveillance for months. Franklin Roosevelt had commissioned a special representative of the State Department to conduct an intelligence investigation regarding the loyalty of the Japanese in Hawaii and on the West Coast, and this was carried out in October and November 1941. In his report Curtis B. Munson described the Issei as "simple and dignified," roughly "lower middle class," and "about analogous to the pilgrim fathers"; he described the Nisei as eager "to be Americans" and "from 90 to 98 percent loyal to the United States." And Munson concluded that while sabotage by "imported agents" was possible, home-grown saboteurs were unlikely. His firm conclusion: "There is no Japanese 'problem' on the Coast. There will be no armed uprising of Japanese." What the FBI in Detroit knew about my father the government knew about Japanese America as a group.

Supporting Munson's report was another, from Lieutenant Commander K. D. Ringle, the Assistant District Intelligence Officer for the 11th Naval District in Los Angeles. Ringle concluded there was no "alien menace," that less than three percent (i.e., 300) of all Japanese Americans could be considered potential saboteurs, and that "in short, the entire 'Japanese Problem' has been magnified out of its true proportion, largely because of the physical characteristics of the people; that it is no more serious than the problems of the German, Italian, and Communistic portions of the United States population, and, finally that it should be handled on the basis of the individual, regardless of citizenship, and not on a racial basis." So the FBI sweeps and wide-ranging arrests after Pearl Harbor were an overreaction according to the government's own findings. Even more so were the impending evacuation and incarceration.

But the Munson and Ringle reports were suppressed by the government, so they could not do for the Japanese Americans as a whole what Kirby's testimony had done for my father. The U.S. had allowed a "surprise" attack by a country that had already shown itself to be ambitious, militaristic, predacious, and clearly disingenuous in recent diplomatic talks. The fleet of Japanese planes approaching Hawaii on American radar had been misidentified. So pressure was intense on both the military and the White House to respond to the attack, to explain how it could have happened, to allay American fears by doing *something*. And in 1942—as at times before and since, when it has been advantageous to use flawed or unsubstantiated "intelligence" or to manipulate or ignore the facts—the government pushed aside the rule of law. Withholding from the public the findings of Munson and Ringle, the Roosevelt Administration bowed to political agendas and brute pragmatism and used "military necessity" as a blanket justification for its actions against a racially stigmatized population of legal residents, two thirds of them American citizens. And with irresponsible eagerness many editorial writers, political cartoonists, and ambitious politicians joined the parade.

The anti-Asian lobbyists and politicians of the West Coast had wanted to rid America of the "Yellow Peril"—especially of those who occupied what was increasingly valuable West Coast crop land—and now, at least when it came to the Japanese, they were about to get their way.

"FEAR ITSELF" AND EXECUTIVE ORDER 9066

Bad is final in this light.

—WALLACE STEVENS, "NO POSSUM, NO SOP, NO TATERS"

In issuing Executive Order 9066 on February 19, 1942, Franklin Roosevelt authorized the establishment of West Coast military zones "from which any or all persons may be excluded," and on March 2 the Western Defense Command declared the western half of Oregon and the western two thirds of

"Waiting for the Signal from Home." Cartoon by Dr. Seuss, first published in *PM* (New York), February 13, 1942.

Washington and California to be Military Area 1, divided into "prohibited" and "restricted" zones. The U.S. Army would decide who was a threat to national security, who had to move or be removed as a "military necessity," who would be arrested and detained. And why. This was the beginning of Roosevelt's deferral of responsibility for Japanese American lives to military leaders, a surrender of civil authority that would eventually extend to the Supreme Court. All civilians within the military zone would now be vulnerable to the biases and decisions of whoever was charged with crafting exclusion policies and procedures—though as it turned out, only Japanese Americans would suffer en masse because of them. "Who," it seemed reasonable to ask, "who is 'the Western Defense Command'?"

The attack on Hawaii created understandable concern for the vulnerability of the West Coast, but the heightened fear of espionage or sabotage by Japanese Americans was never justified. Hoover's FBI report and Lt. Commander Ringle's Naval Intelligence report had independently confirmed that Japanese Americans were overwhelmingly loyal to the United States. In January 1942 the Roberts Commission's report to Congress on the disaster at Pearl Harbor was highly critical of the military command but nowhere suggested the involvement of Japanese Hawaiians or Japanese Americans.

"Wartime hysteria" may have affected parts of the general population, but how could hysteria trump both prior intelligence and the rule of law within the Roosevelt Administration itself? In fact, Attorney General Francis Biddle advised caution for fear that mass evacuation of a race-identified group would violate Fifth Amendment rights, and Eleanor Roosevelt argued that forced evacuation would violate human rights. Both were pushed aside by Roosevelt in favor of Lt. General John L. DeWitt, Colonel Karl Bendetsen, Secretary of War Henry L. Stimson, and Assistant Secretary of War John J. McCloy. Bendetsen (alternately, Bendetson), who held a law degree from Stanford and was on the Judge Advocate General's staff, was the primary architect and memorandum drafter of the evacuation arguments and policies. DeWitt, who had been put in charge of the Western Defense Command in 1939 after rising in the ranks through the Quartermaster Corps, was its military face, advocate, and transmission agent. Stimson and McCloy explained to Roosevelt the merits of selective (not mass) evacuation based on sensitive locations and the legal distinction between the citizen Nisei and the alien Issei, but never got a clear response. In the end they were led to believe that Roosevelt would sign an executive order that would support the plan once the War Department had set it in motion.

As the push for exclusion and incarceration moved forward it became apparent that crucial determinations were coming from desks that were several degrees of legal separation away from the Oval Office, and in the hands of military bureaucrats who could claim "military necessity" but had no legal training (DeWitt) or ignored the legal training they had (Bendetsen). In his 1933 inaugural address Roosevelt had told the country, "the only thing we have to fear is fear itself." In 1942 Japanese Americans had every reason to fear the indiscriminate fear of other Americans, the fabricated fear of

Roosevelt's military advisors, and Roosevelt's own fear of bucking West Coast nativists, lobbyists, and politicians who had no concern for the U.S. Constitution.

Lt. General DeWitt argued that evacuation and incarceration were necessary as a matter of national security—that is, "military necessity." But for justification all he could offer were hearsay, rumor, innuendo, and public paranoia. When asked if there was any hard evidence of sabotage by Japanese Americans that would justify his argument, he answered that it was precisely the absence of any acts of sabotage that "proved" the Japanese were simply lying in wait for the right moment to commit them. It followed from this that preventive detention of the entire Japanese American population would preclude such future actions. When others pointed out that the Issei were legal resident aliens (immigrant noncitizens) and the Nisei were American citizens by birth who had civil and constitutional rights, DeWitt famously replied, "A Jap's a Jap." Any problems with suspect German or Italian Americans could be handled on an individual basis, he said, but the Japanese were "an enemy race" that would prove worrisome "until wiped off the map." DeWitt's almost overnight public posting of the evacuation notices, from Bainbridge Island in Washington to San Diego, showed just how soon he wanted to make this happen. He imposed mandatory "evacuation"—eviction by another name—on a seven-day schedule, from first notice to departure.

Roosevelt's acceptance of DeWitt's opinions as if they were fact served to deflect public focus away from the disaster at Pearl Harbor and the defensive breakdowns of the Western Defense Command—and onto Japanese Americans. But the conduct of DeWitt, Bendetsen, and others was biased and self-serving at best, racist and hostile at worst. And Roosevelt's acceptance of DeWitt's sweeping enforcement of curfew and exclusion on the Japanese but not the other "enemy" ethnic groups was an acceptance of racism as a tool for implementing policy. Congress, marching to the same unconstitutional drumbeat, soon passed legislation that supported Roosevelt's executive orders and, in effect, DeWitt's implementation of them. Most white Americans were willing to sacrifice civil liberties in the name of national security—as long as they were the civil liberties of someone else.

Soon enough, "A Jap's a Jap" and the evacuation order's "all persons of Japanese ancestry, both alien and non-alien" came to mean over 110,000 disrupted lives—all injured, some ruined. It meant legal resident aliens and American-born citizens (DeWitt called them "non-aliens" in order to blur the distinction) who had been charged with no offenses. It meant individuals who were at least 1/16th Japanese. It meant the very young and the very vulnerable, the elderly and the ill. It meant Nisei civil servants up and down the Coast who had been summarily dismissed after Pearl Harbor, simply for "being Japanese." It meant people who would suffer the loss or panic sale of everything from farms and fishing boats to vehicles, home appliances, and store inventories. It meant orphans and foster children, even when the charitable institutions or families involved asked that they not be removed. (Where were they being taken? When would they return?) It meant the 20 Nisei studying at the University of Oregon, and hundreds more at other West Coast colleges and universities, some of whom would never complete their educations. It meant Chiaki "Jack" Yoshihara, a friend of my parents and a member of the Oregon State football team, who was not allowed to travel and play in the 1942 Rose Bowl even when it was moved to North Carolina. It meant my grandparents, who had to leave the Oregonian Hotel and lose a lifetime of savings in the process. And their daughter, my mother, who, even if she had found a way to avoid being locked up, would not abandon her aging parents.

"Camp," then, was actually a flurry of punches, a series of shocks and insults, not a single experience or discrete event. A brief opportunity for "voluntary resettlement" appeared shortly after Pearl Harbor for those who could make plans almost overnight, but forced evacuation wasn't far behind for all those who had had no options or were simply too slow in getting out. And then forced removal necessarily led to the belated practical question of "relocation": where were 110,000 uprooted people now going to live? At first they were put in so-called "assembly centers" such as the Santa Anita and Tanforan racetracks in California and the Pacific International Livestock Exposition Center in Portland. And a few months later they were moved again, by train and bus, to hastily constructed camps with badly built housing, and in locations where they were not particularly wanted. After all, once the West Coast had rejected them, why wouldn't anyplace else? In Colorado, Governor Ralph Carr said that since Japanese Americans had to do their part by leaving their homes, the least Colorado could do was welcome them. But his call for tolerance and a commitment to human rights—in the face of vocal resistance and a flock of "Japs keep moving" billboards—cost him his political career. In any event the federal government placed a major "relocation center" at Granada, Colorado, and built nine similar facilities in six other states: Manzanar and Tule Lake in California, Topaz in Utah, Poston and Gila River in Arizona, Heart Mountain in Wyoming, Rohwer and Jerome in Arkansas, and Minidoka in Idaho. Each was designed to hold at least 10,000 "evacuees." All of this, from eviction notices to barbed wire incarceration, constituted the experience called "camp."

Going forward the Roosevelt Administration would find itself trying to put civil rights toothpaste back in the tube, if only at the level of lip service and platitudes, and making gestures at catching up with America's claim to being a democracy. When Roosevelt authorized the creation of the all-Nisei 442nd Regimental Combat Team less than a year after signing Executive Order 9066, he asserted (with no apparent irony) that "the principle on which this country was founded and by which it has always been governed is that Americanism is a matter of the mind and heart; Americanism is not, and never was, a matter of race or ancestry." But "progress" was perfunctory, fitful, and slow. Even when the now-landmark court cases of Minoru Yasui, Gordon Hirabayashi, Fred Korematsu, and Mitsuye Endo pressed the question. Social historians would later observe that Japanese Americans may have been the only minority group that failed to improve its overall condition by taking advantage of the social changes and economic opportunities brought about by World War II.

THINGS ADD UP: CIVICS LESSON, PART 3

No person shall be . . . deprived of life, liberty, or
property, without due process of law. . . .

—FROM THE FIFTH AMENDMENT TO THE U.S. CONSTITUTION

The onset of war was just a convenient catalyst for accelerating an agenda that had been sustained by xenophobic and nativist propaganda, political demagoguery, exploitive journalism, unfair business practices, discriminatory housing covenants, and decades of prejudicial legislation. The Depression was still not over, and the scapegoat argument that immigrants from

Asia were responsible for many of the country's economic woes was still current. For the get-rid-of-foreigners lobby, forcing Japanese Americans off of "American property" would certainly be a step in the right direction.

Exclusion and incarceration were also the result of some old and supposedly "un-American" habits of mind that were given new expression in the mid-twentieth century. Some "evacuees" would observe that the "1/16th Japanese blood" rule to determine who would be removed and locked up was a legacy of the slavery-segregation system. Some would observe the irony that their "internment camps" were placed on reservations American Indians had been "relocated" to, and that all of them were on land that had been taken from native tribes during the previous century.

In 1942 there were laws linking citizenship to race and country of origin. There were laws limiting and then stopping Asian immigration, and forbidding naturalization. There were alien land laws and anti-miscegenation statutes, and policies that excluded "orientals" from membership in labor unions and civic organizations. And there were countless unwritten but tacitly understood anti-Asian and anti-"other" policies regarding employment, housing, and education. It was a shoddy and shameless network of race-based exclusionary practices, and no less despicable for having been put in place one decision at a time at state and local levels.

When faced with removal and imprisonment after the Pearl Harbor attack, the long-resident Issei were perplexed at being told that if they had been truly committed to the United States, they would certainly have become citizens. It angered the Nisei, many of whom had college degrees but had encountered prejudicial barriers to jobs and career development, to be told that they should have done more to integrate into the social and economic fabric of the country. It galled both groups to know that most other Americans had a far from perfect understanding of the laws under which they expected "others" to live.

1940　On June 29 President Franklin Roosevelt signs the Alien Registration Act (Smith Act), requiring that, in the name of national security, all noncitizen adult residents of the U.S. register with the government and be fingerprinted.

1941　On December 7 the Japanese Empire attacks Pearl Harbor, bringing the U.S. into World War II.

INSTRUCTIONS
TO ALL PERSONS OF
JAPANESE
ANCESTRY

Living in the Following Area:

All of the County of Clackamas, State of Oregon, and all of that portion of the County of Multnomah, State of Oregon, east of the west side of 122nd Avenue and the extension thereof, from the northern limits of the said county to the southern limits of said county.

Pursuant to the provisions of Civilian Exclusion Order No. 46, this Headquarters, dated May 6, 1942, all persons of Japanese ancestry, both alien and non-alien, will be evacuated from the above area by 12 o'clock noon, P. W. T., Tuesday, May 12, 1942.

No Japanese person living in the above area will be permitted to change residence after 12 o'clock noon, P. W. T., Wednesday, May 6, 1942, without obtaining special permission from the representative of the Commanding General, Northwestern Sector, at the Civil Control Station located at:

Administration Building,
Gresham Fair Grounds,
Gresham, Oregon.

Such permits will only be granted for the purpose of uniting members of a family, or in cases of grave emergency.

The Civil Control Station is equipped to assist the Japanese population affected by this evacuation in the following ways:

1. Give advice and instructions on the evacuation.
2. Provide services with respect to the management, leasing, sale, storage or other disposition of most kinds of property, such as real estate, business and professional equipment, household goods, boats, automobiles and livestock.
3. Provide temporary residence elsewhere for all Japanese in family groups.
4. Transport persons and a limited amount of clothing and equipment to their new residence.

The Following Instructions Must Be Observed:

1. A responsible member of each family, preferably the head of the family, or the person in whose name most of the property is held, and each individual living alone, will report to the Civil Control Station to receive further instructions. This must be done between 8:00 A. M. and 5:00 P. M. on Thursday, May 7, 1942, or between 8:00 A. M. and 5:00 P. M. on Friday, May 8, 1942.
2. Evacuees must carry with them on departure for the Assembly Center, the following property:
   (a) Bedding and linens (no mattress) for each member of the family;
   (b) Toilet articles for each member of the family;
   (c) Extra clothing for each member of the family;
   (d) Sufficient knives, forks, spoons, plates, bowls and cups for each member of the family;
   (e) Essential personal effects for each member of the family.

All items carried will be securely packaged, tied and plainly marked with the name of the owner and numbered in accordance with instructions obtained at the Civil Control Station. The size and number of packages is limited to that which can be carried by the individual or family group.

3. No pets of any kind will be permitted.
4. No personal items and no household goods will be shipped to the Assembly Center.
5. The United States Government through its agencies will provide for the storage, at the sole risk of the owner, of the more substantial household items, such as iceboxes, washing machines, pianos and other heavy furniture. Cooking utensils and other small items will be accepted for storage if crated, packed and plainly marked with the name and address of the owner. Only one name and address will be used by a given family.
6. Each family, and individual living alone, will be furnished transportation to the Assembly Center or will be authorized to travel by private automobile in a supervised group. All instructions pertaining to the movement will be obtained at the Civil Control Station.

**Go to the Civil Control Station between the hours of 8:00 A. M. and 5:00 P. M.,
Thursday, May 7, 1942, or between the hours of 8:00 A. M. and 5:00 P. M.,
Friday, May 8, 1942, to receive further instructions.**

J. L. DeWITT
Lieutenant General, U. S. Army
Commanding

SEE CIVILIAN EXCLUSION ORDER NO. 46

Poster for mandatory evacuation, Portland, Oregon, May 1942.

Roosevelt signs Proclamation 2525, stipulating conduct and restricting all travel by alien Japanese residents, and authorizing raids and arrests; approximately 2,000 Japanese community leaders in the U.S. and Hawaii, "deemed dangerous" by the Attorney General, are immediately arrested without charge and incarcerated in isolated Department of Justice facilities (labeled "internment camps").

1942 On January 14, Proclamation 2537 requires all aliens to report any change of address, employment, or name to the FBI.

On February 19, Roosevelt signs Executive Order 9066, authorizing the War Department to designate military exclusion zones on the West Coast and to remove potentially dangerous individuals.

On March 11, Executive Order 9095 establishes the Office of the Alien Property Custodian, with authority over all alien property, business and personal; many assets are frozen.

On March 18, Executive Order 9102 establishes the War Relocation Authority (WRA) to facilitate forced removal ("evacuation") under E.O. 9066.

On March 28, Minoru Yasui walks into the Portland, Oregon police station and demands that he be arrested for violating the curfew, Military Order Number 3.

On May 16, Gordon Hirabayashi walks into the Seattle FBI office to announce and explain his refusal to register for evacuation under Civilian Exclusion Order No. 57.

On May 30, Fred Korematsu is arrested by police in San Leandro, California for not reporting for evacuation.

On July 12, while living in the Tanforan Assembly Center before being sent to Tule Lake and then Topaz, Utah, Mitsuye Endo files a petition for a writ of habeas corpus with the Federal District Court in San Francisco.

By August 12, the forced evacuation and removal of over 110,000 people of Japanese ancestry to ten major "relocation centers" in interior states is completed.

3 ∽ Minidoka, 1942–1945

The promulgation of Executive Order 9066 was not justified by military necessity. . . . A grave injustice was done to Americans and resident aliens of Japanese ancestry who, without individual review or any probative evidence against them, were excluded, removed and detained by the United States during World War II.

—FROM *Personal Justice Denied: Report of the Commission on Wartime Relocation and Internment of Civilians* (1983)

OREGONIANS

Don't forget that a few years ago we came through the depression by the skin of our teeth! One more tight squeeze like that and where will we be?

—THORNTON WILDER, *The Skin of Our Teeth* (1942)

The Oregonian Hotel on the two upper floors at Third and Couch was a Japanese establishment situated on top of a Chinese business in a Romanesque Revival building and thus a paradigm of Portland's lower Alphabet District and a reflection of its history. The "Marumoto Hotel" and the Sue family's dry goods store downstairs also epitomized the goods-and-services economy and restricted livelihood options of an urban immigrant community.

The Oregonian Hotel was two floors of fading wallpaper in narrow hallways and 37 rooms for residents and transients, both individuals and entire families. It was mattresses and beds, tables and chairs, washstands and dressers, blankets and quilts, sheets and pillowcases, towels and curtains, carpets

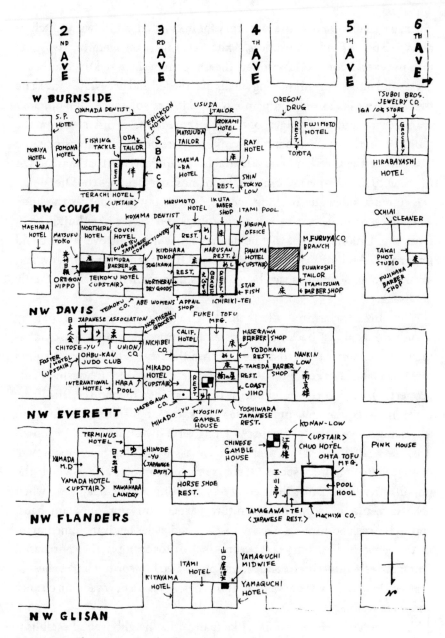

Japantown-Chinatown, Portland, Oregon, c. 1941.

and rugs, chamber pots. The inventory for 1942 listed 53 pillows, 31 pitchers and wash bowls, and 33 cuspidors. And a gas range, a refrigerator, a washing machine, and a commercial ironer. The Oregonian sheltered the overheard noises and intermingled cooking smells of crowded and necessarily intimate lives. Victrolas, a samisen, a piano, fried chicken, soy sauce, daikon, pork chops, bacon and eggs, ginger root. In this sense it was no different from the Quimby (in which the Marumoto children were born), the Greystone, the Teikoku, or the Overland—residential hotels in Portland that marked the Marumoto family's periodic moves. From most perspectives the Oregonian was unremarkable and nothing special. But for my grandfather the hotel was a big step away from railroad tent camps and the farm outbuildings in Baker and Union counties that he'd inhabited while being overworked and underpaid. And for my grandmother the Oregonian meant privacy, and several rooms of family space beyond the single room in which her family got its start.

When Eizo Hayashima sold them the Oregonian for $3,000 in 1927 my grandparents at last became owners and proprietors, with a sense of being in place, rather than sojourners within the city. But because Oregon's 1923 alien land law prohibited them from purchasing land or housing ("real property"), buying the hotel meant only that they owned the furniture, furnishings, equipment, and supplies necessary for operating a business in a building they could only lease. As a long-term investment the Oregonian was, like virtually all of the "oriental" businesses of Chinatown-Japantown, operating in temporary space. Of course the Marumotos also "owned" the opportunity to enhance their equity by painting and wallpapering when necessary, and by adding new furniture, carpets, curtains, linoleum, beds, and all the rest. Scrimping and day-to-day efficiencies made incremental reinvestment possible from year to year—in 1929, for example, they purchased four mattresses and three comforters, in 1931 two box springs and a chest of drawers, in 1937 a hot water tank and two rugs, in 1940 a new vacuum cleaner and some wallpaper.

The Oregonian Hotel was also like many other neighborhood establishments in being a family business where all hands were considered able and all hands stayed busy. And since hotel work was of a series of daily housekeeping tasks, the two sisters were expected to help their mother do it, with occasional assistance from younger brother Yosh. (Assisting with the laundry and other chores certainly made my mother look forward to a day when she would have only her own family's linen to worry about.) Once they were old enough, the Marumoto sisters also held outside jobs, clerical and retail; my mother clerked in a jewelry store and kept the books at the farmer's market. And since the hotel business was vulnerable to seasonal shifts and a transient clientele, my grandfather also had an ongoing job as a "valet"—under the "American" name "Frank"—at the upscale and exclusive University Club. The Marumotos saved and reused everything from string, rubber bands, and cardboard to paper that had only been printed on one side—establishing habits they would pass on to the next generation.

The combination of frugality, family enterprise, outside employment, and interwoven business relationships within the ethnic economy enabled the hotel to make it through the Depression years. The Oregonian was a storm cellar in an economic tornado, and it gave the family a sense of security and place in Portland, and Oregon, and the United States. One measure of this was their commitment to Christmas. Even at the end of the most dreary, touch-and-go years my grandparents found enough money for Christmas gifts, and they made sure there was something for everyone living in the hotel. I once asked my mother if that meant they had a gift for someone who was only there for one night, somebody they'd never see again. "Yes," she told me, "Grandma and Grandpa believed that no one should have Christmas without at least one present, even if it was just a new pair of socks." They were, after all, Christian, and this was, after all, America.

And that's where they were, what they had, and what they were thinking about on December 7, 1941—when the Issei went from being legal immigrants from Japan to "enemy aliens," and many who knew them no longer acknowledged them as friends, coworkers, and business associates. Neighbors in the now pathetically fractured Chinatown-Japantown community began to wear buttons that said, "I am Chinese." The Marumotos' sense of security and belief in an American future were overrun overnight by suspicion, hostility, and political calculation. The spirit of the place soured and the neighborhood began to undergo a radical—and, as it turned out, permanent—transformation.

On January 10, 1942, my grandparents received notice from the property management representative to vacate 105 NW Third Avenue "not later than February 10, 1942." Elmer Colwell had suddenly come up with another use for "this space" after that date, and his terse letter was all they would receive in explanation—although up and down the Coast it was obvious that eviction of Japanese American families was proxy retribution for what Japanese militarists had done half a world away. Some desperate communication between my mother and her brother stationed at Fort Ord led to a letter of earnest intervention from his commanding officer that convinced Colwell to cancel the eviction notice. "Kamish was his name," my uncle would recall years later, "Robert Kamish was my C.O. He was a good man."

Then in late January the Portland City Council began to revoke all business licenses issued to the Issei—thus rendering them unable to make a living. With her brother in the army and older sister recently hospitalized with tuberculosis, my mother was the only one in Portland who might stand between her family and financial catastrophe. So she applied for and received a license to operate the Oregonian in her own name, and on February 9 my grandfather ("a generally licensed Japanese National") sold to his daughter Mary ("a citizen of the United States of America") his entire investment in the hotel, "together with the Good Will of said business." For a purchase price of $10.00, they attempted to put the family's life savings in hands from which they could not legally be taken—a defensive strategy that meant my grandparents were setting aside some core prerogatives of gender and generation at the heart of their culture and sense of self. And from Seattle to San Diego similar desperate measures were taken, further contributing to the rude displacement of the Issei in an America that hardly wanted to recognize even their U.S.-born children as "real Americans."

But on February 19 Executive Order 9066 rendered irrelevant all of the family's efforts and any assumptions about due process—for legal immigrants and Japanese American citizens alike. A curfew to control all "enemy aliens" was selectively enforced on Japanese Americans. On May 6 mandatory evacuation orders were posted everywhere in Portland, with a deadline of noon on Tuesday, May 12. "All persons of Japanese ancestry" had one week to resolve all business matters and arrange for the immediate sale or indefinite storage of belongings. ("What about the car? The sewing machine? The furniture? All these clothes?"). They were told to pack "extra clothing" that would be appropriate for an unconfirmed destination, bedding and linens, toilet articles and table service, and "essential personal effects for each member of the family." But only what they could carry. It wasn't easy to dismantle and disperse an American dream item by item, working nonstop but in fear of violating the curfew, and under an obsessively suspicious public eye.

At least the Marumotos had no vehicles to worry about, and no family dog or cat to find a new home for. But within days of the Pearl Harbor attack my mother had been charged with destroying the small Shinto shrine that affirmed the Marumoto connection to ancestors and family. She broke it into pieces and burned them in the pot-bellied stove, along with a Japanese flag she found in a trunk. No one else would understand the heirloom value and intimate cultural significance of such "un-American" things.

My mother found reliable custodians for the piano, her typewriter, and some irreplaceable family memorabilia, and in this the family was more fortunate than many. (The government offered warehouse storage, but demanded a waiver of liability for any theft or damage that might occur.) Much of the rest of what the family owned was donated to the Salvation Army. That week's issue of *Time* magazine called this traumatic marker in Japanese American lives "Moving Day for Mr. Nisei," and observed (without apparent irony) that this "compulsory migration" would simply amount to a remote resettlement of "the Japs"—and "all they forfeit is their freedom." *Time* was merely one among many. It would become journalistic routine, as well as the norm in government publications and other domestic propaganda posing as "information," to present this mass eviction and imprisonment to the public euphemistically, as merely a wartime curiosity of incidental note.

In 1942 the Marumoto stake in the Oregonian Hotel was as much as $5,000. But in late April, on the verge of being "evacuated" to the Idaho desert, my mother was compelled to sell the remains of her family's investment for $1,100. The purchaser of their life's savings, "one Grace Empee" according to the documents, was among thousands up and down the Coast who profited from war, speculation, and the misfortune of dispossessed Japanese American families—a collective economic disaster that (at 1942 values) added up to roughly 150 million dollars in lost property alone. My grandfather, his life as insecure as it had ever been during his four decades in the United States, was almost 62, and my grandmother was 51.

In 1954, when my grandparents finally were able to file a claim for compensation under the vastly underfunded Japanese American Evacuation Claims Act, the government's response was perfunctory and inadequate— typical of what was offered to tens of thousands of others. They received a

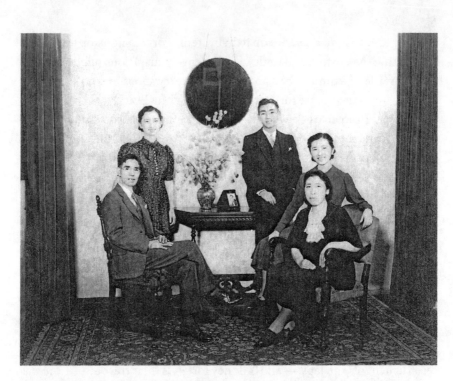

Marumoto family, Portland, Oregon, mid-1930s.

"compromise settlement" of $500, 10 percent of which went to the attorney they had to hire to submit the paperwork.

LOYALTY

Shortly after I turned 13 my aunt drew me away from some bickering horse-play with my siblings to remind me that I was now no longer Neil-chan, but *Oniisan* (oh-nee-ee-sahn), and not only the older brother, but now a young man. My role from then on would be to represent my family well and to set a good example for my siblings.

Three decades later Auntie Fumie took me aside again, this time simply to say, "Always remember, loyalty is important." If she had put this in Japanese, she might have said *chuugi* for "loyalty" and *shingi,* which also means "fidel-ity." By then I knew enough about her difficult life to make me pay attention, and not simply because she was *Oneesan* (oh-neh-eh-sahn), the older sister in her own family. She had endured enough to have a say about loyalty, the loyalty of close friends as well as loyalty to family and country. And she could still recall the many concerns regarding loyalty during the war, particularly at the beginning.

The Marumoto children had been fortunate that during their youth the family was befriended by several *hakujin* or "Caucasian" families and individuals in a Portland that was not always tolerant or welcoming to Asian immigrants. Civic organizations and labor unions, for example, were aggressively exclusive of "orientals" (as well as blacks)—and one of the tocsins of their xenophobia was that the loyalty of the Japanese to the United States could not be trusted. But younger brother Yoshiro was close to Clarence "Buddy" Oliver, a high school teacher who offered him an open house, with study space and recreation in the evening. Cora Oliver, aware that the boy was inclined to roam Japantown too freely for anybody's good, told him that if he and his friends wanted to play poker, they should play at the Oliver house, "not somewhere else." Fumie and my mother were mentored by Miss Mabel Downs during their adolescence and the years following. (The "Miss" became as much honorific as socially appropriate.) Miss Downs was Dean of Girls at Lincoln High School and also worked with the Fellowship of Reconciliation, a pacifist organization. And there was Miss Chase. Jane Chase worked in the local Episcopal bishop's office and was never without her English–Japanese phrase book. Her commitment to the Marumoto family became clear once Fumie was diagnosed with TB and hospitalized indefinitely. When internment removed Fumie's family first to the Portland Assembly Center and then to Idaho, Miss Chase became her regular link to a world she couldn't enter, taking the bus to visit Fumie at University Tuberculosis Hospital every Thursday for four years. Jane Chase was there when Fumie had to say goodbye to her five- and three-year-old daughters as they left for camp with their father. It was a time of emotional isolation when neither Fumie nor her parents could assist or comfort each other. Fumie made clear how she felt about her loyal friend by referring to her after that as "Miss Chase-*san*."

There were other non-Japanese friends of other Japanese American families, people whose friendship withstood the divisive forces turned loose by the war. Friends who promised they'd take care of your car or truck. Friends who helped make sure that the land you had been working would be there for you when you returned. Friends who would protect your church or temple from vandalism. Friends who took on the family pet as their own. Friends who promised that they would be there for you, too, and who insisted that you *would* be welcomed back. When forced evacuation came, Lincoln High friend Rae Hungerford and her family offered safe storage for some of the Marumoto possessions—photo albums, heirlooms, and legal and vital records. But loyal friends like the Olivers and the Hungerfords, Miss Downs and Miss Chase had to be ready to hear from others that they were "Jap lovers." My mother simply put it this way: "Those were the friends who were loyal to us when the war came and we had nowhere else to turn." There were, of course, the many others whom Japanese American families would find it difficult to speak to again.

For my family there would be one more hakujin who didn't blink: in late January 1944, when it appeared that my aunt would finally be discharged from the hospital, Fumie's doctor (no doubt with information and support from Miss Chase) told her that while she was well enough to be released and he knew she wanted to see her little girls, he was going to hold off a while on signing the papers, because "they'll just send you from here to that darn camp, and you'll get sick again." Not too long after that it became clear that the camps would soon be closing, so it turned out that she was the lone member of her family who never went to Idaho. Fumie died in 1999 at age 85, having by then also survived breast cancer. She was the first divorced, full-time working, single parent I ever knew, and she had stared down multiple adversities. I never knew her to be anything but sharper than a tack and tough as nails—what an earlier generation would have referred to (without her liking it) as one tough broad. And she made it clear to us how important it is to have friends whose loyalty is more than skin deep.

THE JAPANESE AMERICAN CITIZENS LEAGUE

I pledge myself to do honor to her at all times and in all places; to support her constitution; to obey her laws; to respect her flag; to defend her against all enemies, foreign or domestic; to actively assume my duties as a citizen, cheerfully and without any reservations whatsoever, in the hope that I may become a better American in a greater America.

—"JACL CREED" (1941)

The earliest venues for negotiating Japanese American life were religious and social organizations—organizations typical of immigrant communities across the country in being related to church missions, business relationships, homeland affiliations, and cultural concerns. These organizations served as places of refuge and legal consultation, informal financial institutions and recreation centers, and liaisons to consular offices. The 1900 Portland *City Directory* listed over two dozen such entities, including churches, clubs, and foreign-language newspapers—and ranging from the "Hebrew" to the German, Norwegian, Swedish, Danish, and Chinese. My maternal grandparents became members of the Japanese American Methodist Episcopal Church, which had been founded in 1893 as a Portland mission.

But the effective limits of Issei-dominated organizations eventually became obvious. A Christian church or Buddhist temple could be nurturing and comforting but not political, and certainly not "activist." And places of refuge reinforced passivity in the face of authority rather than engagement with the core concerns and activities of American democracy. Since the Issei were permanent legal aliens, their larger grievances had to be lodged through the Japanese consulate rather than state and local authorities— reason enough to remain in good standing with the one nation state that afforded them legal and diplomatic status. The Issei had also come from a culture without participatory democracy, and since they would apparently never have voting rights under American law, they had no motive or opportunity to engage with American politics. Unlike the New York and Boston Irish, who were sought out as potential constituents and drawn into local politics from the moment they arrived, the Issei were dismissed as irrelevant. They were simply a population politicians did not have to recognize, and in this respect they were like blacks in the South who were not allowed to register to vote.

In Portland, as elsewhere, the Nisei recognized that their parents had been legislated into political impotence and began to organize in order to take advantage of their own status as citizens. And by 1928 they had created a local chapter of the California-based Japanese American Citizens League (whose motivation and agenda paralleled those of the NAACP, as did its frustrations). The JACL was to be a public voice for the civil rights of Japanese Americans, working within the system to link the Japanese American narrative to the larger American story.

Yet in February 1942 the key social, cultural, educational, business, and mutual aid organizations of Japantown were still dominated by the Issei. And in 1942 the JACL was still coalescing from a group of local clubs that focused on sports and social events into a regional organization with a particular "political" focus on the Nisei as "American citizens of Japanese ancestry." When my mother and father (then still single) became members of the Portland chapter in the mid-1930s, "economic and vocational" matters were among the local chapter's concerns—meaning the difficulties Nisei faced when racial prejudice undermined job searches and career development. Some of the older Nisei also saw the Japanese American Citizens League as a vehicle for asserting their autonomy from their parents and determining the direction of their own lives, while for many Issei such younger-generation organizations were little more than an afterthought.

But the aggressive post–Pearl Harbor FBI sweeps of all "suspicious" community leaders deprived Japanese American communities of leadership. Teachers, journalists, priests, business leaders, individuals who traveled regularly to Japan, and other potential "enemy agents" were jailed and then transported overnight to remote Department of Justice detention camps. The remaining Issei, relabeled "enemy aliens," were powerless and voiceless, yet at the same time reviled and feared. Military and governmental authorities disdained and refused to deal with them. So the Nisei were drawn into the cultural and political vacuum created by the absence of Issei power. Of course the Nisei, too, were impugned at every turn, and for just that reason many were eager to prove that they were loyal American citizens.

Yet fulfilling their roles as citizens was still more concept than practice. The Nisei had their public school civics textbooks and the U.S. Constitution for starters, and they understood that they had rights, expectations, and obligations that their non-citizen parents did not, but many of them were too young to vote. And they had not routinely argued politics around the dinner table; financial concerns, cultural events, and education were the key focuses of their family conversations. So Japanese Americans as a whole did not have what later generations would call a mature and active political consciousness, and given its inexperience and youthful optimism the JACL's strategies were consistent with a belief in equality, a commitment to civil discourse, and faith in American justice. Those strategies were, perhaps predictably, often consistent with the Japanese approach to getting things done through patient discourse over time. Events were to show that JACL erred in assuming that the government's intentions and agenda ever bore any relationship to their own.

The limited political potential of the organization was put to a brutal and divisive test by Executive Order 9066, because the military and the War Relocation Authority saw the JACL as a tool for controlling Japanese Americans as a whole. Since the Nisei were bilingual, it was easy and advantageous for military and governmental authorities to insist on speaking and working through them. Authorities all but anointed the eagerly patriotic JACL as the most tractable and useful organization to speak for all Japanese Americans—even though its national membership only included about ten percent of even the Nisei. In discussions with government authorities JACL National President Saburo Kido and Executive Secretary Mike Masaoka were assertive regarding their capacity to represent all Japanese Americans and welcomed the increasing attention paid to the organization. But in the end, lack of political savvy and the absence of any true leverage probably ensured the pathos of the JACL. Some who cooperated with the government became eager informants for the FBI regarding potentially disloyal individuals—and then couriers to the Issei of government policies and edicts. But in trusting in their citizenship status to help them minimize if not avoid incarceration they were up against the racist irrationality of "a Jap's a Jap." It has become clear that the JACL was led to believe that its "negotiations" with authorities might somehow alter events until it became obvious that the organization's true role would be simple and bleak—to expedite the passive removal and incarceration of over 110,000 people. Kido, Masaoka, and the JACL were manipulated and outmaneuvered, victims to some extent of their inexperience. After the war the JACL would mature into a more politically astute and effective civil rights organization, but the record suggests that in 1942 it was doomed to be overwhelmed and exploited by a government that had its own agenda and was determined to impose it from the start.

THE BIG THREE: KOREMATSU, HIRABAYASHI, YASUI

Deru kugi wa utareru: a nail that sticks up can be hammered down.

—JAPANESE PROVERB

For many years after removal and incarceration the resistance and other disruptive conduct of a relatively small minority of Japanese Americans went largely unacknowledged and unappreciated by the rest. The majority wanted "internment" to become a thing of the past, and found ways to repress feeling and expression. Those who had eschewed confrontation or disruption in acceding to evacuation and imprisonment saw little benefit in revisiting traumatic events, some of which had included Japanese-on-Japanese violence behind barbed wire. That others had resisted was a reminder of divisive intra-family conflicts and unhealed emotional wounds. Those who had served in the military found it hard to understand how the draft-refusals of the so-called No-No boys were an expression of patriotism or a challenge to democracy. My father, with his conviction that emergencies call for practical deeds, once said that those who went to jail for refusing the draft could have served instead as medical corpsmen. When acknowledged, the resisters were often cast as anomalous and embarrassing "troublemakers." Their right to protest was granted, of course, but their contrarian behavior, even when nonviolent, was too high-profile and awkwardly public for many. Individuals who had bucked the system were nails in the collective memory that could be hammered down, like harsh memories from the camps themselves. It would take another generation to start pulling them up.

The nonconformists included three Nisei men who intended their nonviolent civil disobedience to lead to test cases in the courts. Minoru Yasui, Gordon Hirabayashi, and Fred Korematsu are as obscure to most Americans as the 1945 Yalta cohort of Roosevelt, Churchill, and Stalin is famous. But the Japanese American civil liberties cases that came before the Supreme Court in 1943 and 1944—along with *Ex parte Mitsuye Endo,* which focused on the habeas corpus clause in the U.S. Constitution—present some fundamental legal questions that continue to demand attention and concern. The cases also show how much the American legal system, including the Supreme Court, wanted to avoid addressing precisely those questions. And the Yasui, Hirabayashi, and Korematsu cases help us see in perspective the relative passivity of most Japanese Americans in the face of "relocation." They help us understand the socially and philosophically diverse—and therefore fundamentally American—qualities of Japanese American lives.

My father knew the flourishing Yasui family of Hood River through mutual friends who were orchardists in nearby Parkdale, and my mother knew

Minoru Yasui through her work with the Portland chapter of JACL. (In any case there were only 2,454 Nisei in Oregon in 1940, and the younger adult Nisei were generally aware of each other as comprising a modest pool of prospective partners.) Min Yasui was a graduate of the University of Oregon law school. He was strong-willed, at times quixotic, and driven by a belief in the U.S. Constitution. And like many underemployed college-educated Nisei, he found that getting a good education was not enough. For many people, a Nisei attorney was more of a curiosity than a desirable new hire. In order to further his career, Min Yasui had to use family connections to eventually get a position with the Japanese consulate in Chicago. That is, a Nisei who saw himself part of the larger American story found himself working for the Japanese government. (Of course my mother had had the same employer, in Portland, when she succeeded her sister as governess to Consul Nakamura's children.)

On the evening of March 28, 1942, Yasui walked around downtown Portland for a while and at 11 PM turned himself in at the police station for breaking Lt. General DeWitt's 8:00 AM to 6:00 PM coast-wide curfew. Yasui felt the curfew should not apply to American citizens and (if necessary at all) should be uniformly enforced against all "enemy aliens" and not just the Japanese. His trial began on June 12, and on November 16 the judge convicted him of curfew violation and sentenced him to a year in jail and a $5,000 fine—having first erroneously ruled that simply by working for the Japanese government the defendant had forfeited his U.S. citizenship. That is, the court avoided ruling on the legitimacy of the curfew orders that Yasui had wanted to test. Min Yasui was 25. To continue to challenge the curfew he had to appeal, ultimately to the Supreme Court. The JACL distanced itself from the case; it was not interested in legal proceedings that presented Nisei as uncooperative, as anything but "100 percent loyal."

Gordon Hirabayashi, a Quaker who had been granted conscientious objector status, was 24 years old when he challenged the evacuation order itself. He had just begun his senior year at the University of Washington, where he was active in the YMCA and peace-and-justice organizations. On May 16, 1942, he and his lawyer entered the Seattle FBI office and handed an agent a statement that explained his refusal to register for evacuation by citing his Christian principles and his country's "democratic standards." Hirabayashi sat in jail for five months before his case was heard, and then by a judge who voiced inordinate fears of a Japanese attack on the West Coast. With these fears as his premise Judge Lloyd Black rejected the claim that the evacuation order violated Hirabayashi's constitutional rights under the Fifth and Fourteenth Amendments. Black instructed the jury to rule solely on whether the defendant had violated the curfew and failed to report for evacuation. Gordon Hirabayashi was found guilty and sentenced to identical concurrent sentences of 90 days, which he would appeal, ultimately to the Supreme Court.

Fred Korematsu was arrested in San Leandro, California, in May 1942 for not having reported for evacuation under Exclusion Order No. 34. He was a 23-year-old welder who had learned a year earlier that for medical reasons he was ineligible for military service and who simply wanted to go on with his life and perhaps marry his Italian American girlfriend. Ida Boitano was not subject to evacuation, but given California's anti-miscegenation law they were forced to consider a new start in another state. Even prior to the evacuation orders Korematsu had paid for cheap, ultimately ineffective plastic surgery in an attempt to blur his ethnicity and "pass" as a non-Japanese. But once his true "racial identity" was determined he was charged and convicted despite his assertion that he was a loyal citizen whose removal and imprisonment were based on his race and not justified by due process. His case also eventually found its way to the Supreme Court.

The Yasui and Hirabayashi cases were argued in May 1943, and on June 21 the Supreme Court ruled unanimously in both that a curfew imposed on a specific minority group, including citizens, was constitutional, given wartime concerns and conditions. In effect the court accepted the *fear* of potential domestic attacks as valid justification, as well as the unfounded and highly emotional anti-Japanese arguments concerning "wartime necessity" that Lt. General DeWitt had used in justifying his policies in the first place. Because the Supreme Court was required only to rule on one of the charges for which Hirabayashi had been given identical concurrent sentences, it focused only on his curfew violation and avoided addressing the constitutionality of the evacuation itself—the issue on which Hirabayashi had made it a point of getting himself arrested. But the U.S. Constitution was an elephant in the room. Reservations were voiced by Justices William O. Douglas, Wiley Rutledge, and Frank Murphy—and Murphy's statement in concurring with the majority had all the implications of a dissent.

Korematsu v. United States was argued in October 1944 (along with *Ex parte Mitsuye Endo*) and on December 18 the Supreme Court ruled 6–3 in support of the government's position. In this case, too, the majority leaned heavily on the president's powers as commander-in-chief and the military's need to ensure national security in justifying the removal of Japanese Americans from their homes. Yet the majority opinion was a product of rhetorical ju-jitsu, if not legerdemain. And in this decision Justices Owen Roberts, Robert Jackson, and Murphy dissented outright. Murphy was a reliable supporter of Roosevelt's New Deal agenda. But he was also a minority of one as the only Catholic on the Court, and had served earlier as Mayor of Detroit, Governor of Michigan, and U.S. Attorney General—all along strongly supporting social service and legal aid initiatives, workers' rights, and civil liberties. And after what had apparently been agonies of compromise in discussing the Yasui and Hirabayashi cases, Murphy had had enough:

> I dissent, therefore, from this legalization of racism. Racial discrimina-
> tion in any form and in any degree has no justifiable part whatever in
> our democratic way of life. It is unattractive in any setting but it is utterly
> revolting among a free people who have embraced the principles set
> forth in the Constitution of the United States. All residents of this na-
> tion are kin in some way by blood or culture to a foreign land. Yet they
> are primarily and necessarily a part of the new and distinct civilization
> of the United States. They must accordingly be treated at all times as the
> heirs of the American experiment and as entitled to all the rights and
> freedoms guaranteed by the Constitution. (*Korematsu v. United States*:
> 323 U.S. 214 [1944])

Not surprisingly, the unavoidably divisive Korematsu case was scheduled for the same day as *Ex parte Mitsuye Endo*, the one Japanese American case that government lawyers believed they could lose. And losing *Endo* would mean losing justification for maintaining the camps. It was no coincidence that the *Korematsu* decision came one day after the government announced that the camps, now clearly unnecessary as well as possibly unconstitutional, would be closing the following year. Or that the closure announcement from the Roosevelt administration, bound to be unpopular with West Coast vot-ers, had itself been delayed until after the 1944 elections.

In looking at the Yasui, Hirabayashi, and Korematsu cases it is worth noting these ironic contrasts: In acceding with little resistance to the government's demand that they evacuate their homes and enter the camps—thus "proving" their loyalty to the United States—the vast majority of Issei and Nisei were responding collectively and in a passive manner more typical of Japanese than American culture. In demanding their rights in court Minoru Yasui, Gordon Hirabayashi, and Fred Korematsu were conducting themselves in a fundamentally American way, as freestanding individuals asking for justice under the U.S. Constitution. And in using racial condemnation and manipulating the legal system to deprive Japanese Americans of those rights the United States was employing prejudice and coercion of the kind it was supposedly fighting overseas.

The legal cases of the Big Three differed in their origins but their proceedings were all disfigured by politics, misrepresentation, fabrication, and fear. There was some assistance from the American Civil Liberties Union but diffident support at best from the JACL. Yasui, Hirabayashi, and Korematsu all lost in 1943 and 1944 after Sisyphean struggles to resolve their cases. But they were vindicated by the Endo case, by history, and, 40 years later, in the courtroom, when the 1983 report from the Commission on Wartime Relocation and Internment of Civilians energized the movement for redress.

EVACUATION, ASSEMBLY, EXILE (FAMILY #15272)

After Roosevelt's Executive Order 9066 and Lt. General DeWitt's Civilian Exclusion Order 34 my mother and her parents, the Marumoto family, formerly of the Oregonian Hotel, became evacuated Family #15272, under the jurisdiction of the Wartime Civil Control Administration. The bureaucratic embrace of the just-created WCCA was hardly welcome. The government had already declared the Issei to be "enemy aliens" and Nisei students had been dismissed from their colleges and universities. Issei and Nisei alike had been summarily fired from their jobs and business licenses had been cancelled, creating first financial distress, then resignation and despair. And legal aliens and citizens alike were being attacked on the street. Many Japanese Americans were told that it served them right—after what "they" did at Pearl Harbor.

For a few weeks after the West Coast restricted zones were designated, a scattering of individuals and families who had cash, mobility, and a firm destination were allowed to move eastward on their own. But what would become of the rest? The average age of the Nisei was 19, and the typical Issei was over 50, so many families were comprised of the citizen young and the "alien" old, tied together by need and obligation. And what, for example, of the pregnant and the ill? Foster children and orphans? And those merely poverty-stricken, still on the ropes because of the lingering Great Depression? They all had little choice but to hope for the best.

But the Roosevelt administration was playing the politics of the moment, apparently agreeing that the United States had a "resident Japanese problem." So a sequence of increasingly restrictive policies was created on the fly, unjustified by military intelligence or rational goals. Japanese Americans were told repeatedly that any refusal to obey government orders would constitute obvious "evidence" of disloyalty—if only an intention to distract authorities and undermine the nation's war effort. The administration had also gotten ahead of itself, and now had to find somewhere to put 110,000 civilians it had labeled a threat to national security. Who among Roosevelt's military advisors was prepared to acknowledge that misdirected zeal and flawed or misinterpreted intelligence had led to statements and decisions that seemed less defensible by the day? Who among Washington politicians, from the White House down, was ready to say in public that the forced migration now underway had raised some serious Constitutional questions? And who among the race-baiters, oriental exclusionists, and war profiteers who were snapping up "evacuation sale" or "abandoned" property wanted either military or civilian authorities to stop what they were doing?

Japanese Americans were being told that it was for their own well-being that they were now dispossessed and about to be shipped out—they were supposedly being protected from racist attacks. (More than a few of the victims, my mother included, had the temerity to ask why the authorities didn't arrest the attackers instead.) They were a small statistical minority and (as the government knew) not a dangerous one, but by May 1942 racism, exploitation, and political expediency had outrun reason and law.

Those familiar with the protest movements and civil disobedience strategies that have evolved since the mid-twentieth century are often puzzled by the apparent passivity and docile cooperation of Japanese Americans in the face of "evacuation" and "relocation." But hindsight suggests a complex mixture of reasons. The attack on Pearl Harbor had created not only anger and vexation but also a disabling conflict within and across the generations of Japanese Americans—Japan, the country of their cultural heritage and traditions, the country where they had parents and grandparents, siblings in college, and many other relatives, was at war with the U.S., the country of their aspirations and commitment. The FBI sweeps had deprived communities of many proven and trusted leaders—just when those communities needed leaders to help them address unprecedented challenges. Many of the remaining Issei, brought up in a culture where social hierarchy and respect for authority were fundamental, could accept resigned obedience to their government as a necessity: "*Shikata ga nai,*" they were to say many times over before it all ended, "it can't be helped, nothing can be done." Furthermore, many Issei were financially wounded—their property had been confiscated and their assets frozen by the Office of the Alien Property Custodian (Executive Order 9095). For most Nisei, participatory democracy was still largely an abstract conviction, not a lived experience. Meanwhile, the 8:00 PM to 6:00 AM curfew was imposed on "all persons of Japanese ancestry" in the restricted zones (Military Proclamation No. 3, March 24, Lt. Gen. DeWitt). And a few days later "all persons of Japanese ancestry" were prohibited from leaving Military Area No. 1 (Proclamation No. 4, DeWitt, again). And when the angry and bewildered lined up to register for their involuntary evacuation, there was always an armed soldier nearby to watch them do it. Given all this, "passivity" is not hard to explain.

The "assembly center" in which the Marumotos and 3,673 others from Portland and central Washington lived for over three months was the hastily converted Pacific International Livestock Exposition Pavilion, in North Portland, a stone's throw from the Columbia River. The 18 assembly centers, from Puyallup, Washington ("Camp Harmony") to Santa Anita and Arcadia in California, were merely holding pens for people, and many were crudely converted facilities that had been designed for animals. In Portland, families were crowded into stalls or plywood cubicles set up in the exhibition space. Writing to her sister my mother initially referred to their cubicle as a "room"—at first furnished only with cots. The Marumoto family's move-in was greeted by a light bulb hanging from a cord—and in the glare of that naked bulb my mother could see that her life had truly taken a significant turn.

She had grown up an unburdened middle child, and she had gotten used to that role. But in the spring of 1942 brother Yosh was in the army and could only help with family affairs from a distance. And since January Fumie had been confined in University State Hospital as a semi-isolated tuberculosis patient. That left "just Mary" to oversee the piecemeal dismantling of their lives. "Kenny Simpson says they can store my typewriter," she wrote to Fumie, "and Rae Hungerford can take some [of] our other things. Maybe the Hansons still have room for the piano. . . ." Suddenly, she was about to shepherd her parents from eviction to incarceration, and try to mitigate the physical and emotional effects of life in "camp"; to confide in Fumie her concerns about their younger brother, who was being shuffled from one new venue to another by the army; and to help Fumie's husband Jiro care for two young daughters. Mary's role was, necessarily and increasingly, to be her family's spokesperson and its pivotal correspondent. At least she had a fluid, practiced longhand, a fountain pen, an apparently bottomless inkwell, and more time on her hands to write than she really wanted.

With scant access to a telephone, my mother wrote to sister Fumie on a constant basis, and her assembly center (and later, internment camp) letters were a blend of fact and gossip, observation and report, and sisterly confidences—all rendered with sympathy, tact, and respect: "Dearest Oneesan," she would begin, "dearest older sister." The rhetorical challenge was to encourage Fumie to "get well quick" so she could rejoin her family—but urge her not to leave the hospital prematurely and invite a relapse. "Hope this letter finds you in the best of health as is possible," she wrote in her first letter, "I'm sure that you'll improve much faster at the hospital, as there are too many people [and] noise [and] confusion here right now." She also had to keep Fumie informed of the children's health—but needed to sublimate or put off any news that might cause worry. And sister Mary also had to keep clear that, while she was vigilant and could make everyday decisions for Michi and Yuri, she saw herself only as a loving caregiver-aunt, not the girls' substitute mother: "They told us today kindergarten will start Monday also other schools. Planning to send Michi. Will wait for Yuri as she's a little too small, don't you think?" So as Fumie Sakano tried to regain the weight she had lost to her illness and slowly progressed from total bed rest to "sit-time" to brief periods of standing and walking, she read from miles away about Michi's chicken pox and Yuri's eczema, the girls' pastimes and playmates, holiday celebrations (Independence Day!) and birthday parties, and the first day of school.

With its start-from-scratch playgrounds and schools, its improvised post office and infirmary, its public bathrooms and showers, the assembly center was a work in progress—and a sad precursor of the camp in Idaho. There were no furnishings, certainly no creature comforts except for the few household items that "evacuees" might have saved from the bargain-hunters and managed to bring along—"the table, chairs, radio, lamp, rug are certainly useful," my mother wrote. And there were items cobbled together from salvage and scrap. (Soon enough there would be only cobbling, no "bringing along" to Idaho.) There was little privacy, given "apartments" with eight-foot walls and no ceilings, and the loss of privacy was heightened by the awkwardness of being thrown together not only with friends and former neighbors, but with total strangers—other Japanese Americans, to be sure, but people with whom they had little in common. "We have a tag on Yuri," my mother wrote, "so in case she gets lost, anyone can bring her in. I'm glad the children don't play with strangers. We're watching them pretty closely, at first anyway." There were mass meals in dining halls, which meant the loss of family time and occasions for intimate conversation or complaint.

There were contradictions and paradoxes, too. Family members—even my supposedly dangerous "enemy alien" grandparents—were allowed to leave the center in a military vehicle for brief visits to Fumie, though as some evacuees began to take liberties and restrictions increased, the family had to fine-tune its requests: "In order to get permission to go Saturday," my mother wrote Fumie, "will you have your doctor write Dr. S. that for the safety of the people here as well as of [other] individuals, he believes we should be examined at the University Hospital. . . ." But mostly there was unwanted idleness and a need to affirm one's value through meaningful work. "Have been offered good secretary jobs," my mother wrote, "but am taking my time getting settled and besides the children need watching and care and I'd rather do that. . . ." There was always this conflict between what Mary Marumoto might do for her family and what might be possible for her as an individual. Of course, thinking of oneself as a freestanding American citizen was difficult for anyone who had been herded and locked up by reason of race. Meanwhile life went on, even in the assembly centers; children were born, and old people died.

My father, completing his medical training in East Chicago and Detroit, was part of the outside world, and late in the spring of 1942 he decided to make the most of it. Any tentative plans he and my mother had once discussed had been rendered moot; he couldn't travel to Oregon, and now she was about to be sent to Idaho. So on June 23 my mother found herself writing to Fumie, "Kats surprised me with a special delivery air mail advising me to try to leave camp and join him as soon as possible (if that's what I want) before more restrictions are placed on us. Have talked to the folks and the Olivers . . . and everyone is of the opinion that it's best to make my decision and try to get out." Since living together unmarried was a cultural impossibility, this "advice" was a proposal that they marry in Indiana, in the absence of her parents. My mother's habit of subordinating her own feelings and interests (a habit she would never quite set aside) made her delay this announcement until after several pages of news and chatter, and even then she framed it with concern for how her leaving might affect the family: "[Permission to leave] would probably take a few months anyway, so I'm hoping that we would be relocated by that time so I'd know how conditions are in our new center. If only you could join the children there then it would be just perfect. So please, don't worry and try to get well quick." Yet how telling was her next sentence, so qualified and understated: "Now that I've made my decision to get married as soon as permission is granted, I'm rather looking forward to my new life." Of course, with her parents and friends locked up in Idaho, and her brother in the military and her sister an invalid in Portland, her wedding would hardly resemble what she'd once dreamed and planned.

To say that permission to leave was granted but that the bride-to-be deferred her departure ("Mother, of course, made so much fuss about my going so soon," she wrote Fumie), is to say something of Katsumi Nakadate's ongoing frustration. Early on he was able to channel his energy into writing letters of his own and marshaling the help of his local congressman to get his fiancée out of the relocation system sooner rather than later; finally, he just had to wait. In the meantime Mary Marumoto began to assuage her guilt by making sure that the Olivers, Hungerfords, Simpsons, and Jane Chase would provide Fumie with a steady stream of visitors. "I certainly hope you won't feel so lonely," my mother wrote Fumie, "Will promise to write more often." And she dared to begin planning a married life, outside: "I asked Mrs. Oliver to get some things I'll be needing later, a Community Plate—26 piece silverware set, the cheapest one—also several serving pieces of the better grade that I can always buy later and increase." And, as if an afterthought: "Decided to get my rings while I can and get a good one at wholesale, because I'll need it anyway. Must airmail Kats and tell him not to get them himself." The circumstances were already extraordinary, and from here on her responses to them might as well be, too.

Meanwhile, since the now-uprooted Japanese Americans were clearly (and embarrassingly) a civilian rather than a military concern, the Roosevelt administration handed them all over to a newly created War Relocation Authority, directed by Milton S. Eisenhower. The WRA would provide room, board, and incarceration, courtesy of the U.S. government. For Family #15272 this meant suffering the wind and dust of southern Idaho, though for how long, no one knew. The family's resources "for the duration" included my mother's savings and what was left of the $1,100 they had salvaged from the Oregonian Hotel.

By late summer the 550-mile move to Minidoka was imminent, and my mother's final assembly center letters moved briskly and were heavy on essentials. "Dear Oneesan," my mother wrote on August 23, "Am sorry our last visit was so brief. It's always so short, it seems. I never have time to tell you all I want to. I'm glad we went tho', because I'm not sure if I'll be able to go again. . . . [T]he Washington people will be leaving here on the 29th and 30th. The Portland people will be out beginning the sixth but we don't know just what day we will leave. . . . I hope you're fine and that you'll keep on gaining weight. There's nothing to worry about [regarding] us as we'll be fed and clothed and things will be much better in the new center after we get settled as it's going to be our permanent home for the duration. . . . Guess I'll apply for a travel permit from Idaho thru the W.R.A. I just hope it will be easier as I hate to go thru all the trouble again. . . ." The next day she added: "Received letter from Yoshiro this morning so am enclosing it also. Jiro-san found out he can go out tomorrow, but am mailing this letter anyway. I think the children will be going to see you, too. May be the last time before we leave. . . ." And in the midst of it all a passing personal comment: "Mrs. Oliver thinks it a good idea to announce my engagement before I leave here, so maybe I'll do that. After the Washington people leave, about the first. What

KEY

○ **ASSEMBLY CENTERS**
Puyallup, Wash.
Portland, Ore.
Marysville, Cal.
Sacramento, Cal
Tanforan (San Bruno), Cal.
Stockton, Cal.
Turlock, Cal.
Merced, Cal.
Pinedale, Cal.
Salinas, Cal.
Fresno, Cal.
Tulare, Cal.
Santa Anita (Arcadia), Cal.
Pomona, Cal.
Mayer, Ariz.

● **INCARCERATION CAMPS** (often
referred to as internment camps)
Minidoka, Ida.
Tule Lake, Cal.
Manzanar, Cal.
Heart Mountain, Wyo.
Granada, Colo.
Topaz, Utah
Poston, Ariz.
Gila River, Ariz.
Rohwer, Ark.
Jerome, Ark.

△ **DEPT. OF JUSTICE or WAR RELOCATION
AUTHORITY INTERNMENT CAMPS and
"ISOLATION CENTERS."**
Missoula (Fort Missoula), Mont.
Kooskia, Ida.
Bismarck (Fort Lincoln), N. Dak.
Moab, Utah
Leupp, Ariz.
Santa Fe, N.M.
Fort Stanton, N.M.
Seagoville, Tex.
Crystal City, Tex.
Kenedy, Tex.

Assembly Centers, Incarceration Camps, and Department of Justice Internment or War Relocation Authority Internment Camps and "Isolation Centers," 1941–1945.

do you think? I don't know just how to go about it, but I could just wear my ring and let my friends know."

On August evenings, once the sounds of the day died down, Family #15272 and the other Japanese Americans "assembled" in the Pacific Livestock Exposition Center could hear amusement park music and excited shouts drifting over from Jantzen Beach on Hayden Island, not far away. The sounds of other Oregonians—outsiders, outside, free. By the late summer of 1942, even before the internees were shipped off to Minidoka, Manzanar, Topaz, and the other camps, the spiritual, psychological, and economic damage had been done, or had become inevitable.

MINIDOKA "RELOCATION" CENTER: AUGUST 10, 1942, TO OCTOBER 28, 1945

I had at last found the physical Minidoka during a hurried drive-through in 2001—fragments of a chimney and the stone guard house, some cement slabs, and a few starkly misshapen trees, sitting in the midst of some lushly

Orphan Caravan

Three buses approach the desert
and the children inside
watch the green go brown.
Dusty whirlwinds tell them
they are almost home.

Their orphanages, their foster homes
were home only weeks ago, but
the army says they are home
only where they are told is home.

They are being "relocated" once again.

These buses mimic the other caravans—
trainloads of homeless men women
and children, dispossessed and taken away.
An orphan baby is crying. He is
one-sixteenth (at least!) Japanese
American.

Where did Los Angeles go?
What is "Manzanar"?
How long before we are there?

A few hours ago a little girl
decided she would sing
"God Bless America,"
and the young soldier
keeping a watchful eye on them
tried to understand.

irrigated land 13 miles northeast of Twin Falls, just off of Idaho Highway 25. Locals call the area "Hunt." It was a cathartic conclusion to a bewildered and frustrating search, begun 30 years earlier when nothing was marked and I couldn't find a reliable living memory to tell me for sure what Minidoka was, or where it had been. But I made a long stop in southern Idaho in 2003, and on the way to Hunt I took some time in nearby Eden to make friends with Lynn Davis and get reacquainted with Thelma Stone.

Lynn Davis, who had just turned 21 when internment arrived in 1942, was lanky, suntanned, and gray when I met him. He told me about working on the camp before the arrival of the "internees" and, beginning in February 1947, watching it gradually disappear in chunks and pieces when the government decided to liquidate its local "war assets." The assets were assigned, sold, or given away. "Veterans got the first draw," he said, and much of the camp's farmland was snapped up—although some of the acreage allotments weren't large enough and some "homesteaders" weren't able to "prove up on it" with water, fences, and ditches within the required time. The "barracks," Lynn Davis said, were just frame buildings on cement blocks, skirted with 1×12s, so their new owners had to add insulation and other improvements to turn the barracks into livable homes. A doctor from Wendell apparently "turned some of the hospital buildings into several houses, and made some money."

Lynn Davis added, "the stuff not listed as assets, well, you could just take it away"—hand tools, washtubs, pots and pans, picks and shovels, an old wheelbarrow and the once-treasured encyclopedias from the school. (Left-behind pieces of furniture, homemade by the residents from scrap lumber and packing crates, were usually not worth saving.) But the residents had done well with what they had out there, he said. Back then, he recalled, there was only about six inches of topsoil to work with, but they did a good job of growing fields of beans, hay, sugar beets, and "spuds," along with raising chickens. Irrigation came from the Gooding Canal. They kept small family gardens near the housing, he recalled, using water from wells, and they used lava rock for borders and walkways, and in the cemetery.

I had first met Thelma Stone during my brief visit in the summer of 2001. Two years later her sprinklers were still greening up the front of her trailer home and she looked as she had before: a short, sturdy woman with trimmed white hair, combed back in just-washed-no-fuss fashion, a Sunday-white flower-sprinkled shirt and fresh jeans, and a lifetime of wrinkles. Thelma had memories of her husband, her siblings, and a paralyzed son who'd been in a car wreck. And she, too, recalled the building of Minidoka. Constructed overnight in the desert, the camp was pretty much responsible for ending local unemployment and the area's experience of the Great Depression. "My dad was named Charlie Crawford," she said. "The company he worked for was hired to help build the camp. He helped build that place." And then she added, "He'd come home—I wasn't but twelve years old—and he'd tell my mother, he'd say, 'I feel sorry for those people. It's just a dust hole out there.'"

So "Hunt, Idaho" is really nowhere to be in 1942 unless you just have to be at 42°41'N latitude and 114°15'W longitude. Or unless you have to be somewhere between Eden and the railroad siding near Jerome, where trainloads of people can be offloaded—along with coal, food, and miscellaneous supplies—before negotiating the last few miles in trucks and buses. "Hunt" doesn't sound like much, so better to call it by another name, and why not something in the language of the Shoshone people who lived here before. Call it "Minidoka."

♘

Take a space 20 × 24 and around it put tarpaper walls over uncured pine that will soon pull apart in dry air and pop its knotholes, then improvise some partitions (scrap lumber available) or maybe hang a blanket for privacy.

Some nice cots are available and bedding stuffed with straw, and a stove for heat (coal available for the hauling), but (regrettably) no separate bedroom, no kitchen, no living room, no dining room or dinner table, no intimacy.

Then put a number on it for an address (but not the family number they assigned when you were taken from your home), and put six of these rooms under one roof and then arrange 12 of these barracks into a block, and add

a dining hall and a communal lavatory (sorry, no doors or curtains). Gather 36 of these blocks and add buildings for administration (etc.) for a total of 600 structures plus one cemetery, and surround it all with

five miles of barbed wire and eight guard towers placed where you can't miss them (yes, the guns are loaded) and set it down on 950 acres of high (3,950 feet) desert where sand and alkali dust sit on top of cinders and treacherous crosswinds keep particles sifting through the cracks, except when it rains and everything turns to mud, and (of course) you will be looking at 100 degrees in July and a frozen canal in December, but just to prove it's not

a godforsaken place include some interesting flora (sagebrush and grease-wood, for example) and local wildlife (coyotes and rattlesnakes will do). Insert 9,397 residents and some military and civilian staff. Now you have

Idaho's third-largest city in 1942.

✍

But as luck would have it (my mother wrote to sister Fumie) and despite the Depression-ending boom it brought to the local economy, Minidoka was not ready for its residents when they began arriving by the trainload from the assembly centers in Portland and Puyallup. Not a good way to start. But life in the assembly center had prepared my mother for everything from surprise to relief to disappointment, so in the end she included it all in her letters from "camp," the roughest edges softened by her tendency to see hopeful signs in anything good. In her first-impression snapshots she included facts and rumors, updates on Fumie's husband and children, and the news of friends who were also there, at least for the time being:

34–9-A Minidoka Relocation Center
Hunt, Idaho
September 12th, 1942
Dear Oneesan—

Here we are in Idaho's sagebrush country. Jiro-san's probably told you all about our arrival, etc. but he most likely has not written in detail so I'm writing, too. We reached here after 24 hours of rough train ride on an old train with frequent stops and swaying. But they served us very good meals (like baked ham for dinner, creamed chicken for lunch, and good coffee in the diner), which made up for all the discomfort and so it wasn't bad. The children enjoyed their first train ride and were excited and overjoyed at seeing so many cows, horses, sheep, and even a goat or two along the road.

We saw miles and miles of sagebrush country on the way and even had a taste of the dust on the train but were terribly disappointed and very unhappy to be greeted by the dust as we entered the camp on the bus. They have told us that it was unusually windy that day—the worst day as yet. It's been better since although it's very cold in the mornings and quite windy at times. Occasionally the wind sweeps the dust high up in the air like a geyser, so you can imagine how hard it is to keep clean. There's always some dust in our room and even in our suitcases the fine powdery dust has entered. I think much of this will disappear when they start planting trees and grass as they plan to do.

The buildings are built in a crescent-shaped area about 2 ½ miles along the outside. Each block has 12 buildings with 6 apartments in each, also 1 bldg. for the dining hall and one for the laundry, showers, etc. Our room is at one end of the 9th bldg. in block 34. Jiro-san has the room at the other end of the same bldg. in a similar room built for a family of three. We were unable to get adjacent rooms as the others are built larger to occupy 5–7 people. We hope to be moved later when all the residents are in. We hear some families have had to double up and others are still sleeping in recreation halls.

We're very much disappointed to find this center so far from completion. There is no hot water (except in the kitchen) and no lavatories (we have to use outside latrines). The plumbing will be done as soon as fixtures can be obtained. Some bldgs. have no lights yet. We had ours in yesterday. The inside walls are unfinished and no stoves in yet.

But the food has been good and plentiful and we have the much needed privacy and quiet. What a difference from the cramped quarters of our former "camp." Everyone seems to be taking all this fairly well and many are already working.

All the Oregon people who were at North Portland are here now, but we hear others now at Tule Lake will be sent here later as Tule Lake is too near the Coast. When things become more settled, a governing body will be formed and schools and stores will be built. At present there are only 2 small canteens, and Seattle people are doing most of the important work. There are no restrictions of any sort, no fences, either, just a great expanse of sagebrush country around us to separate us from any town or city. . . .

Have met several Wash. friends here. . . . Saw several when we went to meet the remaining Portlanders come in. . . . The Seattle people came first so are living at the other end of this center. I haven't felt like walking so far just to look around and visit. It's quite a walk—two miles or so.

Kiyo lives in block 32, quite near as block 33 is located alongside it and therefore B-32 is only one block from here. After I get a better idea of the set-up here, I'll write more in detail, altho' I don't think I'd get lost now. . . .

I think it's settled that Jiro-san will work with 3 other Seattle watch-repairers just cleaning watches. His is a profession so he'll get $19 a month, which is top wages. Grace and Phyllis [Michi and Yuri] play very well together. Their appetite is good as there's no temptation for candy, etc. between meals. The families between our 2 rooms are the Nakatas (not Dr. N.), Kondos, Shojis, and Akiyamas. The Maedas, Takeuchis and Itos also live in our block.

It rained a little last night and it's very windy today, but the sun is warm. It will take us some time to get used to such freakish weather. . . .

Hope everything's fine with you, and don't worry about any of us as we'll get along with 10,000 others in the same boat.

Love,
Mary

The train ride from Portland had been tolerable but subdued, with decent food and drawn shades. But now, at last in Minidoka, they could look forward to hot water, heated living quarters, maybe a bit more privacy. And, as it happened, watching the barbed wire go up around them.

A THOUSAND WORDS

For reasons of discretion and morale, the polio-stricken legs of President Roosevelt were cropped from White House photographs. What Americans knew of what was happening in the war itself was controlled, when not produced, by the Office of War Information. And a selective "documentary" record of "relocation" was also provided by the U.S. government—although deference toward emotional truth was hardly the point. Uncle Sam wanted pictures and words that reflected American patriotism, resilience, and a can-do spirit in a time of collective sacrifice. With regard to the internment camps the government wanted to show that no one was being abused—that the Japanese in America were simply being asked to sacrifice in an unusual way.

So the official record included the domestic propaganda film "Japanese Relocation," which portrayed the victims of eviction and incarceration as remarkably good-natured and cooperative—latter-day pioneers who were happy to prove their loyalty to America by making a go of it in the desert West. "Colonists," so to speak. The government wanted others to know how well it was treating "the Japanese" and how those industrious residents of "relocation centers" were finding inventive ways to make substandard housing livable, by using shelving made from salvaged lumber, by putting up curtains, by planting decorative gardens. The result was motion-picture "proof" that the "evacuees" were cheerfully engaged in replicating the communities and institutions they had had in Portland, Seattle, and elsewhere—schools and nurseries, sports tournaments and scouting organizations, social events and holidays and traditions—and embracing the "Americanization" classes prescribed for the Issei. The government wanted to present Minidoka and each of the other facilities as a kind of challenging adventure, not a prison camp.

To create its photographic record of the camps the Office of War Information also enlisted the photographers Ansel Adams and Dorothea Lange. But the government insisted on smiles, not images of discomfort, deprivation, and despair; it warned Adams, Lange, and other "outsider" photographers against taking pictures that showed families behind barbed wire or being guarded by soldiers with guns, and told publications such as *Life* magazine not to distribute them. As it happened, Adams was drawn to landscape and portraiture rather than pictures of people in place, particular people trying to live in the particular place called Manzanar. Lange on the other hand was instantly empathetic toward the camp residents themselves and more openly at odds with the government restrictions, but the result was that only a few of her images of life in assembly centers and at Manzanar were distributed before the whole batch was banished to the National Archives. (Like the facts surrounding government conduct in the Yasui, Hirabayashi, and Korematsu cases, the complete file of Lange's images would not be retrieved for decades.)

Life magazine and other news publications never conveyed the gritty texture and monotonous oppression of life in a "Minidoka." Minidoka lacked trees to help place it in the natural world. Minidoka lacked thoughtful and imaginative architecture to suggest a community with personality and soul. It lacked solidly constructed housing to provide a sense of security. Its living spaces were boxes within boxes, boxes that could only be individualized and improved by permission and in authorized ways. Minidoka's communal laundry facilities required a walk outside, no matter the season or weather, and its communal bathroom facilities lacked sufficient walls and doors for even a modicum of privacy. Minidoka was crowded enough to make secrets impossible and fear of communicable diseases and food poisoning a constant concern. It provided three cafeteria meals a day in two shifts each, but this was regimented consumption, not the tradition of appreciation and respect that came with meals cooked by mother and taken at the family table. The food was adequate, but always a reminder that what you ate was not your choice.

So the authorized images of "camp" conveyed nothing of the people's frustration and depression. Or their sense of betrayal and vulnerability. Or their anxiety regarding a future over which they now had no control. Or how easily the spectacle of public humiliation could turn community pride into irrational shame. (In Japanese culture *haji,* or shame, was the conditioned response to public humiliation. Like victims of sexual assault, many internees would give voice to their injury and pain only after years of silence.) The residents of the camps accommodated those who governed their lives only because they had no choice—"Smile for the photographer from the magazine! Smile for the WRA!"—and their efforts to recreate something that resembled a vibrant and authentic community came in response to idleness and otherwise wasted time, and to prove that they were not helpless. The "internees" could not take pictures of their own. After Pearl Harbor Japanese Americans had been prohibited from possessing "contraband" and "spy equipment" such as guns, short-wave radios, and binoculars—and cameras were not included among the "essential personal effects" people were allowed to take to camp.

But the residents found creative ways to express themselves. In the spirit of prisoners everywhere they made hideaways underneath the floorboards of their "apartments," places for intimate personal treasures—a book, some

Witness 13660 (Miné Okubo, 1913–2001)

Artist abroad on fellowship
possessions left in Paris
you fled a Europe about to enter
holocaust, came home only to record
stroke by stroke disbelief in Berkeley,
bewilderment and resignation,
insult and odor of animal stalls at Tanforan,
Utah dust and alkali desert wind,
your own tears. How difficult
Mee-neh, and necessary
to delineate with pen and ink
the sparse textures
of banishment and pain.

The dull eyes
of the other displaced dispossessed
could scarcely register
the truth of what they lived there,
aimless routine of finite spaces
and no place to take their grief.
Forbidden to have cameras and
with numbers in place of names,
others deposited suffering
in a safe niche of memory
for which they would misplace the key.
But you denied denial and recorded
everything—stroke by stroke
anxieties of idleness and regulation,
the death of privacy,
the distracted everyday.

Artist-in-exile, you knew
as you captured that chaos of emotion
how your pictures defied the claims
of *Life* magazine and Uncle Sam,
their cameras, guns, and propaganda gaze,

that your images transcended
the language of your own narration.
Artist-in-residence, Citizen 13660,
you insisted on the testament
of cotton fiber and India ink,
inscribing yourself in every image
of that claustral interrupted life,
missing nothing and saying
over and over
I am here.

"Guard Tower," Kenjiro Nomura, January 1943.

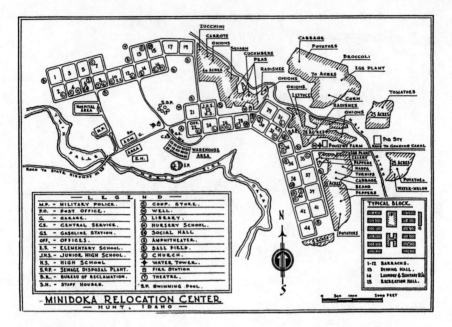

Minidoka Relocation Center, 1943.

drawings or a journal, a stash of sake made from rice taken from the mess hall—but also secret spaces in and for themselves, gestures of rebellion and autonomy. And throughout the camp system professional and amateur artists wove, carved, painted, and crafted, using donated, bootlegged, pilfered, repurposed, or found materials. They made utensils from scrap metal, jewelry from shells, toys from wood scrap, baskets from tule reeds, furniture from salvaged lumber, drawings and paintings on the back of government publications. At Minidoka, Kenjiro Nomura's job was to paint camp signage ("Mess Hall," "Barber Shop," "Lumberyard") but in his spare time he produced watercolors and oil paintings of camp life—often represented by solitary figures moving with purpose under a darkening Idaho sky. At Topaz, Miné Okubo, a Nisei artist who had been studying in France but returned to the United States to avoid the onrush of Nazi oppression, found herself recording camp life in scores of pen-and-ink drawings in which she herself ("Citizen 13660") constantly appears as a witness. At Manzanar, professional photographer Toyo Miyatake smuggled in some key parts and built a camera for documenting camp life from the inside. And Dave Tatsuno, a businessman and home moviemaker, retrieved his camera with the help of friends and shot the intimate footage that eventually became the short film *Topaz*. Some internees wrote, officially for the *Minidoka Irrigator* and the other government-monitored camp newspapers, and in private, unauthorized forms, such as diaries, journals, and of course (although reading and writing in Japanese was supposedly prohibited) *haiku* and other forms of poetry: "Separated year ago today / Chinese quince / must be blooming in my garden," wrote Kikuha Okamoto, a California poet in the camp at Rohwer, Arkansas.

"The trick" Minidoka poet Mitsuye Yamada wrote later, was "keep the body busy. . . . But the mind was not fooled." Staying busy, some residents documented their three-year captivity in a school-yearbook-style publication—complete with a "Sweetheart of Minidoka" and with residential blocks instead of classes—and called it *Minidoka Interlude*. Even so, most camp residents could not express themselves creatively in tangible, lasting ways, could not write the emotional record of what they witnessed and lived or create narratives in which they were the subjects rather than objects to be manipulated for someone else's "truth." In Minidoka, little Michi and Yuri, my cousins, seemed to be growing before everyone's eyes, but their mother would have to take Auntie Mary's written word for it, because Kodak moments were few and far between. Grandpa Marumoto, the family photographer, was without a camera, so in Minidoka they were grateful for occasional outside visitors, "Caucasian" friends deemed harmless by the guards. Miss Chase, for example, who made the long trip from Portland to visit the Marumotos and other friends, made a point of taking a few "snaps." And then there was my mother, who would finally manage to leave Minidoka but would have a Kodak camera in her purse when circumstances forced her to return two years later.

"MILITARY NECESSITY"

My father and my uncle George entered the army under different circumstances and half a continent apart. Yet at the outset, both found themselves in a segregated military that didn't quite know what to do with its Japanese Americans. Ever since the Civil War there had been African American units, led by white officers and typically given menial duties or undesirable assignments. More recently, Filipinos had been used as scouts in specialized combat situations and as kitchen workers at other times. But after December 7, 1941, the Nisei presented a particular dilemma. Where did they fit into the military now, these men whose parents had been labeled "enemy aliens"? What should be done with Nisei college graduates who had earned commissions through ROTC? What should be done with the Nisei who were already in the Reserves or the National Guard? Or in the active army?

Yoshiro "George" Marumoto was shuffled around a lot early in the war. He had just graduated from optometry school in the spring of 1941 when he was drafted, inducted, sent to Fort Lewis, Washington and then on to Fort Ord, then in its final year as a station for over 1,400 cavalry and field artillery horses. He found himself in the company of Nisei inductees from California, with whom he felt an affinity but not always a kinship, and others from Hawaii, who had a Japanese-Hawaiian vocabulary and perspective on life. Regional differences and circumstances had already created diversity among the Japanese in America. But as his letters home made clear, George's Nisei buddies from Portland were now scattered on bases from Colorado to Kentucky, so learning to get along with Californians and Hawaiians, in exchange for being close to Monterey Bay, was fine with him.

Uncle George was the antithesis of my crew-cut, abrupt, hard-driving father, and when I was growing up his easygoing manner, self-deprecating humor, and desire to be dapper—including his mustache and his hair combed back like Clark Gable—endeared him to me. George found the frenetic pace of the wartime military unsettling and the frequent reassignments an inconvenient mystery. For George the army, with its hierarchical structure and khaki wardrobe (they didn't call it olive drab for nothing) and its drill, drill, drill, was hardly a good fit. He was eager to see what life had to offer, but preferred that it be presented in a picnic basket or show up on a dance floor, wearing a dress. The army was also too much like school, which had never captured his attention the way it had his sisters'.

But he was destined to fidget in a classroom once more—and to try to recall the lessons he had not quite absorbed while attending Japanese language school in Portland. The War Department had started intensive Japanese language training for military intelligence as early as the summer of 1941, as relations between Japan and the U.S. deteriorated. And the War Department had come to acknowledge that the U.S. already had a resident population that was tolerably fluent in both English and Japanese, so it began to send selected Hawaiian and West Coast Nisei and Kibei for further training at the Presidio in San Francisco. Men who had been ridiculed for speaking Japanese at home and for attending Japanese school were being groomed as specialists. Like the Navajo Code Talkers who helped lead Marine assaults in the Pacific by using a language that the reservation system and the Indian schools had tried to beat out of them, the bilingual Japanese Americans were going to be useful, after all.

By mid-February 1942 George was among those who had been interviewed in secret and reassigned to the Military Intelligence Service. "No one even knows that this outfit exists," he and the other MIS recruits were told, and any discussion of their interviews would lead to court martial. But after the exclusion from the West Coast of *all* Japanese Americans, including active military, San Francisco was no longer an option. So by the end of March he and others found themselves in a holding pattern at Camp Wolters, near Mineral Wells, Texas, along with, among others, units comprised only of African Americans. George wrote home that Texas was "flat and desolate" and made him long for Oregon, and he reported that the Japanese American soldiers were being assigned "either garbage duty or the rock pile"—what he called "prisoner work." They also felt a new and awkward kinship with *kuro-chan,* the black soldiers or black boys, who were no strangers to the same kind of treatment and the same line of work. Rumor had it that if the army didn't summarily dismiss the Nisei, it might just keep them in north Texas, peeling potatoes forever. His letters home made clear that what George really wanted was a promotion and a higher pay grade, and an occasional home-cooked dinner wouldn't hurt. What he and 200 others got, in May, was security clearance and MIS Language School in Minnesota—an intensive academic regimen aimed at getting their Japanese up to speed so they could translate captured documents or intercepted messages and interrogate POWs.

At Camp Savage George divided his energies between studies and what he referred to as "amusements." He did his best to memorize hundreds of kanji and embrace the intricacies and nuances of his ancestors' language, but it was a constant battle between commitment and bewilderment. It was fitting, then, that in Saint Paul he met Tana Suyama, who was doing domestic work for the owner of a lumber company. By July he was getting serious about the cute orphan girl from Montana and by September he was engaged (a pork chop dinner may have clinched the deal). But by then his Japanese had apparently improved sufficiently for the army to deem him deployable, and shortly after their wedding in November and a brief visit to Minidoka with Tana, he was assigned to ATIS, the Allied Translator and Interpreter Section, and sent to Australia and then New Guinea.

❧

My father had graduated from medical school in June 1939 and on the same day was appointed a second lieutenant in the army reserves. On the heels of his internship in East Chicago he had started his three-year residency in Detroit. But now, halfway through it, he assumed he would be activated any day, and returned to East Chicago to await his orders. "I guess you could say I completed my residency in Europe," he later told me. But when the army didn't seem to be in any hurry to put him in uniform he got testy, and at one point wrote to ask if they anticipated any wounded in the war, which would suggest a need for more doctors. Of course the delay had to do with his being Japanese American (albeit a doctor), although it was not in my father to acknowledge that that could be the case.

He marked time in Indiana by treating walk-in patients and delivering babies, and also used those intervening months to see about getting his fiancée out of Minidoka. Years later he joked that if he hadn't gotten married he wouldn't have had anyone to send his army pay to. But my mother getting pregnant right away probably had at least something to do with his being the only member of his family still in the United States and a part of "America." His father had returned to Japan with his mother's ashes, and his brother Toru was at Waseda University—and after Pearl Harbor, stuck in Japan indefinitely. As far as Katsumi Nakadate knew, he *was* the Nakadate family in the United States—and his first child would be the first member of the family's next generation.

After some training for medical officers in Tennessee, Katsumi Nakadate found himself assigned to the recently created all-Japanese American 442nd Regimental Combat Team and suffering through a season in Hattiesburg, Mississippi. It was hot, humid, swampy, and full of snakes. Along with the other men of the 442nd he shared a dislike for army cooking, although their complaint had an unfamiliar spin: there was never enough rice, not for men who had eaten it twice a day for most of their lives. Eventually the supply officers found they could barter some 442nd potatoes for other units' opportunity to have rice pudding. And as my father saw it, this also made clear that the "*buddaheads*" and "West Coast *katonks*" (pidgin Hawaiian for "pig heads" and "empty-heads") had more than a little in common. At Camp Shelby my father taught first aid to potential corpsmen, removed tonsils, gave penicillin shots to combat venereal diseases, and repaired the damage done by periodic fistfights. It wasn't hard for him and the other doctors to keep up with the patient load, because the segregated 442nd—despite being comprised of the sons of immigrants who had little more than sixth grade educations themselves—had more than its quota of doctors, as well as too many dentists, not to mention more high school and college graduates than the typical unit.

Meanwhile, my father found himself at odds with Mississippi's way of seeing the world through the prism of race. Once, boarding a bus that shuttled servicemen into town, he took a seat in the back only to have the driver remind him that the back of the bus was only for "Negroes" and that he should get back up front, "where you belong." Nonplussed, the lieutenant allowed that he knew he wasn't black, but was tongue-tied to explain why that shouldn't matter. So he told the driver that an officer in the United States Army should be able to sit where he wants. And he did. (Such an exchange was not unique. For example, the record shows that Second Lieutenant and future Brooklyn Dodger Jackie Robinson had a seat-on-the-bus confrontation at another base at about the same time, offered the same response, and was court-martialed for it before eventually being cleared.)

Lieutenant Nakadate was sent to Walter Reed Army Hospital in Washington for several weeks of training in tropical medicine, and this led to the "latrine rumor" that the 442nd was bound for the Pacific Theater rather than Europe—a perplexing prospect for many. But when its orders finally arrived the unit was sent to Europe and into some of the most memorable fighting of the war. And by then my father was not with them. He had been approached during a social event by a higher-ranking officer and told, "Lieutenant, you look like a man who is about to volunteer for reassignment to a unit that needs doctors. Thank you." Segregation notwithstanding, the problem of too many medical officers in one unit was a dilemma the army was finding a way to correct.

We know that ordinary people end up doing extraordinary things in war-time, and that they are driven by extraordinary forces, among them "military necessity." We know that it was a manufactured "military necessity" that led to the displacement and incarceration of over 110,000 Japanese Americans, but also a real need for manpower that eventually made the army create a unit made up of Japanese Americans. And that a real necessity led to my uncle's service in the MIS. And it was military necessity that resulted in my doctor-father's transfer from the 442nd Regimental Combat Team to the 69th Division, and then to the otherwise "all-American" (by which he meant "all-white") 17th Airborne. "And that," my father would say with a laugh, "that was the end of the rice."

"THE HARDEST THING I EVER HAD TO DO"

I can't look at hobbles and I can't stand fences.
Don't fence me in.

—ROBERT FLETCHER/COLE PORTER, "DON'T FENCE ME IN" (1944)

Once she had accepted that college would be impossible, my mother also assumed that marriage was the obvious next step. She was a creature of her time and place. But by her mid-twenties, she had also observed some of the difficulties that could arise in a marriage, brokered or otherwise. And she was enough of a modern girl to believe that in the matter of matrimony she should have a voice and the power to make her own decision—unfettered by cultural expectations and family need. So even though more and more of her friends were getting married she had been in no hurry—and had turned down three earlier offers before accepting my father's proposal. But once he had asked her to join him in Indiana she had to convince her sister, her parents, the War Relocation Authority, and herself that she should not have to stay in Minidoka.

While the family was still in the Portland assembly center she had hoped that "relocation" would evolve into a routine and she would be able to imag-ine another life. And "camp" was in fact becoming somewhat predictable, though hardly a matter of comfort. Heating stoves were finally installed in all the units, and hot water finally came to all the bathroom buildings and laundry facilities by late October. An episode of food poisoning was not repeated, and residents' complaints had resulted in rice being served more often in the mess halls. The camp cooks found imaginative ways of working a wartime overload of Spam and "wienies" into the menus, typically with soy sauce or ketchup. Fumie's girls were settling into a rhythm of school and playground, and it appeared that Fumie herself might be cleared to leave the TB hospital and join them after the first of the year. On the other hand, younger brother Yoshiro, by then stationed in Saint Paul, had gotten very serious very fast about Tana. His sisters wondered about the speed of this courtship and whether easygoing Yosh was even ready for marriage. And since Tana wasn't a Portland girl they had to try to figure her out from her warm letters and their brother's attempts at explaining himself. Given wartime circumstances though, the two sisters had nowhere to go with their concern, and besides, Mary was now about to enter a wartime marriage of her own.

Best friend Kiyo had recently surprised her with a wedding shower, an event poignant both for what it was and what it couldn't be. "There were over 20 girls there at Kiyo's apartment," my mother wrote near the end of October. "We could hardly believe we were at camp, the atmosphere was so much like old times . . . just like a party back home. . . . There were 48 girls in on the gifts—including 14 from outside (Portland, Tule Lake, Heart Mountain . . .)—also 34 girls now at our camp. I don't think Kiyo missed a girl." Most of the gifts had been catalogue-ordered through Sears and Montgomery Ward. In the same letter to Fumie my mother wrote, "I hope you're continuing to improve. We can't wait 'til spring so you can come here and join the children." Yet the camp "hospital" was inadequately equipped and used too many untrained nurses' aides and, as my mother had to acknowledge, "there is rumor that the head physician and head nurse (both Caucasians) are not very kind and so must be anti-Japanese. Wonder why they even came here." And now there were occasional protests, fights, and other disturbances, although not at the level of confrontation and violence reported from Heart Mountain and Tule Lake.

My grandparents told my mother that since she now had a chance to leave the camp for a better life, she should, even if that meant they would not be at her wedding. Cora and Buddy Oliver, the Portland friends who had introduced my parents a few years earlier, encouraged her to go. And so did her friends in camp. You have to think of yourself, they all said, you have to think of yourself. But for someone who had grown up juggling "Japanese" filial obligations and personal dreams of an American life, leaving Minidoka was easier said than done. How could she be an American woman without ceasing to be a Nisei daughter?

The way forward had been opened by wartime necessity and some common-sense second-guessing on the part of the government. The abrupt removal of Japanese American farmers had idled thousands of West Coast acres or put production into unfamiliar and less productive hands. And by the fall of 1942 the military draft was creating a general shortage of farm labor. So ironically enough, residents of the various camps were recruited to do field work—with the added benefit to them of being temporarily free of barbed wire and camp regulations. Men who had been working their own farms in May found themselves stooping over somebody else's crop in September, for the kind of wages they thought they would never face again. (This was also when the government started the Bracero Program, recruiting thousands of Mexican workers to come to the United States; in 1942 4,200 Mexican guest workers entered the U.S., and the numbers would grow tenfold in subsequent years.)

Other Nisei, who could prove that jobs awaited them farther east, applied for releases that might enable them to live there indefinitely. College students who had been expelled from West Coast schools shortly after the Pearl Harbor attack were allowed to apply to complete their educations elsewhere if other institutions would accept them. (For many years afterward, Nisei would often surprise people when they said, "Oh, my cousin went to Beloit," or "I know about Grinnell.") And a young woman could obtain permission to leave camp if she had a fiancé on the outside and was willing to get married far from home and family. Of course more than a few camp residents would observe that if able-bodied men could be allowed outside to do field work in Idaho or take jobs in Wisconsin, if college students could attend classes in sociology and physics in Iowa or Pennsylvania, and if brides-to-be could get permission to travel on their own by bus or rail, that would seem to leave behind barbed wire only the security threat presented by younger children and 50-year-old grandparents. For its part the government could see that piecemeal resettlement of low-risk individuals was one way to begin dispersing the Japanese American population.

Given her recent history of having visited Japan and her twelve years of Japanese language school my mother's application for leave clearance might have raised some eyebrows—but since she, like others, considered the government's mandatory "loyalty questionnaire" gratuitous and offensive, it is not clear how she actually responded to individual items. "Loyalty questions" 27 and 28 had been reworded with gender in mind and now asked women if they would serve as nurses or in the Women's Auxiliary Army Corps, as well as renounce any allegiance to Japan. To her this all seemed coercive and obvious and pointless at the same time—bureaucratic patriotism getting in the way of life. "I'm wondering if I ever thanked you," she wrote to Fumie in October, "for the *Bride's Magazine.* Looking at the dresses sure makes me wish I were going to be married in satin and veil at a church...."

But her application was approved, and her departure was timed to coincide with that of another Chicago-bound bride-to-be—neither of them would have to endure a long, solitary journey under suspicious, if not hostile, eyes. By mid-November my mother's letters were reduced to crisp observations on quotidian matters and the tentative future. "Dearest Fumie," she wrote a few days before leaving Minidoka,

> It's getting colder here. We had our second snowfall this morning, but it's fast melting away and the ground is awfully soft and messy to walk on. We're glad we can get plenty of coal at present, we are only to stay indoors near the stove to keep warm....
>
> Mother and I have finally made the curtains and draperies for both rooms and put them up. Father has built some cupboards and things, and now the rooms look much cozier. With most everything done that can be done to improve the inside (without much expense) I feel better about going.
>
> I can hardly believe I have only a few days left here—after such long waiting.... Tana seems very anxious to meet me—I can't wait to see her, either. I hope things work right and I can make the trip before Yosh is assigned someplace.
>
> It's very inconvenient that mother can't read English. Guess I'll have to brush up on my Japanese and write to her after I leave. Try to write her, too, as I won't be here, and Jiro-san, being as he is, won't tell mother anything. Anyway, let's do our best to write often.

Two days later, on November 17, waiting for the afternoon train out of Sho-shone, she wrote a final note from Idaho:

It was really sad parting, but it had to be sometime—

Kats will meet me in Chicago. He wired me today. He certainly waited a long time for me. In his letter today, he says the Bicknells suggested we stay at their house, so we may until we can find a suitable apartment.

I should reach Chicago on Friday morning sometime. But at the rate the trains are now being delayed, we may not reach [it] until much later than the scheduled time—which is 8:30 A M Fri.

Hoping everything's fine with you. Don't worry about the children. I know they'll get along fine and there are others close on hand whenever help is needed. Just get well quick and join them soon.

Will write you as soon as I arrive.

Love,
Mary

Vitality and youth seemed to leave Minidoka on a daily basis, and indeed it appeared as though only the very young and the very old would remain to endure dust storms and imprisonment with dignity and patience.

"The hardest thing I ever had to do," my mother would say later, "was leave my parents behind in that camp." My father, of course, was happy and relieved that she had finally been able to take that step—even though when he greeted her in Chicago she weighed only 99 pounds, having lost 15 since her family had been forced out of their home in Portland. A week later they were married. The Methodist ceremony took place at the minister's home, with a dozen witness-guests, and the honeymoon was Thanksgiving in Min-nesota, with the bride's brother and his own new wife.

GREYHOUND

When Auntie Tana testified before the Commission on Wartime Relocation and Internment of Civilians in 1981, she was still angry and unhappy. And who could blame her? She wanted her brother back, the big brother who had left four siblings and a stateside army assignment for combat duty with the 442nd Regimental Combat Team and ended up permanently MIA in France. And she wanted the memory of stigma to go away. She recalled that while he was over there trying to prove that Japanese Americans were good Americans, too, his brother and sisters were objects of hostile glances, verbal abuse, and spitting incidents, though they were far from the Pacific Coast.

But the exceptions were also worth remembering, Tana would remind us. There was the time when her sister Mary (we called her "Little Mary," to distinguish her from my mother, and because she was only a little over four feet tall) was pulled off a bus to Twin Falls and tossed in jail in Butte. During a rest stop someone had warned the local sheriff that there was a "Jap" on board. But as soon as the driver found out he stormed in and demanded that they release his passenger immediately, and they did. Another time Tana and sister Betty were enduring the usual mistreatment—"It was worth it," Tana said, "because we were going to see my husband's mother and father"—when the bus driver had finally heard enough and made a point of standing with them to buy sandwiches at a diner when they had to leave the bus. "They're my passengers," he told the manager, "and I want you to serve them. They're American citizens, with relatives in the service." "I wrote a letter to the company," Tana said, "to let them know that those drivers took care of us."

Tana made a half-dozen of those expensive and challenging wartime trips to Minidoka from Minneapolis and Chicago. What rankled her most, though, occurred on the Thanksgiving trip she made with my uncle just before he was sent to the Pacific Theater. Her soldier husband was in full army uniform, but the guards searched him anyway, for security reasons, as he entered the gate.

JIM CROW, 1943

My mother was pregnant for the first time when she rode the train from Northwest Indiana to Mississippi to visit my father, at that point still assigned to the 442nd Regimental Combat Team. She was young and "only" a woman, but it was 1943, a time of major social shifts and permanent changes in where and how Americans worked, and who they lived with, and how they conducted their lives in a wartime culture of upheaval and flux. For my parents it was the interlude of love and fragile plans between their getting married and his shipping out. Love's not time's fool, the poet says. Now, traveling alone, cherishing her moment, and carrying her future, she rode the *City of New Orleans* into the Jim Crow South.

When the train pulled into Hattiesburg she needed to find her lodgings—the arrangement was for her to stay in the home of a local minister—and then see her husband, but first she needed to find a bathroom, a "lavatory" she would have called it. There were, of course, two sets for both men and women, marked "WHITE" and "COLORED." She had grown up in Oregon in the twenties and thirties, and fully understood what it meant to be labeled by "race." As "resident aliens" her parents had been required to keep a current registration with the INS: Country of origin, Japan. Race, Yellow. In Portland, my mother had been a member of a long marginalized and now excluded group, the "Oriental," the "Asiatic." But now? WHITE? or COLORED?

She, who later taught us always to wash with soap and hot water and to put tissue down on toilet seats in public bathrooms, chose the less unappealing of the two doors, the door that, in Mississippi, suggested that at least passing attention had been paid to cleanliness and order. And then? Life in Hattiesburg continued to drift its way through the summer of 1943. No word or gesture acknowledged her presence. No objection or cough or accusatory turning of heads. It somehow didn't matter there, where there was no clear and absolute category for a woman of color who was not "colored."

A single, unaccompanied Japanese American woman, of average height and modest carriage steps down from a train. She stops, looks around her, and walks unheeded into one of two clearly labeled public facilities. The eyes of Jim Crow observe only what they have been trained to see, and they see that she is white.

I'M YOUR NATIVE SON

It might have been a telegram, but my father remembered it as a long-distance phone call—in those days either a luxury or a necessity—from O. L. Marks, M.D., his wife's obstetrician: "Jim, we've run into some complications with the delivery, and figured you'd want to know right away, and maybe you should see about finding a way to get up here. . . ." Any doctor would know that the term "complications" can cover any number of unwelcome possibilities. And a young doctor who had lost his mother to kidney disease four years earlier, who faced another huge loss if "complications" turned childbirth into a catastrophe, would surely have to get up to East Chicago and see for himself.

This was near the end of August 1943, and his commanding officer at Camp Shelby said, "Lieutenant, there's a war going on, in case you didn't notice, and letting you run home right now just isn't in the cards." My father, respectful by upbringing and no-nonsense by conviction, nevertheless put up an argument, finally declaring that he didn't see himself sitting around in Mississippi, just waiting. It was somewhere between a stare-down and insubordination, and the C.O. waffled between protocol and sympathy. It came down to a three-day pass and an ultimatum.

Hattiesburg to Chicago was 750 miles and the better half of a day on the *City of New Orleans,* packed with wartime travelers, cargo, and mail. All the seats were taken. He stood in a vestibule all the way, kept alert by rocking clatter, held up by fear and hope. Through daylight, high noon, twilight, and darkness, through Jackson, Yazoo City, Memphis, Fulton, Carbondale, Effingham, Kankakee, a litany of stations on a landscape flickering with urgency. He rode track rattle in an air pocket of noisy speed. Then at last Chicago's Union Station, then out to East Chicago on the South Shore Line, then the news that a few hours earlier O. L. Marks, M.D., had successfully addressed the complications, slapped the baby, sewn the mother up: "Congratulations! It's a boy, and they're doing fine. They're both fine."

The new father stayed with his family less than 24 hours before surrendering himself to the army. At Camp Shelby the C.O., relieved to have his headstrong but now euphoric medical officer back on time, shook his hand. "Sorry you couldn't make it to see your son born, Doc," he offered, "but it's great news that they're both O.K." And then he added, "Besides, as long as you were there when they laid the keel, you don't have to watch 'em launch the ship."

The next time my father saw me he was on the verge of being shipped overseas with the 17th Airborne to catch up with the D-Day invasion and spend the winter in Belgium. In a photo dated June 1944 he is holding me with the pride of a man who doesn't want to set his baby down but knows he will have to, the grip of a man who knows he might never see his son again.

Katsumi and Neil Nakadate, June 1944.

He is proud, and being brave, but he knows that might not matter in the end, and I am sure this is why he could never recall that moment. Decades later he claimed he never saw me between my birth and his return from Europe, when I was walking and talking and old enough not to recognize him when he walked through the door. He would be there when his second, third, and fourth children were born, and would eventually deliver over 200 babies himself. But I think he knew in the summer of 1944 that we two together were about to become casualties of the war.

THE 100TH INFANTRY BATTALION AND THE 442ND REGIMENTAL COMBAT TEAM

When Momotaro was about 15 years old, he went to his father and said: "Father, you have always been very kind to me. Now I am a big boy and I must do something to help my country."

—FROM "PEACH BOY," A JAPANESE FOLKTALE

Overview and cliché obscure individual identities and lives. Even the recognition eventually brought to the performance of the 100th Infantry Battalion, the 442nd Regimental Combat Team, and the Nisei in the Military Intelligence Service (MIS) encourages us to forget that the conditions and reasons for Nisei enlistment in the military varied. My uncle George Marumoto was drafted months before the United States entered World War II, after which he was both warehoused and shuttled around until the army decided there was a job he could do. My father was in the Army Reserves but inactive on December 7, 1941, then was started and stalled to the point of goading the army into putting him to work. George Suyama, my Uncle George's Montana brother-in-law, had enlisted on his own but found himself stationed in Missouri and insisted on being given a chance to fight overseas with the 442nd, to make a point.

The 442nd Regimental Combat Team and the 100th Infantry Battalion themselves had separate identities before being combined by the War Department and homogenized by history. The 100th Infantry Battalion came first, in June 1942—a renaming of the Hawaii Provisional Infantry Battalion, which had descended from the deactivated Hawaii Territorial Guard. People of Japanese ancestry made up over one third of the population of the Territory of Hawaii, so despite Hawaii's demonstrated vulnerability because of its proximity to Japan, and despite the arrests of some individuals, its Japanese American population as a whole was never incarcerated. Locking them all up would have been economically disruptive and logistically unworkable, not to mention a violation of their constitutional rights. So the Hawaiian Nisei continued to hold their jobs and their positions in the National Guard, and were never removed from their homes—an irony that never escaped their counterparts from Oregon, Washington, and California. It was in this context of relative freedom and largely undamaged self-esteem that the men of the largely Nisei 100th Battalion entered wartime service. The 1,400 men of the 100th referred to their unit in pidgin Hawaiian as the *one-puka-puka*, and their motto was "Remember Pearl Harbor." They had Hawaiian pride and were willing to prove it.

They went from island beaches to Camp McCoy, Wisconsin; Camp Shelby, Mississippi; and Camp Claiborne in Louisiana—and prejudiced skeptics had them under constant scrutiny for signs of disloyalty and incompetence. They entered the war beginning with the Italian Campaign, having first been rejected for another deployment by General Dwight Eisenhower. In the fall and winter of 1943–44 they fought their way up the boot of Italy from Salerno to Monte Cassino, where they faced brutal resistance and became known as the "Purple Heart Battalion," and then to Anzio and the outskirts of Rome. There, in June 1944 they were permanently attached to the 442nd.

The 442nd Regimental Combat Team was activated on February 1, 1943 and was to draw recruits from both Hawaii and the "relocation centers." The unit was formed partly in response to the army's ongoing need for manpower, and since the earliest Nisei MIS recruits were already proving themselves uniquely valuable in the field there was more support and less resistance to additional Nisei soldiers. Still, to some in the military and in the Roosevelt administration the 442nd was just an experiment, worth trying on grounds of political expediency and military necessity. And the Nisei had to deal with some old prejudices—for example, that non-white soldiers would only perform effectively (and without "creating problems") in segregated units. Conventional army wisdom also had it that non-white troops were only capable of serving in supporting roles. And of course the army believed the Nisei could only succeed if the officers assigned to lead them were white.

The formation of the 442nd was also a response to demands from many Nisei themselves, and their reasons for enlisting were personal as well as collective. Many were fervently patriotic. Many had argued from the outset that they deserved a chance to fight for their country like everybody else. Their loyalty to the United States had been called into question by the firestorm of rhetoric that followed Pearl Harbor, and now they wanted to prove their detractors wrong. Some young men in the camps were more than restless and wanted to escape a demeaning and unproductive life. But whatever their motivations, the thousands who wanted to go from the camps to the military had to be willing to serve unconditionally, entering the war even though the government insisted on keeping their families locked up.

The proof of a man's patriotic fitness to serve was supposedly found in his responses to the one-size-fits-all "loyalty questionnaire" cooked up by federal officials early in 1943 and required of all residents of the camps. Questions 27 and 28 became the focus—often a perplexed focus, depending on gender and generation. Question 27, concerning a willingness to serve combat duty in the armed forces, was not confusing for the young men, but it was for their sisters and their aging parents. And while many young men found it easy to "swear unqualified allegiance to" and "faithfully defend" the United States, and to "forswear any form of allegiance to . . . any foreign government," their parents did not, since renouncing the country of their birth would leave them without legal and diplomatic status. Would deportation follow? And what would happen to a family if the citizen children and noncitizen parents provided different answers to these or any other questions? Would family members be split up and sent to different camps? It should have surprised no one that as they viewed America anew through barbed wire, a vocal minority of draft-eligible Nisei rejected the paradox of being "free" to serve their country. Let us out of these prison camps, they tried to argue, and we'll be happy to wear a uniform. Let our parents go home. Unheeded, that minority resisted the draft as a matter of conscience or rebellion: *No,* they said to Question 27, and *No* to 28, and so came to be known as the No-No boys.

Yet thousands said *Yes.* They averaged 5'4" and around 125 pounds, and some supply officers referred to the 442nd Regimental Combat Team and 100th Infantry Battalion as a quartermaster's nightmare. Mocking detractors wondered aloud how men who couldn't fit standard-issue uniforms would do in combat. But the men of the 442nd/100th weren't about to complain or

Go for Broke

Upon the unveiling of a memorial to the 442nd Regimental Combat Team/100th
Infantry Battalion, and other Japanese Americans who served in World War II
(Los Angeles, June 1999)—and remembering Gwendolyn Brooks and John Okada.

> The exploits of the Nisei vets
> outlast their humanity. Their battle cry,
> their selfless conduct on the Arno and the Po,
> in the rescued villages of France
> and shrapnel-splintered forests of '44
> play well now in Peoria, even better
> in towns from Seattle to San Diego
> that once exiled their patriotic blood.
> The L.A. memorial calls the roll
> of the Four-four-two and One-puka-puka,
> invokes their fighting against all odds
> and reason, shooting the works against
> fascism on one hand, bigotry on the other.
>
> But no accounting there for blind energy,
> idealism betrayed, cynical hope,
> a chance to leave Hawaii for the States
> or escape in Europe the barbed-wire camp
> that was not a home. Why must we believe
> the needs and motives of their youth
> were not like those of Dorie Miller
> or the Tuskegee fliers,
> their love of country less confused
> than that of Ira Hayes? Even Audie Murphy
> was just some mick from Texas
> until Italy and France, when Hollywood
> saw something in the risks
> he had to take.
>
> Without conflict we glory in their glory—
> old men parsing granite letters,
> barely recalling the bewilderment

of youth, and those forever lost and young,
who served ambiguous visions once
and died in their embrace.

*"Naw—we don't hafta worry about th' owner comin' back.
He wuz killed in Italy."*

Cartoon by Bill Mauldin Copyright by Bill Mauldin (©1945).
Courtesy of Bill Mauldin Estate LLC.

make excuses because of their size, and my father recalled more than once (as always, a story to teach me a lesson) that when they trained they always made the smallest man in the squad carry the heaviest weapon—for example a Browning Automatic Rifle that, with bipod and bandolier, weighed almost 40 pounds—because "in combat he might have to do it." At 5'5" and 145 pounds my athletic father stood out a bit and would have fared better than many in such a test, but not by much.

They occasionally fought among themselves, friction sometimes arising between the Hawaiians and mainlanders because the Hawaiians thought the mainlanders were overly proud of not speaking pidgin and because many mainlanders who had been inducted from the camps seemed to welcome confrontation. It took some weekend leaves with West Coast comrades—to visit families a lot like theirs except for being locked up in a "relocation center"—for the Hawaiians to understand why their bunkmates wore resentment on their sleeves.

Like thousands of other "colored" American infantry in World War II the Nisei soldiers were aware that they were discriminated against as civilians and treated as an expendable commodity on the battlefield. But like the Tuskegee Airmen and the "Triple Nickel" 555th Parachute Infantry Battalion the Nisei were finally able to show that they could do more than manipulate a grease gun, load cargo, and haul garbage (the work that both Nisei in training and German POWs were frequently assigned, as my Uncle George Marumoto had observed.) The 442nd/100th unified under the crapshooter's motto "go for broke"—pidgin for "shoot the works"—and it carried them from Italy to Germany, by way of France. In the winter of 1945 they would forge a lifetime bond with a batch of Texans. A few months after that one of their artillery units found itself liberating Jewish survivors in the smoky shadow of Dachau. And by the end of the war the 442nd/100th would become the most decorated unit for its size and length of service in the history of the U.S. Army.

LOST

George Suyama's mother had died after a hard life in Montana, leaving five young children, among whom he was the older son. George's father, Ichiro "Harry" Suyama, a railroad laborer turned successful farmer, had once enlisted to fight in the Spanish American War because Teddy Roosevelt had said citizenship would be granted to all veterans—a promise that was never kept, at least as far as Japanese immigrants were concerned. Harry had died less than a year after his wife. By all accounts, their oldest child George was smarter than a whip and bound for success—and already in the army and guarding military prisoners in Missouri when he insisted on being reassigned so he could fight overseas. He had a kid brother and three sisters, and he wanted to keep his siblings from being branded with the stigma of Pearl Harbor. Before he left for Europe he told them, "Mary, Tana, Betty, Frank, never be ashamed of being of Japanese descent."

In late October 1944 he was killed in the Vosges Mountains, a casualty of the 442nd Regimental Combat Team's rescue of a battalion of Texans from the 36th Infantry, a former National Guard unit that had been surrounded by the Germans. The Texans were slowly being wiped off the map, and losing them was becoming a morale killer and a public relations nightmare. When other units failed to break through to save them the apparently impossible task was given to the 442nd. They engaged in a five-day firefight, from tree to tree, in a cold, wet forest, with rifles, machine guns, and mortars. Artillery blasted canopy and limb into a hail of splinters and cordwood. But the Nisei finally broke through the German lines on October 30, and approximately 210 men from the Lost Battalion were rescued. By that measure the mission was deemed successful. But over 800 men from the 442nd were casualties, including 200 killed in action. George Suyama's name is etched on the Wall of the Missing at the nearby military cemetery at Epinal, because his body was never found.

The 442nd rescued the Lost Battalion, liberated Bruyeres, and captured Biffontaine. By the end of the war they had received five Presidential Unit Citations. So they earned the right to be considered heroes by other Americans, including many in Texas and tens of thousands in the camps. The army cartoonist Bill Mauldin paid homage in the face of others' ignorance, and eventually the Nisei soldiers had their exploits written up by historians. But they paid a high price to earn recognition and respect—and some would say they had to sacrifice too much. "Twelve of my boys from Troop 123 eventually signed up for the 442nd," my father told me many years later, referring to scouts in the Portland troop he had mentored while he was in medical school and that later ended up in Minidoka. "Two of them are still in France."

By the late fall of 1944 there were stars in our windows, as in the windows of American families across the country: two stars in the window of my grandparents' unit 34–9-A, in the internment camp at Minidoka, Idaho; and three stars in our apartment window in Indiana—a blue one for my father, a blue one for my uncle Yoshiro "George" Marumoto, and a gold one for my uncle-by-marriage, Sergeant George Washington Suyama of Lewis and Clark County, Montana, the missing uncle I never got a chance to know.

"WAKARIMAS'"

It was not until 1974—a year after my mother began to "declassify" her memory and her feelings about being removed from her home in Portland and sent to "camp"—that we learned what Uncle George and the other MIS Nisei and Kibei had done during the war. Before that, we had only been told that he had been overseas for over three years, that he had served in the Pacific, and that that was all we were going to get. The formal prohibition against discussing his service record sat somewhere between my father's disinterest in discussing the Battle of the Bulge and my mother's reluctance to explain to us what "Minidoka" meant to her. The story remained sequestered there for two decades, except for an anecdote or two relating to monkeys. But in 1974 the government began to release various World War II military intelligence records, among them George Marumoto's.

Once he had been interviewed as a potential student for MIS Language School, George disappeared from the public version of military history, and he existed for his family only in the form of occasional correspondence. By March 1942 he was in Texas and by late May in Minnesota, and by April 1943 he was "somewhere in Australia," where he could confirm his well-being only through chatty letters regarding food, clothing, and family matters—and an occasional telegram to confirm simply that he was alive and well.

George chafed under the detail-driven task of turning Japanese military talk and writing into a useful English equivalent. He sought relief by taking swimming breaks in the warm Pacific. He got himself a pet monkey that tore up his letters one day, along with a half-dozen cartons of cigarettes. Of course he took his work seriously, but the translations were not particularly interesting in themselves—after all, he was contributing discrete pieces to a patchwork of information that others would knit together and determine the larger meaning of. George was most in his element when he could be the good-cop interrogator of Japanese POWs—an American soldier with a face that reminded them of a friend or neighbor. A fellow who was doing his duty, too, but might have been just as happy doing something else. He would offer them a smoke and a smile and tell them that he simply wanted to ask a few questions, and he assured them that, Japanese propaganda notwithstanding, they were not about to become victims of barbaric American torture. "*Wakarimas*'" they might have said, nodding back, "I understand." And then they would talk to him.

At times George was assigned a personal bodyguard, so he wouldn't get shot by mistake, and since battlefield identification was only uniform-deep, this concern was not a frivolous one. He once recalled for me a time when the Nisei translators were called together in order to find a volunteer for a highly unusual assignment. Some enemy units were apparently on their heels, and the allied command needed a volunteer to strip down to his skivvies, wade out into the river between the opposing armies, claim he was officer so-and-so from the Imperial Japanese Army, and order "his" soldiers to surrender. While George was pondering the odds of succeeding at such a mission— good enough, as it turned out in this case—another soldier raised his hand.

For George and others in the MIS there were certainly opportunities to exercise ingenuity and courage as well as to endure tedium and routine. But by making the plans and orders of the Japanese military accessible to the Allies, the Japanese American linguists helped shorten the war by months and saved thousands of lives. And while they were at it, George and his Nisei colleagues helped nurture and solidify allied camaraderie: "Those Aussies," he explained, "those Aussies sure could drink!"

A WHOLE LOT OF BELGIUM

The paratroopers were barely tolerated by some of their own generals, and knew it. They were aware of being patronized among the high command even as the Army Air Force itself was considered indispensable. George S. Patton apparently didn't think much of the Airborne. An armor and artillery man, General Patton favored tanks over parachutes—and word was that he considered airborne units both useful and expendable, helpful enough until Third Army muscle could roll in and finish the job. This despite the record of units such as the 101st Airborne, which had performed with distinction at Normandy. For their part the Germans, and the SS in particular, were said to have neither love nor respect for the American paratroopers, and it was understood that their orders were to take no airborne prisoners. Hearing this, the Americans were prepared to return the favor, and my father always said that if the Germans ever decided to attack his medical unit he was prepared to prove that his marksman's rating (rifle and pistol) was no fluke.

On the ground, his command amounted to two jeeps and a trailer containing tents and over 250 pounds of medical supplies. They drove with the jeep's windshield down to avoid reflections off the glass, pulled off the road for fast-moving caravans and occasionally got stuck, and otherwise slogged toward a memorable winter on the Rhine. The doctor and his corpsmen dogged the forward margins of the battle and set up their aid station a few hundred yards behind, performing first aid and triage, saving the soldiers they could and sending them back to a field hospital. Once when he and I were watching an episode of M*A*S*H, I asked my father if that series was anything like what he'd been through, and he answered, "Well, to some extent, but we were closer to the front and it always felt like somebody was trying to shoot me."

By the fall of 1944 Katsumi Nakadate was less an idealistic patriot than a pragmatist trying to do good work in a bad situation. The war had begun to change him, and his need simply to do his job well had to contend with his usual impatience with anyone who did not know how to do things right or who got in the way. "Doing my job" was what he believed in, never mind the agenda of the German army or a gaggle of Allied officers pointing at a map. Not surprisingly, *his* generals—the generals most respected by many other GIs—were Omar Bradley, known as an enlisted man's general, and the no-nonsense, no-pretentions A. J. McAuliffe. (McAuliffe was only weeks away from acknowledging to his troops at Bastogne that "We're fighting, it's cold, we're not home"—and in the same breath telling them that he had just rejected a German surrender ultimatum.) By now my father was a captain, but his affinity and affection were for soldiers like Willie and Joe, Bill Mauldin's unshaven and sardonically irreverent foxhole stoics, and into the next century he could tick off the names of his aid station comrades in the 681st Glider Field Artillery Battalion as if they had been the lineup of the

New York Yankees: Richard Shaw from New York, Arnie Severson from Wisconsin, Charles Love from Pennsylvania, and a buck sergeant from New Jersey named William Twigg, his driver. At one point Twigg resorted to tying a chunk of rope to him to make sure the doctor wouldn't fall out of the doorless jeep when he dozed off as they traveled at night: "Sorry to have to do this, Doc, but I'm in a lot of trouble if anything happens to you."

It was on a day late that fall when my father's three-vehicle aid unit found itself knee-deep in Belgian mud, somewhere west of Bastogne, having been forced to give way to faster traffic. Twigg was at the wheel and my father and the corpsmen were heaving and shoving on a jeep, when a high-riding, high-horsepower vehicle with stars to spare pulled up with a jolt. The big man himself emerged, glared at the airborne insignia on the doctor's sleeve, and wondered aloud, "Captain, why are *you*, an officer in the United States Army, standing here in the goddamn mud, pushing on a jeep?" A rhetorical question, really, if you are a general wearing a distinctive-looking sidearm, but a vexing interruption if you are a battalion surgeon. "*Sir,*" my father answered, "my orders are to set up an aid station several miles up this road and maybe save some soldiers' lives, and I've got to take care of *this* problem before I can do my job . . . *Sir.*" In return he got a look of dismissive impatience, and then the general disappeared into his vehicle and took off. "Did I ever mention," Dad told me in recounting that passing moment—my father, who never swore in public beyond a well-placed *dammit* but certainly knew how to use ellipses—"that I never did care much for that . . . Patton."

As a boy I asked my father what countries he had been in during the war. "Oh," he said, "we started from Boston, and you already know I ended up in Germany, but we went over to England on an ocean liner that had to zigzag a lot because we didn't have an escort to protect us from submarines, and then over the English Channel to France, and at one point I was in that little country, Luxembourg. And of course there was a whole lot of . . . Belgium."

"GOTT MIT UNS"

The snow was black.
The corpses stiffened in their scarlet hoods.

—LOUIS SIMPSON, "THE BATTLE"

By late 1944 rumor had it that the Germans were booby-trapping their own dead officers—so the Americans would get blown up when they searched the bodies for maps and battle plans. That meant my father found himself unable to treat them. This distressed and angered him, because when it was feasible he did what he could for wounded Germans—speaking to them in the pre-med German he had learned in college. He was not alone, of course, in trying to act humanely even under brutal conditions—but he thought of it as a natural progression from being an Eagle Scout and "doing a good turn daily." And it was perplexing when he heard the wounded Germans mumble the phrase "*Gott mit uns*"—"God with us." "It kinda hurt my religion," he would try to explain, "to think that we believed in the same God and here we were trying to kill each other." When we were growing up he would remind us from time, "I wasn't there to kill people . . . I was there to save people's lives." And then he'd stop.

After its relatively easy introduction to the war in France the "Sightseeing 17th Airborne" got rid of its condescending nickname in Belgium. It was during the Battle of the Bulge that my father overheard a soldier being told that the fighting was so desperate that there was no one to spare for guarding several captured Germans—so his orders were simply to "march them out of here and come back in ten minutes without them." And it was in the Ardennes that my father got wounded the first two times. After that the 17th was part of the "Operation Varsity" nighttime assault over the Rhine River near Wesel, where he got hit the—nearly fatal—third and fourth times. He didn't parachute into Germany with the rest of the 681st Battalion, but came down in the vulnerable belly of a glider, along with a jeep and his medical supplies—either the medics and their equipment would all land safely together, or they wouldn't—and was hit in the hip and back by shrapnel before the glider hit the ground. So he first performed first aid on himself and then patched up paratroopers until he was ordered to report to a field hospital before he could bleed to death. "There was another doctor, on a second glider," he told me, "but I never saw him again. . . . Somehow the Germans knew we were coming." During his two months of recuperation in hospitals in Belgium and England he had time to remember how many wounded soldiers there had been for whom nothing could be done. "I patched up boys your age," he would tell Portland high school students on Veterans' Day visits 50 years later, but he was thinking about the ones he had lost.

In the English hospital he also had time to worry about what might be happening to his brother and his father—noncombatants who had ties to America, living in an increasingly desperate Japan. Baseball was forbidden then, Toru recalled much later, as was the teaching of English, and there were severe shortages of rice and other staples, as well as clothing. When the war had started Toru was working as a bookkeeper, but by early 1945 he and his new wife and child had left the soon-to-be-bombed Omori District in Tokyo for a short stint with Nakadate Denki in Kofu—with the American B-29's soon to follow. *Yanagimachi* (Weeping Willow District) "was flattened," he said, including the electric company, and so, as he wryly put it, "I had to look for another job." Eventually we learned that Toru had actually kept such a low profile that he was under virtual house arrest—concerned that if the Japanese government decided he was an American spy they would throw him in prison, and if they decided he was truly loyal to Japan they would draft him into the army. But the only part of this my father learned in 1945, in a message conveyed through the Red Cross, was that his brother and his family had successfully fled Kofu for the family's homestead in rural Ya-manashi. From there they could see smoke from the burning city.

By the time my father had recuperated enough to leave England in search of his unit, Germany had surrendered, and the 17th Airborne had been moved out in preparation for being sent to fight the Japanese. Only a mop-up crew was left in Germany when he showed up to recover his footlocker and found that it had been emptied of everything but his uniform and a few incidental items. "A sergeant who never did seem to like me apparently decided I wasn't going to be back," was all he said about it. But the footlocker thievery stuck with him, especially because my mother's letters were among the missing items. So at that point he finally removed himself from combat. He agreed to be reassigned to the 82nd Airborne and the occupation of Berlin, where a black market and prostitution were already taking hold amidst the rubble and his job was to treat the flu and routine illnesses, injuries from accidents, and the damage GI's incurred from fistfights, sometimes with their allies, the Soviets. "Borscht," my father would say, "in Berlin I tried borscht . . . and I didn't care for it much." For their part the allies apparently had trouble comprehending an Asian face in an American officer's uniform. "The Russians," he said, "would glance over from their side of the line and look at me kinda funny." The way my father looked in 1945—thinner than at any other time in uniform—was documented by a German artist who did colored pencil portraits for GI's in order to keep from starving.

In Berlin Dr. Nakadate also found himself treating German civilians from time to time, children included—perhaps the closest he came in Europe to practicing the kind of everyday medicine for which he had entered the profession. Certainly it was his least traumatic work since training with the 442nd, the most prevalent complaint of the Berliners being head lice. He enjoyed recalling the time when a young mother brought in her injured child. She pushed her son toward him, but when the doctor with the Asian face asked, in German, where the pain was, the boy turned in puzzlement and asked her, *"Mutti, bist du sicher* . . . are you sure he is in the *American* army?"* Such a passing moment was a bulwark against squalor, the kind of story my father preferred to tell in later years, when harsher memories were about to break in.

Perhaps the footlocker, the artist, and the German boy—and my father's growing sense of what could befall Japan now that the war in the Pacific was nearing a conclusion—were at the heart of another incident, which he mentioned only once. On short notice he had agreed to be the officer in charge of a half dozen men on R&R, and at some point in the adventure realized that their vehicle was suddenly short on space. The problem was "souvenirs" the men had been "liberating" from German houses. It was an awkward moment for a Japanese American Methodist Eagle Scout, having to put a damper on that party, but he came up with a solution he could live with: he ordered a rest stop between two towns and before stepping away told the men to remove any unauthorized material from the truck, saying that when their break was over he didn't want to see anything in the vehicle "that wasn't issued to us by the United States Army." Whatever he literally couldn't see when he returned no doubt ended up somewhere in the U.S., but he did witness a cairn-like stack of miscellaneous possessions as they drove away. Perhaps something of an offering to the German people.

His end-of-the-war souvenir for me was a V-mail birthday message from Berlin in September 1945, a gift that began in apology and ended in hope. "My Son," it began, "Your 2nd Birthday and daddy is still away, not able to do what a dad ought to do for his Son. I hope on your 3rd Birthday I'll be present. . . . You are lucky to be living in America, where there is plenty to eat and good clothes to wear. You know that many children in Europe will

A World War II Doctor Visits High School Students, Veteran's Day 2004

The war this time is one of sun and dust
that some call a quagmire. Men are dying
in sand. But I don't know Iraq,
or even Vietnam, their fathers' war.

These could be the grandchildren of men
who didn't come back from Belgium
and France—went all that way
and never made it home.
After England it turned bad,
but especially '44 and '45,
the worst winter in Europe in fifty years.
Just our luck. And the Germans,
in the Bulge, and
when we crossed the Rhine.
No secret weapons, or smart ones
on either side, just rifles, mortars, artillery,
fear. Not like an hour on T.V. or
two at the movies, but six weeks short of food,
ammunition, sleep.
                                And heat, of course.
There was frostbite, and some of the wounded
froze. We never had enough people
or medical supplies. Well,
I couldn't have done my job with gloves on,
anyway. There was a red cross
on my helmet and another on my sleeve,
to show I was only there to help,
but I don't think the Germans cared.

Anyone who was there
would tell you it was tough.
I want to tell these students
just how tough, if that would
do them any good.

I have no feeling in these fingers
anymore.

starve this winter." And he ended, "May you never have to fight overseas as your dad had to do, under unhappy circumstances." As I grew up, he would retell his few wartime stories of comedy and redemption several times, but the tragic and pathetic stories only once—seemingly out of nowhere, on long-drive fishing trips when my brother and I were alone with him in the car. But the stories were there, and the nagging pain of some irremovable shrapnel near his spine kept his memory sharp.

In 2003, as we watched Bradley Armored Vehicles storm their way into Iraq and across the TV screen, he looked over at me. "Just remember," he said, "in a war there are no winners."

UNDER THE APPLE TREE

My father went into the war with a medical degree, an uncompleted medical residency, and his harmonica, which he called a "mouth organ." Six decades later he could still play "Don't Sit Under the Apple Tree (With Anyone Else But Me)"—a reminder to his assisted-living contemporaries of the hopes, fears, and brutal truths of 1942. Nostalgic and brave and playful at once, "Don't Sit Under" was less a prohibition (unenforceable, in any case, from overseas) than a poignant plea to save the fragile intimacies of courtship and marriage for the guy who, given time and luck, would eventually be marching home. Life was full of uncertainty, "for the duration," and anything but reassuring correspondence from home was hard to take. A Dear John message could be as disabling as a piece of metal flying through the air.

From her new home in Indiana my mother continued to be the key link in a network of family correspondence, at times a translator, at times an explicator or mediator, at times the bad news messenger with a thankless task. She corresponded with her parents in Japanese, and in English with her husband, sister, brother, and friends in other camps. She read between the lines when she had to and received and forwarded updates and gossip from East Chicago to Minidoka, Portland, the European Theater, and "somewhere in the Pacific." That, taking care of a baby, and sending my father socks and other necessities should have been enough to keep her busy. Her new sister-in-law Tana, only 23 herself, moved down from Minneapolis and found a job, and the two young army wives kept each other company while East Chicago settled into its own version of civilian life—sustaining wartime production of petroleum and steel with a draft-drained labor force, living on staples measured in ration stamps, salvaging and recycling aluminum and rubber and steel, following the progress of the war in the papers, writing lots of letters, and waiting for the mail.

But my mother's life took another turn during the summer of 1944 because of what my father later referred to in a diplomatic euphemism as "certain family problems": Fumie's husband Jiro had "found a new friend" in camp and was on the verge of getting himself released to start a new life in Salt Lake City—and simply leaving their daughters with Grandma and Grandpa. This was upsetting on its face, but for my incarcerated "enemy alien" grandparents, trying to help Fumie avoid the shame of a failed marriage while also caring for two young children under camp conditions was more than they could handle. Yet something had to be tried. Once again younger sister Mary was the only one in a position to act, who knew and could speak to all of the principals, who would be able to consult at length with an outside attorney. Officially, my mother had only been allowed to leave camp in order to live in Indiana, so it wasn't clear how freely she would be able to travel. But it was obvious that she would want to consult in person with Fumie and with Jiro, and it became clear that she could only help her sister and her parents by first signing herself back into Minidoka—and hope that any restrictions on a "voluntary long-term visitor" would be minimal. The only obvious benefit of this upheaval was that she would now be able to introduce her parents to their first grandson. Along for the ride, I entered Minidoka shortly after my first birthday, and lived there as another innocent resident for the next six months while my mother negotiated the security gates and traveled by train and bus between Minidoka, Portland, and Salt Lake City.

It proved a fool's errand, with forgiveness and hope on one side and unrepentant intransigence on the other, and Fumie (who never remarried) finally had to sign off on a divorce from her hospital room. As always, my mother had done her best in what finally turned out to be another *shikata ga nai* situation. When she had done everything she could and nothing else was possible her parents told her to pack up, reclaim her freedom, and take me home to Indiana. So she left them behind for a second time. It was a particularly painful time for a family imprisoned by illness and prejudice, during an era of fixed gender roles and expectations of marriage that seem curiously rigid today. Fumie never dropped the "Mrs." from her name and in our family infidelity and divorce were not discussed.

Western Union delivered well over a million "regret to informs" regarding U.S. military personnel who were killed, wounded, or missing in action during World War II. One of those telegrams arrived at our apartment on West Chicago Avenue a few days before we returned from Idaho—shortly after Easter 1945. The neighbors had accepted the envelope and placed it on top of other mail, knowing that we would be there in a matter of days. Many years later, when asked to recall the fall and winter of 1944–45, my father allowed that the Battle of the Bulge and crossing the Rhine were "tough . . . real tough," and that getting shot up wasn't much fun, either. "It was no picnic." My mother—who had just completed her own demanding mission, alone and in a hostile land, and was about to learn what it means to have a husband "severely wounded in action"—would not have been blamed for saying the same.

HABEAS CORPUS, 1944: *EX PARTE MITSUYE ENDO*

At the age of 22 Mitsuye Endo had been dismissed from her job as a typist working for the California Department of Motor Vehicles and had been forced from her home in Sacramento. She would eventually be sent to the camps at Tule Lake, California, and Topaz, Utah. She could not speak or read Japanese, had never been to Japan, and had a brother serving in the U.S. military. She had complied with the exclusion and evacuation orders—had not broken any laws, even in peaceful protest—and therefore had passed the "good behavior" loyalty test that the government imposed on Japanese Americans. In July 1942, while living in a converted horse stall at the Tanforan Assembly Center, she petitioned for a writ of habeas corpus, asking that she be discharged and restored to liberty. In her petition she asked that the United States show proof that it had a right to lock her up, and she appealed the subsequent denial. At one point the government offered to make it easy for her to be released from camp if she would drop her case before it could reach the Supreme Court, but she refused the bribe, pursued her suit, and remained behind barbed wire for two years in the meantime. Finally, on

December 18, 1944, the Supreme Court ruled unanimously, in *Ex parte Mit-suye Endo,* that the government cannot detain a citizen that the government itself concedes is loyal to the United States. (The court's tortured handling of the internment cases as a whole was reflected in its 6–3 decision, on the same day, to uphold the conviction of Fred Korematsu for not *reporting* for detention.)

Since the War Department and the Supreme Court supposedly worked independently of each other, it seems far from coincidental that one day prior to the *Endo* decision, the Roosevelt administration announced that, effective January 2, 1945, the West Coast exclusion order against the Japanese would be revoked. The announcement seemed oddly timed in that it was made on a Sunday, unlike most other noncombat information. But the government had suddenly decided it had no reason under the law to keep the Japanese Americans in a camp, so it might as well let them all go home. Of course, for many Japanese Americans, this was problematic, since "home" no longer existed. But "coincidence" and irony invite the question: what if Mitsuye Endo had, in the name of national security, been deprived of the right to petition for a writ of habeas corpus? The authors of the U.S. Constitution had, of course, anticipated the answer 150 years earlier.

The camps did close during the coming year; my grandparents left Minidoka in July 1945 and the Idaho camp would be empty by the end of October. But by the time the Endo case was decided over 110,000 lives had been permanently damaged, not only by the war that Japanese Americans suffered through with the rest of the country, but also by scapegoating, "evacuation," and imprisonment, which had singled them out.

My grandparents, Minejiro and Hatsune Marumoto, were experiencing their third winter of incarceration at 34–9-A, Minidoka War Relocation Center, Hunt, Idaho.

My cousins, Michi (age 7) and Yuri (5), were now living with their grandparents and had not had contact with their mother since leaving Oregon.

Their mother, my aunt Fumie Sakano, was nearing the end of her third year of TB hospitalization in Portland, and her second without seeing her children.

Fumie's sister Mary had left her home in Indiana to rejoin their parents in camp, in order to help them care for Michi and Yuri under chaotic conditions and then to help Fumie negotiate her impending divorce.

I, wrapped in the innocence of toddlerhood and a warm winter coat of a kind that was not available in camp, was oblivious to both the immediate hardships and the larger story.

Meanwhile, my father and the 17th Airborne, and over a half million other American soldiers, were engaged in the six-week Battle of the Bulge, although he also understood where and how his wife and son would be spending Christmas.

My uncle Yoshiro "George" Marumoto was translating intercepted messages and interviewing Japanese POWs in Brisbane, Australia, but due to censorship restrictions and distance was finding it difficult to communicate with his own family.

My uncle-by-marriage George Suyama, who had asked for combat duty as a way of fighting home-front discrimination against his siblings, was missing in action with the 442nd Regimental Combat Team and presumed dead in the Vosges Mountains.

COMING HOME, STARTING OVER

Nana korobi ya oki: Seven times down, eight times up.

—JAPANESE SAYING

The war ended in Europe on May 8 and in the Pacific on August 15, 1945. But these dates obscure the difficulty that many experienced in "coming home," let alone starting over. The U.S. alone had over 1.1 million killed, wounded, or missing in action, and many veterans, including my father, did not get stateside until 1946. And Japanese Americans, like astronauts re-entering Earth's atmosphere and surrendering to gravity, found it necessary to accept what had changed while they were "in camp," and what had not, in the places they had known before the war. This was when tens of thousands of Japanese American internment stories entered a soundproof room, surfacing afterwards only as oblique and misleading responses to questions and

Minidoka, Idaho, Winter 1944–45

Across this hostile unclaimed land
uprooted people struggle to believe
in windy desert spaces. Here
the numbered barracks of the dispossessed,
watched by soldiers and barb-wired
for safety all around, are leaking grit
and cold. Bleach-green sagebrush
gestures at survival
as far as the Sawtooth Range.

This is no place for angry faith, and
to prove themselves as American as Gehrig
and DiMaggio, to take a hack at Hitler,
Mussolini, or even "those damn Japs"
many young men have left for the 442.
At Hattiesburg they met water moccasins,
swamps, and Mississippi heat,
learned to fire a service pistol and a BAR—
and were told to mind
the back of the bus
when going into town. Overseas,
from Anzio to Biffontaine, snipers
and shrapnel have cut their ranks in half,
and Purple Hearts and telegrams
become their families' valentines.
Here people can count on casualty lists
from week to week, censored mail,
and letters of regret. Ennui and empty days
accumulate for mothers, fathers,
and lonely brand-new brides,
busy with worry in a place that offers
little room for hope, no future
but what the past has given.

Gold stars shine in the desert night,
and dust settles on the windowpanes.

Still Life with Goldfish, East Chicago, Indiana, April 1945

Creaky stairs and a snug hallway,
cozy radiators, scuffed linoleum, an icebox,
a small wooden table, a goldfish and
pebbles in a flat-sided bowl. A three-
room walk-up above the Huber
Funeral Home. Outside, ladies in babushkas
bustled from A&P to evening meal, with
kielbasa or pot roast to complete the day.

My mother's future marked time
as my childhood toddled on, past
Reid Drug and vanilla shakes, past
neo-Gothic First Methodist, past
protective walls of Inland Steel, past
St. Catherine's where I was born and
Lewin's where my doctor (now army
surgeon) father once bought dapper ties
to impress the nurses. On quiet walks
to Kosciusko Park we waited for
no news good news regarding
the Third Army, one telegram away
from having to start
a whole new life.
                    After six months
in Idaho we returned at Easter
to stuffy-quiet rooms, no goldfish,
a week of un-forwarded mail
and a "regret to inform" from
the Department of War. "It came
a few days ago," the neighbor said,
"you'd have missed it if we'd sent it on."
At least "wounded in action" offered
some take-it-or-leave-it for going on.
907 W. Chicago Avenue, a place

for writing letters, measuring sugar, meat,
and butter, waiting for what came next.
On the ground floor the dearly departed lay,
suspended between last rites
and their eternal rest.

Katsumi (James), Mary, and Neil Nakadate, 1946.

comments in postwar conversations: "Oh, we knew their family in camp . . . what did you do in school today?" Or, "I think I had Spam for the first time in camp . . . pass the butter, please." Such awkward evasions were the tip of an emotional iceberg. For decades, passing references deflected stories of trauma and damage due to removal and incarceration, in my family and many, many others.

There was still, of course, anti–Japanese American sentiment on the West Coast—the product and residue of war, racism, misinformation, and decades of discrimination—and there were more than a few who didn't want "the Japanese" back: "If those people hadn't been guilty of something, the government wouldn't have locked them up in the first place!" Still, about half of Portland's Japanese Americans returned, some because they knew nowhere else to go. My grandparents returned in July 1945, after three years in Idaho. After demonstrating their loyalty to the United States by cooperating with "evacuation" and "relocation" orders, after enduring insult and deprivation. But now Minejiro and Hatsune Marumoto had little in the way of cash, and no equity in America, and they could only hope that looking up prewar non-Japanese friends would enable them to recover cherished possessions that had been entrusted to them. With them were my cousins, Michi and Yuri, who were finally reunited with their mother, at last released from the hospital. But their family had been a casualty of infidelity and wartime disruption, and their father was . . . gone. It was the moment, Fumie said later, when "we all started over together." In Salem some legislators sponsored initiatives to oppose the return and resettlement of Japanese Americans, advocating deportation instead.

The Oregonian Hotel was now in other hands, of course, and there was no Japantown, only remnants of the multicultural prewar community they had called home. My grandparents, my cousins, and my aunt, along with many other refugees from Minidoka, again found themselves in challenging surroundings, this time a barracks-like public housing project in St. John's Woods. They would be in that holding pattern for seven years, slowly rebuilding their economic lives and becoming Oregonians again. My grandfather, then 65, found himself accepting part-time work that would have suited him only as a desperate young immigrant—janitorial work and clearing tables in a restaurant. Fumie, her TB now treatable with antibiotics, made fitful progress through a series of service agency and civil service jobs that eventually led to a long-term position at Portland State University. Like other Nisei whose parents' economic lives had been ruined, she became the primary breadwinner as the family recovered. Finally, just before Christmas 1952, they were able to buy a house, in the Irvington District, where my grandparents planted snap peas, tomatoes, and roses in a backyard garden— "For you a rose in Portland grows," the city had been telling the world for years—and could finally think of themselves as "home."

Meanwhile Uncle George was discharged from the army under orders to say nothing about his work in military intelligence, and returned to Portland with Tana, the girl he had married and then been separated from for over three years. He and others organized the Oregon Nisei Veterans, since the American Legion had made it clear that they were not welcome there.

My father, Captain Katsumi Nakadate, M.D., finally returned to East Chicago in January 1946, having been declared 30 percent disabled, and with a Purple Heart (and three oak leaf clusters) to account for it. At Camp Grant he suffered a discharge physical during which a young private made several futile attempts at taking a blood sample. When the captain learned that the private had been stabbing at veterans for less than two weeks he grabbed the syringe and drew his own blood—his final act as an active-duty doctor. (His physical rehab would continue for eight more years.) Separation papers in hand, he took the train from Rockford to Chicago, and from there the South Shore Line. In East Chicago the former multisport athlete limped down off the car, crossed West Chicago Avenue, climbed the stairs at 907, and greeted the woman he had lived with for only half a year before going off to witness a lifetime's worth of carnage. It was fortunate that we happened to be home when he got there. He had neglected to phone ahead to let my mother know he was finally on his way.

I think he wanted to surprise his future before it surprised him. But during the war my mother had gotten used to asking her own questions, and the first words out of her mouth were, "Where did you come from?" (As time passed, confusion set in as to the precise phrasing—or which word got the emphasis.) Years later there was no mention of what, exactly, she was wearing when she saw my father for the first time in two years—but those were the days of housedresses and aprons, so I'm sure it was not what she had planned. Captain Nakadate also found himself being stared at by a toddler son who had started to talk but didn't know him from the muffin man, the muffin man, who lived in Drury Lane—or, for that matter, the cheerful man who climbed our stairs once a week with giant tongs and a block of ice that dripped on my mother's linoleum. But we began to resume our lives together, my father attempting to restart his medical practice and my mother carrying the burden of re-establishing a domestic life. My brother Jim appeared ten months later, the first of our family's three Baby Boomers. And safe and sound and reunited, we began to send money and packages to Japan.

My now permanently expatriated Uncle Toru—still in shock from how quickly he had lost the "dual" in his citizenship—along with his wife Tomiko and infant daughter Katsumi, had survived the endgame of the Pacific War by fleeing to the village his father had once left for the United States. The Nakadate homestead was a crowded refuge, also sheltering two aunts, cousin Norio, and of course Grandpa himself. They were in Toyotomi-mura when the nuclear age began—and it was there that, for several years after the war, we sent "care packages" of commodities and clothing. Earlier that summer Toru had witnessed wholesale devastation in Kofu and had seen the electric company's offices destroyed by American bombers. Carpenters were called in as soon as hostilities ended, and the family began to rebuild, and of course Toru pitched in on the reconstruction. But his days with the family business were numbered.

The Allied Occupation Forces had shut down the Japanese government's Foreign Office Radio Room in Tokyo, but a group of expatriates from Oregon, Washington, California, and Hawaii took over the facility and made themselves immediately useful, creating an organization they called Radiopress. The Nisei/Kibei grapevine connected Toru with his cohort ("Somekawa, Ogishima, Nikaido . . . ," he recalled), and Toru, a Japanese American (now American Japanese) city boy, was liberated from both rural life and electrical contracting by his bilingual skills. In 1946 Radiopress began to monitor international broadcasts and distribute translated transcripts by subscription to the major Japanese newspapers. Around the clock it was Radio Peking, Radio Australia, All-India Radio, Radio Pakistan, the Voice of America, and the BBC. (Soon enough, Radiopress would become a primary conduit to the West for news out of Communist China, North Korea, and Vietnam.) Toru, working in the English section, listened through headphones and typed news and editorials onto mimeograph masters, renewing daily his acquaintance with the language of his youth and the country he had lost. He looked forward to the commentaries of Alistair Cooke, the BBC correspondent in New York City, whose observations on American life were two or three times the average column length. Occasionally, transported by the language and the voice, Toru forgot to keep typing.

For the next four decades Uncle Toru would take the 5:00 AM train into downtown Tokyo, so he could sit with headphones and a typewriter, listening for America. With his binational, bilingual perspective and his listening post in a devastated Japan, Toru was repeatedly reminded that history is written by the survivors, and that silences and omissions can be the most telling part of the record. As the decades passed, the Sansei, my generation, would come to recognize the same, and begin to recover the experience that was "camp."

4 ～ Sansei

If we are always arriving and departing, it is also true that
we are eternally anchored. One's destination is never a
place but rather a new way of looking at things.

—HENRY MILLER, *Big Sur and the Oranges of Hieronymus Bosch* (1957)

SANSEI DREAMS?

The Sansei were the second Japanese American generation born into citizenship. Some Sansei, including my cousins Michi and Yuri, were born before the war and spent three childhood years behind barbed wire. Some, like my lifelong friend Keith Nakayama, were among the 6,000 born in the camps (or nearby hospitals) and were toddlers there. Many Sansei, like my siblings, were Baby Boomers who grew up after the camps had closed, and some of us, by chance and the luck of geography, had only passing or oblique relationships with the camps because we grew up outside the West Coast exclusion zone. But over time most Sansei were alike in being both enveloped by the euphoria and prosperity of postwar America and nagged at by the censored memories of thousands.

Many Sansei inherited the lost dreams of Issei grandparents and the interrupted ambitions of Nisei mothers and fathers. For the Issei it was dreams of owning their own farm or business. Dreams of buying a house and living as their achievements and income justified. Dreams of engaging in the American political process. Dreams of voting, not just paying taxes. For many Nisei the dream was achieving a college education. Or applying that education to a job that actually required the degree—not being underemployed or relegated to "traditional" employment for "orientals." The Great Depression had certainly created private as well as great public losses everywhere, but the ordeal of "camp" was a blow from which many Japanese Americans could not recover. For the Issei there was not enough time, not enough energy. My grandfather and grandmother were 65 and 55, far from being able to pick up and start from scratch. And after the war many Nisei took on their version of a promise that had governed their own parents' lives: "kodomo no tame ni," "for the sake of the children." They would push wartime trauma aside, find belated success, and give the next generation a better chance than they had had. This was not necessarily expressed in words, but for many Sansei it was tangible and clear.

The Sansei grew up in gradually resettling rural communities and cities up and down the West Coast—and in families scattered across other time zones by the diasporic force of "relocation"—and it felt to some as if they carried the Issei's broken hopes to high school in notebooks and book bags, brought the Nisei's lost aspirations along to college dorms from Seattle to San Diego to the Ivy League. Many Sansei still tracked toward math and the sciences, planning to be doctors or engineers. But now, two generations away from the immigrant need to survive and one generation removed from the obligation to find a stable niche, there was also a sense that it might be possible to study almost anything. Departures from the safe and reasonable path were not always easy for parents and grandparents to accept—"Major in English?" my doctor-father responded with skepticism, "I thought you already knew English. And what are you going to do with it?" But the Sansei were usually good students, hardworking and reliable, and as a group well-behaved. Over-achievers some called them—except that for many that only meant meeting their parents' expectation that they work at the top of their potential. The exceptions were easy to overlook, and soon the Sansei found themselves stereotyped in their own right, as Exhibit A of a so-called model minority.

INDIANA, OUR INDIANA

The first word I ever read was INLAND, high on a factory wall in East Chicago, and every time I looked up at it through our car window it evoked comfort and awe. It was solid, it was there, it was *In-Land*. (Surely I was not the only child there who heard security in that name—as with "The Region" and "The Midwest"—and to whom it seemed unnecessary to add the word "steel.") Before and during World War II the Calumet Region was the epitome of American productivity and strength, and postwar the Region was fused by its smelters and refineries to the chassis and engines coming out of Detroit. Inland Steel was iconic, indeed necessary, like the Chicago stockyards or the Board of Trade. And while there were other key businesses between Chicago and Gary, Indiana (Standard Oil, in Whiting, for example), Inland was the first and only industrial monolith that mattered to me. (The Rust Belt decline of the seventies and eighties, like the disappearance of the Union Stockyards, was on nobody's list of things to come.)

My family's presence in East Chicago seemed consistent with the determined diversity of the place. "Nakadate" lived side by side with Bartos, Benchik, Karwasinski, Zandi, and all the rest. My ears grew familiar with such all-American names, and the appearance of the very newest newcomers, the refugees from the war, simply made me feel secretly secure, since they were the "displaced persons," not I. So whether I was sipping a milkshake on a stool in Reid Drug or being doted on by the St. Catherine's nuns while my father made hospital rounds, I considered myself at home. When I was three our growing family moved out of the cozy East Chicago apartment and into a small house on Calumet Avenue in Hammond, "right next door." My boyhood there was infused with fascinating aromas and sounds—our milk came from Jim Patterson's ice-dripping, creamy-smelling Prairie View Dairy truck, and the double doors of Tom Balio's green panel truck opened up on fresh vegetables and fruit. At night, while falling asleep with my brother Jim in the next bed, I could hear the mechanical lullaby of train cars being coupled and uncoupled in the Monon Railroad yard. To my boyhood mind Hammond was yet another comforting place where people were willing to give you a chance to figure things out and do something with life.

By 1951 we were a multi-child postwar family with two boys followed by two girls—a number and order of offspring my father had always wanted and took a bit too much for granted. And we had moved yet again, this time two blocks away and into a recently built three-bedroom house, the first one my parents owned. (My mother found the timing of our increasingly difficult moves somewhat vexing; she was always well into a new pregnancy when my father recognized that the current housing would no longer be adequate.) On 173rd Place the ethnic blend of the neighborhood had a familiar ring—Anderson, Wainwright, Vomish, Miyofsky, Ohr—and my purple Monarch bicycle and I found ad-hoc playgrounds accessible and inviting: grassy hills beside highway viaducts that my friends and I slid down on corrugated cardboard; "vacant" lots lush with milkweed, ragweed, dandelions, and wild grasses, filled with antic grasshoppers and palettes of butterflies; sandlots for baseball, full of rutted and dusty promise; alleys with hoop after basketball hoop stretching (it seemed) to Indianapolis. This was Indiana in the 1950s, and basketball the secular faith, so participation in pick-up games and shot-making contests in the alley helped validate my presence in the neighborhood. The only thing worse than not being chosen was not taking part. We were not a good fit, basketball and I, but learning to dribble was as vital to my well-being as wrestling would have been in Iowa or football in Ohio.

Little League baseball arrived in Hammond just in time to rescue my summers and help sustain me for the rest of the year, and hours of playing catch with the wall of our house and stoopball in front focused my energies. My goal would be to throw the ball accurately and catch it without error 20, 30, 40 or more times in succession—or start over. It was a solitary compulsion, not in order to reach the major leagues but merely to seek perfection. Such dedication even made my buying baseball cards acceptable. And when my father took me to see the White Sox and their breakthrough Latin/Caribbean core (Rivera, Minoso, Carrasquel . . .) I found the presence of non-Anglos in the lineup compelling confirmation that my respect for baseball was not misplaced.

That Northwest Indiana valued elbow grease and tenacity suited my father just fine, since that was also the ethos of his immigrant parents and Japantown neighbors in faraway (and apparently long-lost) Portland, a culture that saw no profit in complaint. "So what do you expect *me* to do about it?" he would respond whenever I lamented some unfairness of my boyhood world. A teacher's pronouncement that my school's inventor-namesake had defined "genius" as "one percent inspiration and ninety-nine percent perspiration" sounded familiar enough to me; Edison, it seemed, concurred with my father. This, combined with my mother's Depression-inspired frugality, made for a family belief-and-behavior system that I later discovered was called the "Protestant ethic." Our parents believed in achievement over the long haul, and above all in delayed gratification and the distant rewards made possible by education. And the economic setbacks of their youth caused them to value learning all the more. "Once you have your education," my mother would say, "no one can ever take it away." Their loss of college savings in the Depression had made them wary of bankers and banks, and their wartime loss of property and status due to evacuation and internment made them wary of government assurances, even when the "peace and prosperity" Eisenhower years arrived. Our catechism was simple and direct: go to school, listen to your teacher, stay out of trouble, save for the future, sit up straight. And don't make excuses.

Accordingly, my father (like his father before him) had little patience with the incidentals that gave cultural texture to children's lives—candy bars, comic books, Saturday matinees. Of what educational value were Superman and Captain Marvel? Or (on television) Captain Video and his Video Rangers? Or frivolous movie musicals like *Oklahoma!*? In his book they were distractions, a waste of money and a waste of time. And so it was with fads. When a friend of mine got a pair of blue suede shoes and I wanted a pair of my own, the "discussion" quickly arrived at *No* (neither of us could have anticipated the disagreements over popular music that were yet to come). Meanwhile, it was all right that I collected butterflies, since that was "science" and therefore educational, or even postage stamps, which taught me something of geography, history, and accomplished lives. And (son of an Eagle Scout) I joined Cub Scouts and then Boy Scouts, and not incidentally, took swimming lessons at the Civic Center: "Did you know," my father offered by way of inspiration, "that some soldiers drowned on the beach at Normandy because they didn't know how to swim?"

Such harsh declarations were tempered by my mother's gentle diplomacy: You can accomplish things without causing others to feel defeated or lose face. Rules and expectations should serve teaching and learning. What is learned and understood now will affect the future. I see now that this ethos was not simply maternal, but also very Japanese, and that it was natural that my mother became the translator and mediator between her husband and her children, negotiating between his pronouncements and our needs, and at times even persuading him to see things another way. (If she had been a legislator, she would have made short speeches and then done wonders in the committee room.) After all, she wanted a family, not an autocracy. And she became a volunteer—serving as a "room mother" at the school, telephoning for the PTA, helping to lead our scout organizations, canvassing our neighborhood for the March of Dimes. Cookies and punch, wiping noses, character-building, fighting polio, encouraging us to persevere when the homework was difficult—all of it.

Meanwhile she would draw from current events and the recent record for public role models to set before us—although at that time the successes of America's minorities were scattered, and sometimes dismissed as almost freakish exceptions. Jim Thorpe, the Gershwins, Jesse Owens, Marian Anderson, Jackie Robinson, Ralph Bunche. These and others were mentioned in passing and occasionally as possible subjects for school reports. We were taken to see *The Jackie Robinson Story* at the drive-in theater. A few "orientals" had made a mark—actress Anna May Wong and diver Sammy Lee among them—but there, too, the focus seemed to be limited to entertainment and sports, and it would be more than a decade before Asian Americans became visible in politics. The virtual absence of Japanese faces was awkward, and for me puzzling. Where were they?

During our vacation trips to Oregon to see my mother's parents and siblings (and my five cousins), I might have sensed that perhaps we were but sojourners in the Midwest and my Hoosier boyhood a matter of borrowed time. During a summer visit to Portland shortly after the passage of the legislation that made it possible for my grandparents finally to become citizens, I helped them study for their citizenship exam, reviewing American history and civics in a language that I found easy and they still found difficult enough that their mispronunciations struck me as either humorous or embarrassing. I copied down the Pledge of Allegiance in Japanese (the kanji were alien to me, of course, vexing in their intricacy and number), and was perplexed that Grandma and Grandpa had to suffer such frustration in order to have something I took for granted. "You were born here," my mother explained, "you are already an American." But surrounded in Portland by the food and language and memory of my heritage, I was the one who felt somehow displaced. Even our close friends the Nakayamas, with whom we had shared weekends at the Indiana Dunes, had by this time left Chicago and returned to Portland. In Oregon I was among people who looked like me, yet somehow felt I didn't belong. Or perhaps I didn't know where I was from.

My father always said that Indiana had been a good place for our family. He had been drawn to East Chicago in 1939 because St. Catherine's had offered him an internship, and my mother had found shelter there during the war. But it was also true that ten years later my parents were increasingly conscious of the distance between themselves and their Oregon roots—and a Japanese community that was gradually re-establishing itself. I was too busy with baseball and school to see that we might be on the verge of returning to the West Coast, and that I, who had known it only as a curious visitor, would soon be going back. (In one of those odd twists of education I would one day also return to my Hoosier roots, for graduate work in Bloomington.)

ECHOES OF THE WAR

After posing for a homecoming family portrait my father had placed his ID cards, dog tags, paratrooper's "jump watch," and medals in a dresser drawer, along with the trauma and behind the tee shirts and ties. His boots, officer's uniforms, and Eisenhower jacket went back into the footlocker that had been shipped to "Capt. Katsumi Nakadate . . . East Chicago, Ind." Like other veterans he wanted to store the war in a secure place and get on with civilian life—making a living, re-entering a marriage, catching up in general. My father was determined to do what he had promised himself he would while experiencing extreme discomfort in Belgium, in Germany, and in a hospital bed in England. My three younger siblings were one expression of this desire, as was a postwar progression of family cars, from Studebaker to Pontiac to Oldsmobile.

But no sooner had he declared himself back in the saddle ("K. James Nakadate, M.D. announces his return from overseas military service and resumption of practice at . . .") than it became clear that the shrapnel that remained in his "backside" and back would keep him from resuming his prewar medical practice at his prewar pace—surgeries every morning, walk-in afternoon and evening office hours, 2 AM calls to deliver babies, and all the rest. So he returned to the classroom for another three years, this time under the G.I. Bill, to be an anesthesiologist. (He was, it turned out, on the leading edge of a transition in which modern medicine would become a bewildering roster of specialists, making a relic of the family doctor who treated patients at home.) In this way and others, to be a child at that time was to be surrounded by aftershocks and echoes of the war, the war, the war, everyone's conversation marker for time and place and people: "Before the war he was . . . During the war she had to . . . He got called up in . . . was wounded in Italy . . . You couldn't buy that in 1944 . . . a sole surviving son . . . war widow . . . war bride

. . . V-E Day . . . V-J Day . . . Pearl Harbor. . . ." Of course, in my family any references to Japan-as-enemy brought with them an awkward pain, since for us Japan was also cultural heritage and my grandparents' place of birth. And all but buried by all other talk of the war were those occasional, seemingly accidental references to "camp"—my family's experience of exile and imprisonment, censored into obscurity.

The war. When I started school at Edison Elementary in Hammond, there up on the wall outside Principal Robaska's office, along with the portraits of Washington and Lincoln, was Joseph Rosenthal's already-iconic photo of U.S. Marines raising the flag on Iwo Jima. A few grades later we brought to class school supplies and small personal items such as toothbrushes to put in Red Cross boxes for children in countries still recovering from the devastation, and the Marianas Islands were added to my sense of remote geography. Occasionally there were "all-school movies," paid for by "paper drives" that mimicked wartime collections of scrap iron, rubber, and the like. At home, my friends and I found ourselves "playing war," naively mimicking the experience our fathers had just endured—wielding stick-rifles and imitating soldiers by diving into dirt piles and hiding behind bushes and trees. I always found myself hoping we would decide to role-play against the Germans this time, not the Japanese.

The war. For five years after V-J Day my family sent food and clothing to my grandfather in Yamanashi and my Uncle Toru and his young family in Tokyo, living under the American occupation of Japan and suffering in a black market economy. We boxed up commodities from wool yarn to Hershey's cocoa, and Toru, having no way to compensate, would enclose with his thank you letters a few colorful Japanese stamps for my collection.

The war. In 1949 ABC television aired the documentary series "Crusade in Europe," making cultural currency of General Eisenhower's personal narrative, and three years later NBC offered "Victory at Sea," six full months of Sunday afternoon segments that we watched religiously. (The events of the Pacific war were a revelation for my father, too, of course, since he had been in Europe.) I stared at the black and white footage in silence, enthralled and bewildered by the sudden power and sheer inventiveness of death, and by the alien and sometimes grotesque images of Japanese faces not unlike my own. The orchestral soundtrack of "Victory at Sea," a counterpoint of strings and percussion, took its place in the soundtrack of my childhood, its

Hoosiers

I grew up short, slight, and a step slow,
where iron hoops hung from most garages,
and rusty bracket holes claimed
almost all the rest. What they now call
"walking" we called "steps," and
palming the ball was among the major sins
we knew. With two or three
we played H-O-R-S-E, spelling out jumpers,
hooks, and lay-ups as the days shortened
and a twilight chill blew in off the lake.
With four or more
we faked and passed
in ad-hoc alliances,
breathing in
the fading light
and breathing out
warm clouds and truancy,
forbidden by the code of the alley
to go home and break up the game.
Better to face an inquisition
than be mocked for the rest of the week.

That was Northwest Indiana in the Fifties,
in the shadow of smelters, refineries,
and Branch McCracken,
so no chance of avoiding it
any more than an occasional fight
or the neighborhood grit that made the ball
unruly. I was never any good, of course,
but to be in the right place at the right time
to screen for the sure-handed and the quick,
a natural at going from slow to stop
so the game could go on and on. Jackets
in a heap, we scuffled into suppertime
and the wrath of our fathers,

dribbled and drove until fingers tingled
and sweat made us shiver,
until darkness came on
and the rim we shot at
was just a memory
and a sound.

marches and maritime lullabies associated in my head forever with bodies floating in the sea.

The war. One evening we were hustled into the car for a quick trip to the frozen custard stand on Calumet Avenue, and hustled as quickly home with our five-cent cones so as not to miss a speech on television in which General MacArthur—who had supervised the occupation in Japan but had just been relieved of his most recent command by President Truman—told us that old soldiers never die, they just fade away. I never knew whether my father sided with the stubborn war hero or Harry Truman on the matter of Korea, only that the occasion involved a general from my father's war, and that war itself was not letting go of us anytime soon. People talked of "Commies" and "the Iron Curtain," and for several years a closet in our basement was stocked with canned milk, soup, flashlights, and other fallout shelter supplies.

The war. As I learned to read I took to the Sunday comics, where "Terry and the Pirates" and "Steve Canyon" offered some all-American adventures in exotic locations—and enough offbeat and exotic secondary characters to populate a carnival sideshow. These latter included stereotyped render-ings of devious and hostile "oriental" women that were without reference points in my experience. (My mother and my aunts hardly resembled the Dragon Lady or any of her sinister sisterhood.) Steve Canyon was a reminder that our world was one of war veterans facing new challenges, and the strip about Italian war-orphan "Dondi" reminded me never to take my family for granted.

The war. World War II propaganda cartoons such as "Bugs Bunny Nips the Nips" were thoughtlessly recycled into the afternoon playground of chil-dren's television, and they would appear unannounced to abuse my imagina-tion. (My siblings and I were too young to have seen any of these cartoons in the movie theater, and the older Sansei, such as my cousins, were spared that trauma to the extent that almost all of them were locked up in the camps.) I found myself fascinated, confused, and hurt by the cartoons' portrayals of slant-eyed, buck-toothed, glasses-wearing "Japs"—grotesquely offensive as manic and hapless monkey-men who jabbered incoherently and scuttled, vermin-like, over "rising-sun" airplanes destined to crash and burn. The fear and panic of the ridiculous monkey-men became mine. I was particularly sensitive to the ubiquitous black glasses as part of the stereotype—usually large round glasses, to contrast with the exaggerated "slanty" eyes—since my own near-sightedness became a problem by the time I was eight. Fearful of being ridiculed not only as a "four-eyes" but also as a "Jap" for wearing even the wire-rimmed equivalent, I would leave for school with my glasses on and arrive with them shoved in my pocket for the rest of the day. This was good for my self-esteem but bad for my schoolwork, until my teacher commented on my constant squinting and my mother insisted that I tell her how the frame and earpieces got so bent out of shape.

The glasses were in my pocket at recess one day when an older boy from another class came up and asked me, with accusation in his voice, "Hey kid, are you a Jap?" (There was, of course, no way to escape this inevitable playground question.) My mother had told me that "Jap" was a slur, but she had not explained what to do in response, except perhaps to turn and walk away, and I was only redeemed from my stuttering mumble by a classmate's words: "Nah—he's an American, just like us." Which of my friends from that United Nations of a class (Howard, Stillson, Jongsma, Latour, Lasota, DeBoer, Lewallen, Kolanko, Popagin, Zweig . . .) had spoken up so directly, so fast? I only recall that I was grateful for the loyalty and the intervention. But even then I understood that my friend's protective answer only begged more confusing questions. It was also at that time that I began to recognize the expectations my parents were placing on how well we did in school, with me as the role-setting big brother, necessarily wearing my glasses all the time. And it was then that I began biting my fingernails down to the quick.

With great affection John Updike called it the time when everyone was pregnant. But for me the 1950s were when I first began to understand that I knew little about what had happened during the war to the people I cared about most. And when I realized that I did not understand what it meant to be "an American, just like us."

CITIZENSHIP: CIVICS LESSON, PART 4

Three related facts of my youth were that my parents seldom discussed politics (except to say that voting was a right and an obligation), that my parents voted Republican for many years, and that my mother and her sister spoke regularly and seldom argued. But Auntie Fumie was a Democrat, and she was well-read, thoughtful, and unafraid to argue her case, and this threatened the equilibrium. As when, in both the 1952 and 1956 elections,

Made in

After Hiroshima and
MacArthur's return
the store shelves offered scraps
and the black market did quite well.
My uncle's refuge was Yamanashi-ken
and the village Grandpa had left
for America many years before. Once
the Red Cross located him
Dad sent letters and money. For five years
we spent occasional weekend time
packing boxes to send there, too. Not
gifts exactly, but offerings
assembled with care—coffee,
cocoa, sugar, children's clothes
and shoes—the store value
less than the postage. My mother
covered the cartons with
brown paper tied with twine,
attached a declaration
for the customs people.
                           Meanwhile,
since we had won the war
we rode new bikes to Dairy Queen,
dozed off at the drive-in movie, took
weekend Oldsmobile rides. At school
we filled Red Cross boxes for refugees,
(toothbrushes were my forte) and
at birthday parties our airplanes,
trucks, and cars were made from
cheap and colorful tin
on which small printing told us
they had been Made in
Occupied Japan.

DP's, Northwest Indiana, 1950

"That's Mrs. W_____,"
my mother said, "from Poland,
a refugee."

Middle-aged, heavy-set,
in a bulky brown coat,
in clunky black shoes,
crossing the street,
babushka tight against the wind.
"Some people call her a DP,"
my mother said, but that was not
a word I should ever use,
like saying "K-Y's" for people
from Kentucky who had come
north looking for jobs. "It would
make a person feel bad,"
she said, "who had already
left everything behind."

"DP's," she said, perhaps
remembering
Japantown before the war,
"DP's have lost their homes,
their country."

she supported the "intellectual" Democrat Adlai Stevenson rather than war-hero Dwight D. Eisenhower.

In explaining her own voting my mother noted that a person has every right to keep such matters to herself, but then observed that Franklin Roosevelt had personally ordered the forced evacuation and imprisonment of her family and almost all other Japanese Americans, that Harry Truman ("another Democrat"), had chosen to drop not one but *two* atom bombs on Japan, and that Truman, adding insult to injury, had opposed the legislation that finally made it possible for her parents to become citizens of the United States, legislation that became law only because Congress overrode his veto. This list of grievances made it impossible for my mother to support Democrats generally. (The notable early exception was Richard L. Neuberger, a fellow Lincoln High graduate and liberal journalist who had spoken out on behalf of Japanese Americans and later became a U.S. Senator.) My father would have added that the Republicans were more likely than the Democrats to ward off the specter of "socialized medicine."

My mother maintained that her sister was forgiving of the Democrats because Fumie had not personally suffered the humiliation and pain of life in "camp" (given her hospitalization for tuberculosis)—somehow forgetting that Fumie had been a Minidoka victim of a different kind, separated for three years from her children and helplessly suffering the betrayal and termination of her marriage from 400 miles away. For her part Fumie argued that the Democrats were nevertheless the party of the New Deal and had otherwise stood up for America's minorities and working class. As for the McCarran-Walter Act, the Immigration and Nationality Act of 1952, Fumie could have mentioned Truman's veto message to Congress, which pointed out that the bill maintained the highly discriminatory national origins quota system of 1924: "This quota system—always based upon assumptions at variance with our American ideals—is long since out of date and more than ever unrealistic in the face of present world conditions...." And, Truman added, "The greatest vice of the present quota system ... is that it discriminates, deliberately and intentionally, against many of the peoples of the world.... The basis of this quota system was false and unworthy in 1924. It is even worse now."

Truman was right, of course. McCarran-Walter extended discriminatory policies concerning immigration and the rights of resident aliens, as well as some objectionable provisions of the Internal Security Act of 1950—so the sisters' disagreement finally exemplified the perfect at odds with the good, or at least the tolerable. Truman's desire for an immigration policy stripped of the old biases was at odds with a flawed piece of legislation that offered a modicum of progress. For my mother and many other Nisei, that modicum included long-sought approval for immigrants from Japan to become naturalized citizens, and it was clear that McCarran-Walter might provide the only such opportunity in their parents' lifetime. So they found it hard to forgive the president who didn't want it to become law. (The prejudicial features of McCarran-Walter would remain in place until passage of the Immigration and Nationality Act of 1965—although arguments over immigration policy would hardly disappear from American life.)

Meanwhile, the badly conceived and underfunded 1948 Evacuation Claims Act had virtually guaranteed inadequate settlements for Japanese American losses suffered between 1942 and 1945. My grandparents, though, took what crumbs they could get at the time, and a few years later, under McCarran-Walter, finally acquired their citizenship.

1943   On December 17 the Magnuson Act, or Chinese Exclusion Repeal Act, is signed into law by President Roosevelt, allowing immigration from China (now an ally against the Japanese) to resume on a highly limited basis and permitting Chinese immigrants in the U.S. and Hawaii to become naturalized citizens; restrictions on property ownership remain in place.

1944   On December 18, the Supreme Court rules in *Korematsu v. United States* that the exclusion order leading to Japanese American internment was constitutional. The Supreme Court also rules unanimously in *Ex parte Mitsuye Endo* that the government cannot detain a citizen that the government itself concedes is loyal to the United States.

1948   In *Oyama v. California* the Supreme Court holds that alien land laws violate the equal protection clause of the Fourteenth Amendment.

The Japanese American Evacuation Claims Act authorizes payment for economic losses due to evacuation and internment.

1951   Oregon repeals its anti-miscegenation law.

1952   On June 27 Congress passes the Immigration and Nationality
        Act of 1952 (McCarran-Walter Act), which nullifies racial
        restrictions in the 1790 naturalization law and some restrictions
        of the Oriental Exclusion Act of 1924. Immigration from Asia
        resumes, and Japanese immigrants can now become U.S.
        citizens. (However, McCarran-Walter retains "country of origin"
        quotas and severely restricts immigration from the "Asia-Pacific
        Triangle." Japan is allotted 185 immigrants per year.)

                        UNDOCUMENTED

In May 1953—nine presidents, two world wars, and one internment after
they had legally entered the United States and my grandfather had worked
for the railroad—my mother's parents graduated from the "Americanization
School" (sponsored by the Japanese Ancestral Society of Portland!), and not
long after that applied to become citizens of the United States. They did so
without hesitation and with no expression of resentment. My grandmother,
Hatsune Marumoto, was on the record as having arrived in 1913 as the wife
of Minejiro Marumoto. But since their joint status hinged on his, who was
he? The government required that my grandfather show proof of his U.S.
residence and employment prior to 1906, the year before Theodore Roosevelt
signed the "Gentlemen's Agreement" that severely restricted immigration
from Japan.

"Dear Mr. Kimmell," my grandfather wrote on May 15 (through Auntie
Fumie) to the superintendent of the Oregon Division of the Union Pacific
Railroad Company: "In order to complete my application for naturalization, I must submit evidence of my residence in the United States prior to
1906. As I recall, I worked with the Oregon Railroad Navigation Company
from about 1900 to about 1905 in the vicinity of Arlington, The Dalles, and
Hood River. . . ." Two weeks later, Kimmel responded that "Payroll records
have been checked but we were unable to locate service for Mr. Marumoto;
however, if Mr. Marumoto will furnish the following information, we will
be glad to re-examine. . . ."

"Dear Mr. Hopkins," he wrote near the end of the month to the superintendent of the Southern Pacific Railroad Company office in Portland, "I
must submit evidence of my residence in the United States prior to June 29,

1906.... I worked with the Southern Pacific Railroad, Extra Gang... about 1905 and 1906. Will you please check your files to see if my name is included in your employment records...." A week later Hopkins allowed, "We have no record here from which to verify such service. To enable us to have payroll check made at San Francisco, will appreciate advice as to whether you recall the name of your foreman or foremen, whether entire service was in vicinity of Canby, Oregon, and what this gang was doing there...."

After 50 years he couldn't be sure of the foremen's names. He did remember Sakai and Omata, two of his coworkers, and certainly what the crew was doing—raising track, clearing slides, and "burying bridges"—in the vicinity of Canby, Aurora, Oregon City, and Woodburn. Whether the offices responsible ever corroborated his railroad work is not clear; it is possible that (as with plantations in the antebellum South) there were records of workers and wages, but with the names not fully or accurately listed, or even retained. But despite this difficulty in establishing his American history, Grandpa and Grandma Marumoto were eventually granted their citizenship—after first demonstrating that they could recite in order the names of the presidents, including the nine under whose administrations they had lived as legal but marginalized resident aliens, and the one who had exiled them to the Idaho desert. I was in elementary school then, and new to the history myself, but I remember trying to help them pronounce names like Lincoln and Polk and Coolidge.

I marvel at their dignified insistence on making this last important statement near the end of their stubbornly American lives. In studying the group photos that document the swearing-in ceremonies we can see that the Issei are gratified, dignified, and proud. They are diminutive, and physically compromised by their ordeals, but mostly erect—as great a generation as their adopted country could deserve.

LITTLE AMERICA

In the summer of 1955, the year before Congress authorized construction of the Interstate Highway System, my family moved across the country. My father was going to be the new chief of anesthesiology (he was most of the department, it turned out) at the Veterans Administration Hospital in Walla Walla, Washington. Jim and I rode along for three days and 2,000 miles in the family car, towing an aluminum boat on a trailer with undersized tires, loaded with bags and boxes. The tires blew out and were replaced somewhere in Nebraska. My mother and sisters stayed behind to complete the sale of our Hammond house and finish packing, catching up to us by plane just as the yellow and green Mayflower van pulled up to the door.

I suffered a 12-year-old's losses because of that move—schoolmates, several close friends, my Boy Scout troop, part of a season of Little League baseball. And my collection of baseball cards, which my mother deemed not worth saving when she found them in our room. (It was after that when my father first mentioned to me that his own card collection had been lost during the war.) In exchange, I got some moving snapshots of my country, an introduction to trout fishing, and a few insights on identity and place.

We drove west on the Lincoln Highway, through corn, taking the measure of Illinois and Iowa (including Ames, where I would later live and work for over three decades); through wheat, oats, and cattle succeeding each other across Nebraska; through mile after mile of Wyoming rangeland, complete with clusters of antelope staring at the highway traffic. And after scores of Burma Shave signs, and landscape less barren but more relentless than anything I'd seen in T.V. Westerns, we pulled into Little America. Little America, Wyoming was a glorified truck stop and gas station, with motel space and a restaurant, and it was being successfully hyped by highway signage into a place to visit even if you didn't need to stop. Well before the logos of McDonald's and Kentucky Fried Chicken replaced shaving cream jingles in making travelers feel good about being on the highway, Little America insisted that road food, simple shelter, and cross-country driving were essential to life in the U.S.A.

When U.S. 30 cut north into the high desert of Idaho the "Little Skunk" images of the Stinker stations took over, and local humor was writ large on middle-of-nowhere signs: "This ain't sagebrush, it's Idaho clover!" And then we passed through Twin Falls, only a few miles from the now-abandoned Minidoka camp. My father neglected to mention that, ten years earlier, my mother and I had actually lived amid that same Idaho "clover"—or for that matter that he, Jim, and I were approaching the territory his father had covered fifty years earlier as a salesman for the Furuya Company. And at last we entered the Columbia Basin in eastern Washington, where billboards welcomed us to the "Inland Empire" and I realized that I was still more than a step away from the ocean.

Walla Walla was where my younger sister started school and my brother tried his hand at violin, and where we lived with other administrators' families on a residential loop within the hospital post itself, well beyond a security guard at the entrance to a long drive. Our house was large and blocky and white, like all the others, with screened-in porches front and back, and big open rooms with high ceilings that held too much of the winter cold. A small creek at the bottom of our hill held small trout and marked the perimeter of my summer explorations. But for me our year there was a blur of early adolescence, memorable for fishing interludes with my father, weekend station wagon trips to Portland, and the abrupt appearance of Grandpa Nakadate.

The trout fishing getaways usually began with my father calling home on the afternoon of a summer day of too much paperwork and not enough medical practice, in hopes that my being available on short notice would be reason enough to take leave of his desk. The phone would ring, he would tell me to catch some grasshoppers for bait (I stunned them with a flyswatter), and 20 minutes later he would walk in the door. Another 20 minutes after that we were on the Little Walla Walla River, in the shade of cottonwoods and alders. One weekend we accompanied a friend of my father's who fished for sturgeon on the Snake River. On another weekend we crossed into Oregon to fish for trout in the Wallowa River—"It's a really beautiful stream," he said during the drive, "It's hard to describe. But you'll see." And the Wallowa was indeed powerfully serene (much later I realized he was hardly the first to make that observation). But those spontaneous interludes still hold me, grasshoppers and flyswatters and all. It was then that I began to understand how much my father needed fishing to regain his equilibrium at difficult times. And much later I caught on that our fishing time together meant that he was in some way catching up on the years we had lost while he was held hostage by the war.

For my mother, though, fishing was just something to tolerate, and Walla Walla was still too far from home. This became clear during our bimonthly weekend trips to Portland, when she could again be close to her sister and parents. In Portland I was surrounded by a nonstop blend of English and Japanese. "*Pan*," Grandma Marumoto explained, "*pan* is 'bread,'" and I listened in awe as my cousins code-switched with ease, chatting with their friends in one language and with our grandparents in another. (Indeed, they were Grace and Phyllis to me, but still Michi and Yuri to our grandparents.) There was a network of the Marumoto family's longtime acquaintances—a few new ones, but most the resilient remnants of prewar associations. And tagging along with one or another grandparent, I was introduced to various Issei friends and Nisei merchants, the people who made tofu, and even one elderly couple that had found a way to re-enter the hotel business. A few even remembered my father's family from well before the war. At the midsummer Japanese *undokai* or community picnic I ate more kinds of Japanese food than I knew existed, and saw more Japanese faces than there were Poles in Chicago, or so it seemed. In the living room of my grandparents' house there was a 24-inch doll of a Japanese woman in a gold-embroidered red kimono, her deft gestures protected by a glass case. And in her kitchen my grandmother tried without success to show me how to make sushi, even though my boyhood desire to be outside made me impatient with the pace and nuance of the craft. "Whatsa matter you?!" she would say, slapping affectionately at my misbehaving hands, "too fast . . . more slow, more slow!" Much later I learned that I had, in fact, blown my best chance to learn from one of the sushi mavens of Portland.

Then, in the spring of 1956 my father's father came to live with us, appearing suddenly out of the distant reality of a Japan I knew only by name. How this came about was never clear to me, nor was the intended duration of his stay—nor my mother's response to the sudden presence of her father-in-law amidst a busy family with four children, although according to Japanese custom she was obliged to welcome him into her household. Several moves and a decade beyond the war my parents were finally settling in, and my mother didn't need a reminder of where my father's patriarchal habits had come from. But there was Bun'ichi Nakadate, fierce-eyed, taciturn, broodingly authoritarian, and (to my mind) humorless. A part of me that I had little understanding of and, at that point in my life, little interest in getting to know. "Weren't you afraid to come to America when you didn't know English? What was it like to learn a new job and a new country at the same time? What did you do in Japan during the war? Why didn't you come back to the U.S. after it?" Taking refuge in seventh grade and stumbling into adolescence, I never tried to ask. But my bewildered ignorance and any ongoing family tensions were pushed aside when my father accepted a staff position at St. Vincent's Hospital in Portland. Methodist boy that he was, he was returning to Portland by way of yet another Catholic institution, and my mother was finally returning to the hometown she had left, unwillingly, for Minidoka. Grandpa Nakadate moved to Portland with us, and stayed long enough to see how unfamiliar it had become. He returned to Japan within the year, taking with him the answers to my unasked questions.

THE SANSEI SUBURBS AND THE MANAGEMENT OF PAIN

Ambrose "Bucky" Shields had respectfully declined the chance to take over a Depression-strapped family farm near Lawrence in order to attend the University of Kansas and become a doctor. A war veteran and a surgeon, he had arrived at St. Vincent's Hospital shortly before my father joined the anesthesiology staff in 1956. They became a crackerjack surgical team, fishing partners, and fast friends. Bucky wielded the scalpel, my father kept the patients breathing and managed their pain, and in order to step away from the burdens of mortality they went trout fishing together. No-nonsense, no-frills sons of the working class, they had no pretensions and little patience with those whose egos outran their skill set, whether in surgery or on the river. And a close friend didn't have to work too hard to get an honest opinion out of Bucky, whose locutions were feisty and time-tested. "Those guys were as useless," he would say, "as the buttons on the back of a coat." And 55 years after the fact he could still get his Irish up when recalling the problems my parents had had upon returning to their hometown—a few of which my father had confided to him during one of their weekends on the Deschutes River.

At first my parents had hoped to build a house near Beaverton, but for unexplained reasons the developers vetoed the builder's agreement. Then, when showing them a finished house near Sylvan, the realtor admitted that some neighbors had voiced objections to the "Japanese family." "Well, I could still sell it to you," he told my parents, "but...." This was ten years after Hiroshima, of course, but wartime hostility had not disappeared. For some people it was still "our enemy, the Japanese"—or at least convenient to think so. This was over half a century since Bun'ichi Nakadate had arrived, when he had experienced racism from his first day in Portland, and now he had to

Chief Joseph Slept Here

(Hin-mah-too-yah-lat-kekt, on the hundredth anniversary of his death)

Until surrendering in 1877 Chief Joseph and a band of Nez Percé resisted the U.S. government's demand that they move to a reservation. Despite being told that he would be allowed to return to the Wallowa Valley, Joseph was taken first to Kansas and then Oklahoma Territory, and in 1885 was finally sent to a non–Nez Percé reservation in northern Washington. He died in exile there.

Have you ever fished the Wallowa in the crisp sunrise,
with raspy magpies peppering the trees?

Have you stood there at midday, when tiny insects, motes
of dust, and the sun's glare converge, making eyes water?

Have you been there in pebbled afternoon,
with redwings dipping among the reeds and bushes?

Have you felt cool shadows sliding down canyon walls,
the breeze billowing a line into elegant loops of grace?

Have you had the white-tails query your presence
before flickering into the pines, leaving you,

a buzzing fly, and swirling current?
I fished there once, age 13, and even then knew

it was more beautiful than my father had promised,
more peaceful than sleep. Some time later

I learned that it all belonged to someone else,
whose eloquence came from a sacred place, who had wished

only to return there and rest forever where I stood.

wonder what difference there was between his being prohibited by law from buying a house in 1924 and his son's not being able to buy one decades later because "someone" had objected, somewhere along the line.

My parents were conflict-averse in different ways—my father preferring to push past it with a "damn the torpedoes" attitude, and my mother inclined not to insist on staying "where we weren't wanted"—but now they had to insist on being . . . there. "Kodomo no tame ni," their parents would have said, "for the sake of the children." They were two thousand miles from Northwest Indiana, with its working class ethic, its recent immigrants and war refugees, its relative tolerance of a diversity of cultures. They were in Portland, at that time a city overlooked and ignored, "somewhere between Seattle and San Francisco" and fighting an inferiority complex as wide as the Columbia Gorge. They were in Portland, with its dominantly white population (96.5 percent in the 1950 census) derived primarily from North Atlantic Europe, and its history of wary ambivalence toward Asians. They were home.

They were also of the generation for whom the West Coast suburbs were invented, from King County in Washington to San Mateo and Orange Counties in California, acre after acre where citrus groves and strawberry fields, truck farms and corner groceries disappeared, and carports, strip malls, and shopping centers took their place. But it became clear that in some people's minds suburban middle-class American life was not for "just anybody"—anybody's education, work ethic, credentials, and accomplishments notwithstanding. Yet it was important for us to be close to my father's work, with good schools nearby, and little crime, juvenile or otherwise. After single hotel rooms in Japantown and tiny apartments in East Chicago and Minidoka barracks and modest houses in Hammond and box-like V.A. housing in Walla Walla my parents were looking forward to several bedrooms, a dining room and perhaps a den, more than one bathroom, a dedicated place to do the laundry, a garage. They wanted rhododendrons, rose bushes, and a lawn. They wanted their Sansei children to grow up *there*. Mary and Katsumi Nakadate were not alone in this, of course, and they were among the Nisei who had managed to hold their own during the Depression and found ways to move forward despite the war and the camps. (They were also sad to see housing discrimination shadow upwardly mobile American minorities into the next century.)

So a house on Sunset Boulevard—teal-green, three-bedroom, one-and-a-half bath, split-level, two-car garage—became my family's third shot at buying a home in the southwest suburbs. An independent builder had designed and built the house for his daughter and son-in-law, but when the son-in-law was transferred it went on the market. "They're Japanese," the realtor said to Joe Gersch, "Should we sell it to them?" "Why not?" Joe answered, at the beginning of what became a long friendship with my parents. This was the context in which they paid $23,500 in cash for outright ownership, no mortgage in the mix to foul up the dream. For my parents the name "Sunset Boulevard" was an unanticipated statement, something out of a movie, out of California, but in the end an allowable extravagance since the neighborhood was not ostentatious and the house itself far from over the top. That house, in that place was, after all, what they had been working toward for much of their lives. A nice turn of events, given the way things had started.

In fact, just as Joe Gersch was saying *Yes*, someone else was ringing doorbells. He was "concerned" regarding the people who were planning to move into the neighborhood—and couldn't something be done about it? It was, it turned out, a "Raisin in the Sun" moment that might have gone either way. But in response, another neighbor (a feisty Scotsman named Macnab and a journalist by trade) started a campaign of his own. "That family has a right to live here, too," he told whoever would listen, "and incidentally, wouldn't it be silly not to want another doctor in the neighborhood?" So when our unloaded moving van pulled away there were no scenes or incidents, and neighbors from next door and across the street dropped by with handshakes and smiles. My family would be there for the next 55 years. During the first week of eighth grade Gary Severson—who would become my best-friend-for-life—invited me to transfer my Boy Scout membership into his troop, which met at St. Andrew's church, right down the street.

My mother had had all the training she would need to be the perfect suburban mom. Her mother had taught her how to shop and cook, and she had done countless loads of laundry at the Oregonian Hotel. She had taken home economics classes at Girls Polytechnic. She had taken some Latin and French along with the math and chemistry at Lincoln High, shorthand and bookkeeping in "business college." She had worked as a governess for Consul Nakamura and had helped care for my cousins in Minidoka. Some might have said that she was unsystematically trained or underemployed, but intuition had suggested that she would use it all in the coming years, and she did. Her long-range goal was to make sure that we all benefited from higher education, especially her daughters. Meanwhile, she drove us in a station wagon to dance lessons, swimming practice, and baseball games, served as a Girl Scout leader and made phone calls for the PTA. The calendar was crowded, but it was probably her way of achieving post-camp, postwar stability and fulfillment, and some social historians of the period would say she was hardly alone.

So there we were, four kids in the middle-class suburbs. Like millions of others we just accepted our postwar circumstances as entitlements, our new schools and textbooks, our energetic and committed teachers. There we were, four Sansei kids with only a sketchy sense of "evacuation," "assembly centers," and "relocation." And with only vague intimations that there had been "a few problems" concerning the first two houses our parents had "looked at." (I only learned about the doorbell pusher decades after the fact, from a high school friend.) There were the Nakadate kids, with only a vague sense of what it had taken to get from Japantown to Sunset Boulevard. Of course, that ignorance made it easier for us to embrace our neighbors and our friendships, to believe in our schools and teachers, to focus on doing our best from day to day, than if we had known there were people nearby who had not wanted us to have the chance.

When we finally sold the Sunset Boulevard house after my father's death it looked modest by twenty-first century standards, with its low ceilings and snug bathrooms, its concrete-slab patio and partially finished basement. It looked modest even when emptied of the dividable, donate-able, recyclable, and dumpster-worthy items that our Depression-wounded mother had saved and stored, and which, in ritualized devotion to her, we took the time to sort and distribute. But when we locked the house for the last time before turning it over to the realtor, we removed the door to the kitchen closet on which Mom had marked and dated the growth of four children and their close friends, and we put it in the truck.

When they were both in their eighties Bucky Shields had occasion to give my father a physical exam, and only then saw the scars from the nearly fatal wounds his fishing partner had incurred in Germany in 1945, and only then learned that "Jim" had left the army with a handful of medals. "So all that time," he said at my father's memorial service several years later, "there were

Thank You

(my father said on the phone)
for remembering,

yet perhaps not recalling the poetry we read
of rock and snag and riffle, of Wilson, Wallowa,
Nestucca, and Zig Zag, Necanicum, Deschutes.

And did he remember when rivers were
his solace and retreat—eddies and pools,
cascades, rivulets, and sliding currents of grief?
Grim hours in surgery made flowing water
needful—and line unspooling in hope,
like Whitman's spider's thread.

At 90 did he remember
the snarled reels of my novice days,
or the day when, grateful and almost proud,
I could finally cast on a dime,
taking pleasure in a bright lure
dropping to the water,
line sweeping downward, and
the sinker tapping pebbles
in a perfect drift?

Did he remember
the brilliant winter afternoons
when I drove us home
on a learner's permit, flickering
through shadowy corridors of Douglas fir
with the Big Band saxes of his youth on the radio
and luminous fish scales cradled in the trunk?

"Thank you," he said from many watersheds away,
"for remembering when we did those things together."

the rest of us in the operating room going on about our war exploits, and there he was, not saying a word, but having done more and gone through more than anybody else." And in a conversation shortly after that he added, "And there were your dad and your lovely mother, and you kids who did so well in school, and to think there had been people who didn't even want you to live in the neighborhood because you were 'Japanese.'" A bad situation, he allowed, nothing to like about it.

"Bad liquor," Bucky would say from time to time, "bad liquor makes bad tunes."

A MINORITY

Comparing our stories decades later, a Chinese American classmate and I realized that both his parents and mine had been thwarted when they first tried to build or buy homes in southwest Portland near where we attended high school. Something to do with the contractor, or maybe the realtor, or perhaps the family across the street. The old anti-Asian prejudices still circulated in the world of 1950s real estate and neighborhood formation, still undercut the aspirations of both Chinese and Japanese Americans. During the recent war the Chinese (and Chinese Americans) had supposedly been the "good Asians" while the Japanese and many Japanese Americans had been labeled "enemy aliens," but a decade later both groups might have expected to be on stable footing once again. It was an interesting time. (The fall of 1957, when we entered high school, was also when President Eisenhower ordered federal troops to enforce integration in Little Rock, Arkansas.)

How telling, then, that Jim Lee and I could not recall experiencing overt racial prejudice at Wilson High during our four years there—though many years later we could not rule out faulty or selective memory. It seems obvious, though, that we had our teachers and classmates to thank, and of course we had stayed busy with activities that included service clubs, baseball, football, cheerleading, and student government. But we had also been aware of being the only two non-white members of our class of 444. Jim and I had a few things in common, but we were not "typical" or representative of anything, even with our experiences combined. Yet there we were, a highly visible Asian American minority of two, and all but invisible at the same time.

Given that, how could we live the everyday lives of teenagers without constant self-consciousness? How could we continue to respect family and heritage while being expected to assimilate into a melting pot? How could we strive to succeed as individuals yet avoid being seen as exemplars of something far beyond ourselves? How could we have a social life without tripping irrational triggers in the parents of the girls we dated? How could we begin to find out who we might become? Somehow we managed to address at least some of those questions without asking them in so many words. Perhaps to everyone's surprise and no one's, I was elected president of my senior class, and Jim later married one of those girls. (Meanwhile, perhaps inevitably, the summer before college the father of a classmate advised me that, going forward, I would do well to "look for a nice Japanese girl to marry.") It was an interesting time, indeed.

When I first walked in the door, the school was only one year old, one of thousands being built across the country to accommodate the baby boom. But while my parents thought of Wilson High—an excellent school in a safe community—as the anchor of a suburban dream, I simply entered it as a nurturing reality. I understood I would be going to college, and it was a good place to prepare. Of more tangible significance was that the Soviet Union launched the first space satellite in October of my freshman year, an act of Cold War one-upmanship that immediately raised the ante on American education. The response was the National Defense Education Act, drafted and passed in eleven months by an unusually efficient Congress. American education was deemed a vital element of national defense—and educational achievement something of a patriotic act—and this coincided with the earnest ambitions of many Asian American families. I may not have anticipated taking five years of high school math in four years, or studying both physics and chemistry, or joining other students in newly-minted honors classes, but suddenly it was all there to be done. We were in the embrace of a national agenda that fit my parents' agenda exactly.

My parents expected me to excel academically—and in the process to set the bar for my brother and sisters. (It took a while for me to understand what a problem my "setting a good example" created for them.) "Always do your best," was the way my mother would put it, and "I expect you to earn good grades," my father would say, more pointedly. He wanted me to become a doctor, while she just wanted me to be successful and happy; but in the end "do your best" and "earn good grades" both meant "be sure to end up near the top." To the extent that I wasn't gifted in a particular subject, I was expected to spend extra time on it to make up the difference. When excellent grades actually materialized, it was understood that satisfaction in them was reward enough for the time being. When specific assignments or teachers seemed particularly challenging, I knew that whining, giving up, and failure were all part of the same slippery slope. And that perfection was always possible. (Once I handed my father report cards containing five A's and one B, and his response was, "What happened?") But while the need to "catch up with the Communists" in math and science made honors courses in English and history mere afterthoughts for many, that was hardly the case for me. I did well enough in science and math, but found myself enjoying Dickens, Cather, Rölvaag, and *The Human Comedy* much more, and taking three years of German.

Of course, being conscientious also mattered, since neatness and precision reflected respect for the process as well as for the project at hand, not to mention my teachers themselves. And personal conduct had more than individual implications; it would necessarily reflect on both our family and the Japanese American community at large. "Good deportment" (as my father called it) was to be assumed in our family, along with handing over our report cards as soon as Dad got home from work. Not incidentally, since school friendships would affect academic performance, I was expected to pick appropriate companions, and in this regard I was both smart and lucky. Gary Severson and Larry Veltman, my closest friends and academic rivals, had parents with similar expectations, and were obliged to toe a similar line.

None of this was expressed to us as a single statement, but rather inserted into passing moments and absorbed over time. Yet it was as real as the rice or the fried chicken on our plates, as constant as the Portland rain. It was the way things were going to be. Eventually it became clear to us that this severe and ambitious agenda was driven by the loss of my mother's chance for higher education because of the Great Depression, by my father's memory of working two jobs in college and completing medical school even as his mother was dying of kidney disease, and by their Nisei conviction that Sansei success would testify that the family was still on track. I think we were like many postwar Sansei in that what was expected of us was made clear, but the legacy behind the expectation was only hinted at.

Then, roughly between 1957 and 1973—the year I started high school and the year my younger sister graduated from Stanford—the lives of Japanese Americans as a group again began to shift, and again due to changes in international relations and in domestic politics and social life. Within our family the shift was most poignantly seen in what we learned of Japanese. My brother Jim and I had started school in the Midwest and too close to the end of the war and its raw emotions and cultural push-back to learn and use Japanese, even at home, if we wanted to be considered "real Americans." So along with learning how to hold a rice bowl correctly and how to wield chopsticks we picked up only a few essential Japanese words and phrases from our mother, who insisted on teaching us that much at least—and then we studied European languages in school. Sisters Jean and Ann, on the other hand, entered middle school in Portland as the multicultural tide began to turn ("Black is beautiful!" "Yellow is mellow!"), and were encouraged to study not only French but also Japanese, offered through Saturday language classes at the Portland Buddhist Temple. (It seemed no accident, then, that Ann ended up majoring in Japanese and that after college Jean went to study under a master potter in Japan.)

The broader-impact changes were political. President Truman had ended segregation in the armed forces in 1948, and the McCarran-Walter Act of 1952 enabled the Issei finally to become citizens. And then under Eisenhower, Kennedy, and Johnson, Japan grew as an ally and emerged as a trading partner—and produced a postwar economic miracle to rival Germany's. Hawaii was admitted to statehood in 1959 and became the first state to be represented in Congress by Asian Americans. Shortly after that a new Immigration and Nationality Act was passed, finally abolishing the national origins quotas for immigration that had been crudely camouflaging racial and religious bigotry since 1924. The Japanese were among the good Asians, again, and again welcome to come to the United States.

Academic success at Wilson High took me to Palo Alto rather than Eugene or Corvallis. In 1961 I joined what seemed an academic diaspora that began to pluck many Sansei from their hometowns and communities and spread them across the country, often at "elite" institutions. (Brother Jim chose Eugene, but our sisters were also drawn to California.) At Stanford I was in awe of the talents of my peers, grateful for opportunities that opened up like palm fronds over the Inner Quadrangle, and a bit intimidated by the expectations the place invoked. And I was once more among a small minority cohort, of which Asian Americans seemed the largest part. Passing others on the Quad or seeing them in class I would wonder if we had followed similar paths in order to get there, if we were driven by similar urgencies and parental imperatives. But I also noted that most other Asian Americans at Stanford came not from the Pacific Northwest, but from California, and the signature ethos Californians projected led me to conclude that my being a fellow Asian American was more coincidental than definitive. At core a humanist, I abandoned pre-medicine after a year and majored in English, finally trusting my talents enough to disappoint my father and resist the Sansei tendency to track (or be tracked) into a technical or scientific field. (In chemistry lab I once found myself partnered with the only other Asian in sight—but was thankful that at least he understood what we were supposed to be doing there.) I also spent six months studying in Germany—where a guard at one border crossing saw in my passport that my birthplace was "Indiana, U.S.A." and called his buddies over to stare at what they believed was a genuine American Indian. And then I left the West Coast for the doctoral program that appealed most to my desire to teach American literature, coincidentally the program that took me back to Indiana.

Meanwhile the movement for civil rights accelerated and protestors against the war in Vietnam demanded that the government justify its policies and behavior. The racist implications of the war became a salient aspect of the discussion when Muhammad Ali famously said, "No Viet Cong ever called me a nigger," and signs at subsequent West Coast antiwar rallies conveyed sentiments like, "No Viet Cong ever called me a dumb Chinese." Cultural frustrations and generational division infused the air, and misinformation bred mistrust. But even my father, decorated World War II veteran that he was, acknowledged some unease regarding the conflict in Southeast Asia. When I asked him in 1968 (after much hesitation) how he felt about the antiwar protests and the young men of my generation who did not believe in the war and were hesitant to serve, he surprised me when he glanced up from his newspaper: "This Vietnam," he said, "this Vietnam War is not the same thing. This Vietnam is different."

Something else was different, too: by the mid-1960s Japanese Americans (often linked, as earlier, with Chinese Americans) had been dubbed a "model minority"—in part because many entered the academic honor roll as

Kodomo no tame ni

At Portland *Ikoi no kai,*
over the loaves and fishes
of their senior years,
over Tuesday sushi
and Friday pasta
of memory-rich communal
meals, Nisei parents
offer each other stories
and photos—*dozo, dozo*—
of sons daughters,
clippings from Boston Chicago,
postcards from Tokyo Rome,
grandchildren saying cheese
in Berkeley New Haven—
and so remember braces
homework piano lessons,
scrimping and saving
and doing without
as their own parents had,
"For the sake of the children."
How wonderful that success
has taken them
so far.

freshmen and were still there as seniors, in part because Asian Americans tended not to be "troublemakers." Asian Americans tended to fit in and not rock anybody's boat, and the exceptions proved the rule. When a free-spirited Sansei friend of mine got crosswise with a P.E. teacher at Madison High, he was pulled aside and asked, "Hey, kid . . . why can't you be a *good* Jap?" while the "model minority" tag promoted a positive stereotype, it was a stereotype nevertheless. Like all racial or ethnic stereotypes it ignored and obscured differences—among the Asian groups, between communities in different regions of the United States, in the varying circumstances of "becoming American." The model minority label skewed even further the notion of what Asian Americans should aspire to do (engineering! computer science!) and how they should get there. When applied to Japanese Americans "model minority" seemed appropriate and appealing, because the visible resilience of many suggested that as a group they had recovered from the damage done by removal and incarceration. But this made it possible to overlook the many, especially the Issei, who had never recovered economically or emotionally from what they had suffered during the war. For some Issei and Nisei there had been angry renunciations of citizenship (followed by deportation), depression and suicides, and intra-community resentments and violence. And finally, the model minority stereotype was being paraded before black Americans, Latinos, and others—like the teacher's pet before a misbehaving or knuckle-headed class—to indicate what they themselves might accomplish if they only had the focus and commitment. But there was unease in being the teacher's pet, discomfort in being a buffer group that was reflexively wedged into larger arguments over ethnicity and race.

Not long after these and other social and political elements came together, the movement among Japanese Americans—now sometimes preferring the term "Nikkei" as one that acknowledged all the generations at once—to seek redress for the World War II injustices began to coalesce. There would be some rocking of the boat, after all.

5 ∾ Unfinished

that is the painful precision

of exile, details' mound of exact increase,
not as one thought or read, of dimming vision

by distance, but its opposite.

—DEREK WALCOTT, *Tiepolo's Hound* (2000)

"KANPAI!"

In 1967 my parents flew to Japan to visit relatives on both the Yamanashi and Wakayama sides of the family, my father for the first time. It was two years after my grandfather's death in Yamanashi-ken, so the trip was also an important occasion to pay respects and affirm family ties. There was a medical convention in Hawaii that would get them halfway there, my mother pointed out, and if they didn't go at that time, then when? My father, for whom international travel had all the attraction of a tatting circle (Belgium and Germany having satisfied any youthful cravings), knew that the convention was hardly the point. He was the older son of the oldest Nakadate son.

With Uncle Toru accompanying and my younger sister in tow, they made the rounds in Yamanashi—both the Ashizawas and the Nakadates—and everything went well enough. Except that my mother (ever sensitive to nuance and gesture) detected a bit more formality among the Nakadates than seemed necessary, even accounting for Japanese protocol and family members not having been in touch on a regular basis. As if an awkward question hovered over every polite conversation, yet no one wanted to acknowledge it. But during a bedtime conversation my parents figured out what was going on, and at the next dinner gathering they found a way to make Nakadate Denki a topic of conversation.

Toru himself had never been comfortable in the business world and, disappointing his father, had disengaged himself from the electric company after the war by going off to Tokyo to work for Radiopress. But what about Katsumi, the first son of the man who had helped capitalize the company in its early days and at one point held a controlling interest? Nakadate Denki was doing quite well, my parents were told (this much they already understood), benefiting from Japan's flourishing economy during the highly productive years since the war and occupation. Thanks, of course, to the money that had been sent to Japan long ago by the recently deceased oldest brother . . . and thanks to the acumen and hard work of his siblings. Yes, Nakadate Denki was doing well. At that my father—in the best Japanese he could muster after years of only sporadic use—offered congratulations to his uncles, and his gratitude for the success they had made of the business. And he added (with regret, of course) that, as a doctor devoted to a demanding medical practice in the United States, he lacked the time and expertise to take a responsible role in company matters. Furthermore, in his judgment the company was already in capable hands, and it might be best for the family if that were to continue to be the case. The question had been answered. And (as my mother reported) the next thing said was, "*Kanpai*," and by more than one person: "Cheers," they said, raising their cups with serious energy, "cheers!"

By comparison, the visit to my mother's people in Wakayama, the Marumoto-Imoto side of the family, was long on conversation and short on drama.

REDRESS; OR, THE SENSE OF AN ENDING:
CIVICS LESSON, PART 5

"In city after city, the Commission heard testimony from former evacuees who for the first time openly expressed pain and anger about evacuation and its aftermath. Many had never articulated their feelings even to their children, or within the ethnic community which shared their experience. It became obvious that a forty-year silence did not mean that bitter memories had dissipated; they had only been buried in a shallow grave."

—FROM *Personal Justice Denied*

The right to petition the government for redress of grievances had been there from the beginning, but after the war the possibility of compensation for removal and the trauma of "camp" was the subject of only intimate, and muted, and scattered conversation among Japanese Americans. In 1948 there had been the Evacuation Claims Act, but only 10 percent of the former internees had sufficient spirit, stamina, and financial records even to submit a claim for their economic losses—or to claim the privilege of wrangling with lawyers representing the very government that had incarcerated them. Many had all they could do simply to restart their lives. Almost three decades passed before redress began to take shape as a viable movement.

Some had gone "home," like my grandparents and my aunt and cousins, only to live in minimally adequate housing for several years. Some resettled far away from the West Coast, often in the place that had offered them their first refuge outside of barbed wire—cities like Denver, Chicago, and Seabrook, N.J. But even as postwar recovery gave way to "peace and prosperity" few spoke freely of where they had been between 1942 and 1945, and why, and how they felt about it. Like amber-encased insects of a lost time, the anger and resentment, pain and grief, and core-deep psychic injury of "camp" lay buried by almost 30 years of everyday life.

But the need to do something—lest all settle for nothing—concerning redress became obvious. The Issei and older Nisei began to die, and with them the living memory of internment. (My grandparents, whom I was first able to meet only after being carried through the gates of Minidoka, died in 1963 and 1966.) At the same time the Yonsei, the great-grandchildren of the Issei, were arriving in increasing numbers, with no recollection at all of life behind barbed wire. What redress might involve, how it could be achieved, and who would help bring it about were open questions. But nothing could be done without a change in the way Japanese Americans related to the camps as a part of their personal and shared history. Perhaps it was time to set the "shikata ga nai" mindset aside.

Enryo, respectful submission to authority—whether parent, teacher, employer, or government leaders—had come to the United States with the Issei and skewed the reaction of many Japanese Americans to Executive Order 9066 and much of what followed. And even when the Issei finally became naturalized citizens, after which they could and did vote, they were hardly prepared to "petition the government for a redress of grievances." But passive acceptance waned as Issei leadership shifted to the Nisei, and as the Sansei came of age. By the end of the 1960s the more outspoken and activist Nisei and Sansei had come to believe that a redress initiative had to be undertaken. The larger context of their redress efforts was the convergence of several social, cultural, and political phenomena, including Hawaiian statehood and the election of Asian Americans to Congress, the successes of the civil rights movement, the impact of the accompanying women's movement, vigorous public protests against the war in Vietnam, and passage of the 1966 Freedom of Information Act.

The campaign began with a resolution submitted to the 1970 JACL national convention by Edison Uno (and passed but not acted on) that the U.S. government pay monetary reparations to victims of removal and internment, followed by Henry Miyatake's proposal for monetary reparations at a JACL meeting in Seattle in 1973. But progress was fitful, given ambivalence in some members toward redress as a project and disagreement among others regarding goals and tactics. Among yet others there was ambivalence concerning the JACL itself, the oldest and most widely recognized Nikkei organization, in part because of its history of "accommodation" in helping the government carry out forced evacuation in 1942. The campaign for redress would take another fifteen years and involve several high-profile individuals, a coalition of legislators, local and national organizations and work groups, and countless grassroots volunteers—reflecting a range of Japanese American values and goals across three generations, values and goals that emerged from an increasingly diverse and at times divided "community."

The National Committee for Redress (of the JACL), the National Council for Japanese American Redress (in Seattle), and the National Coalition for Redress/Reparations (Los Angeles) reflected the variations in personality and region that had distinguished Japanese American communities since the beginning of the twentieth century. Did redress require a class-action suit against the government? Should redress involve monetary payments to individuals? Since any payment would be token and symbolic, would $20,000 or $25,000 be appropriate and sufficient? Would any amount of money paid to an individual—in the face of stigmatization, emotional pain, and psychological damage—be an insult? What about community or block grants, or an educational fund? And, given the wide range of prewar conditions and circumstances for Japanese Americans, who should be eligible for redress?

Ironically, given the way Japanese Americans had been manipulated and overpowered by government officials in 1942, the individual agendas of the various Nikkei groups were all displaced in July 1980 at the urging of Washington politicians. The difference was that in 1980 the U.S. Congress included four Japanese American members—Democratic Senators Daniel Inouye and Spark Matsunaga from Hawaii and Democratic Representatives Norman Mineta and Robert Matsui from California—who recommended that redress be pursued through legislation rather than the court system. And for strategic reasons any proposals would be preceded by the work of a congressional Commission on Wartime Internment and Relocation of Civilians (CWIRC). The commission would formalize and elevate the discussion, and the hearings would attract attention and publicity. The commission's charge would be to review Executive Order 9066 and its impact, and to recommend to Congress any appropriate remedies. Some opponents of the commission as a strategy believed that it could stall redress into oblivion—justice further delayed would be justice indefinitely denied. And in fact, the commission's work eventually included 20 days of hearings in cities across the U.S. and took over two years. But even though former internees were dying with every day of testimony and every week of debate, the tradeoff proved a good one—time in exchange for credibility and education.

The CWRIC hearings in the summer and fall of 1981 served to activate and focus the energies of individuals and groups, and the commission's invitation to testify opened emotional doors that had closed as the internees emerged from the camps. Anticipation of the hearings invigorated local organizations across the country, as evidenced in Portland by the re-energized pages of the mimeographed JACL newsletter. And anticipation of the hearings catalyzed grassroots action, including redress surveys and fundraising, as epitomized by my aunt Fumie's work on the Portland redress telephone committee—Auntie Fumie, who had never set foot in Minidoka because of her TB hospitalization but whose parents and children had been taken to it. The phone calls urged community support of redress resolutions and legislation, and helped identify potential witnesses for the hearings.

Seeking support from Oregon politicians, Fumie's friend Susie Sakai testified to the legislature in Salem that "The poverty of the [camp] environment and the paucity of the ordinary conveniences of life did not bother me as much as the knowledge that we had been stripped of our civil rights without due process, deprived of our freedom of mobility, and confronted with the fact that the government we had trusted and loved had turned its back on us. The pain of this abandonment and the agony of total rejection continue to be a part of our lives, even forty years hence." Across the country phone calls, letters, and office visits lobbied individual members of Congress, and at local events where politicians expected to discuss farm policy or defense, they ended up hearing about Manzanar, Heart Mountain, Tule Lake, and Minidoka. Across the country Nikkei organizations urged letter writing and Op-Ed pieces, and held meetings and workshops to prepare witnesses for the CWRIC hearings and to nurture the resolve of individuals who were about to testify for the public record to a pain they had never before spoken of. *"Ganbatte,"* friends would say, echoing their parents and grandparents, *"ganbatte!"*—"Do your best."

For many Nikkei the hearings were more than a venue for testimony. They were a request by the government for speech, after a very long silence. In August 1981, testifying before the commission in Seattle, Tana Marumoto told the story of her "big brother," George Washington Suyama, who requested active duty so he could give the lie to the wrong-headedness and racism that led to internment, and was killed in France. "For two years," she said, "those letters and packages we had sent to him came back. . . . What kind of a price tag do you put on my brother, on the members of my family whose lives were shattered because of this incarceration and the shame? . . . What kind of reparation do we deserve after 41 years of bearing the guilt of Pearl Harbor?" This was Auntie Tana, who had been able to meet her new parents-in-law only by visiting them in Minidoka and had to watch as her new husband was searched by guards at the gate, army uniform notwithstanding.

Whether or not the Nikkei in Congress or the redress activists had fully anticipated their emotional dynamic and impact, the CWRIC hearings became the liberating *sine qua non* of redress.

When the commission report, titled *Personal Justice Denied,* was issued on February 22, 1983, its 467 pages were underwritten by the testimonies of over 750 witnesses. They had spoken of lost jobs and lost incomes, abandoned farms and machinery, repossessed vehicles and boats, permanently interrupted college educations, family pets left behind. They had spoken of ostracism, verbal abuse, and physical confrontations. They had spoken of depression, feelings of insecurity, and other forms of emotional distress. They had spoken words they had never spoken before. *Personal Justice Denied* concluded that "a grave injustice was done to Americans and resident aliens of Japanese ancestry who, without individual review or any probative evidence against them, were excluded, removed and detained by the United States during World War II." The Commission made several recommendations to Congress, among them that the government acknowledge and apologize to Japanese Americans for their unjustified removal and imprisonment, that a research and education fund regarding the wartime treatment of civilian populations be established, and that each surviving victim of the government's violation of constitutional rights be offered a symbolic one-time payment of $20,000.

Only a month earlier, Fred Korematsu, Gordon Hirabayashi, and Minoru Yasui—aided by historians, legal experts, pro bono attorneys, and the Freedom of Information Act—had filed petitions to overturn their convictions for test-case violations of curfew and evacuation orders, as well as petitions for writs of error *coram nobis,* charging legal misconduct on the part of federal officials. The government vacated all three convictions and only Yasui was not granted his *coram nobis* petition, having died while waiting for a resolution. In 1983 facts and reason finally displaced the racial bias, emotion, and mythmaking of 1942.

Still, some in Congress refused to recognize a distinction between what Eleanor Roosevelt had called "the American Japanese" and the Japanese who had attacked Pearl Harbor and perpetrated the Bataan death march. Iowa's senior senator told me he was against redress because "those people were our enemy," and he eventually voted against the redress bill. Republican Senator S. I. Hayakawa stubbornly defended internment policy and categorically rejected the concept of redress—a reminder that minority positions existed even among the Nikkei themselves. But others were open to dialogue, and for many who had known little or nothing about removal and internment, the testimony from the hearings and the commission's findings were crucial.

So after dying in congressional committees in 1983 and 1985, redress legislation finally came up for a vote in the 100th Congress, and passed the House in the fall and the Senate the following spring. The country would now "accept the findings and implement the recommendations of the Commission on Wartime Relocation and Internment of Civilians." President Reagan finally signed the legislation four months after that, and in 1989 Congress approved and President George H. W. Bush signed the legislation that authorized funding. A year later, in October 1990, the first redress apologies were offered and the first payments received by the oldest surviving former internees. It had been an imperfect process and a long slog, under three presidential administrations.

Redress meant different things to different people, even among Japanese Americans. For my father it meant a chance to document that family keepsakes and mementos of his youth (including those vintage baseball cards) would never be passed on to his grandchildren because he had been prohibited from going to Portland to retrieve them. For my mother it meant that she could finally convey the full meaning of "camp" to her children—and lament that her parents had passed away without knowing that the destruction of their American Dream had finally been acknowledged. But the government's admission of its violation of human and constitutional rights was the crucial refrain, cutting across individual Nikkei stories with their themes of anger, irony, shame, resentment, despair, stigma, humiliation, and shaken or lost faith. "Redress" was a fifteen-year conversation—among Japanese Americans and between Japanese Americans and the U.S. government. In the end approximately two thirds of those affected by removal and imprisonment had survived to receive apologies and compensation.

What redress means, going forward, to the vast majority of Americans will depend on their understanding (or not) of the token $20,000, and the ongoing relevance of the apologies the government made, on their behalf, to people they will never meet.

1959   Hawaii is admitted to statehood.
        Hiram L. Fong (R-Hawaii) becomes the first Asian American and
        first Chinese American to serve in the U.S. Senate.

Daniel K. Inouye (D-Hawaii) becomes the first Japanese American to serve in Congress.

1963 Daniel K. Inouye (D-Hawaii) becomes the first Japanese American to serve in the U.S. Senate.

Spark M. Matsunaga (D-Hawaii) begins service in the U.S. House of Representatives; he succeeds Hiram Fong in the Senate in 1977.

1965 Patsy Takemoto Mink (D-Hawaii) becomes the first Asian American and Japanese American woman to serve in the U.S. Congress (1965–76, 1990–2002).

On October 3 President Lyndon Johnson signs into law the Immigration and Nationality Act (Public Law 89–236), which abolishes the national origins formula for immigration in place since 1924.

1966 On July 4 President Johnson signs into law the Freedom of Information Act (supplemented and amended in 1974, 1976, and subsequent years).

1970 Edison Uno introduces a resolution at the JACL national convention for the U.S. government to pay monetary reparations to victims of removal and internment (adopted, but no action is taken).

1973 The "Seattle Plan" for winning redress is proposed by Henry Miyatake and others.

1976 On February 19, with Proclamation 4417, President Gerald Ford rescinds Executive Order 9066.

1978 The National JACL convention adopts a resolution calling for redress for internment.

1979 JACL representatives meet with Sen. Matsunaga, Sen. Inouye, Rep. Norman Mineta (D-Cal.), and Rep. Robert Matsui (D-Cal.) regarding the proposed redress initiative.

The National Council for Japanese American Redress is created, to be headed by William Hohri of Chicago.

1980 Congress passes a bill establishing the Commission on Wartime Relocation and Internment of Civilians (CWRIC), to review Executive Order 9066 and its impact, and to recommend any appropriate remedies; the CWRIC is appointed by President Jimmy Carter near the end of his administration.

1981 Between July and December the CWRIC holds hearings across the U.S.

1983   On January 19 Fred Korematsu, Minoru Yasui, and Gordon Hirabayashi file petitions to overturn their World War II convictions for "test-case" violations of curfew and evacuation orders. All three convictions are vacated, but Yasui dies without his petition for a writ of error *coram nobis* being decided.

On February 22 the CWRIC releases a 467-page report, *Personal Justice Denied,* which concludes that Executive Order 9066 was not justified by military necessity and that a grave injustice had been done.

In June the CWRIC makes its recommendations to Congress. Redress bills are introduced in Congress, but all die in committee.

1985   Subsequent redress bills die in committee.

1987   On September 17 the U.S. House of Representatives votes 243 to 141 for passage of the redress bill, H.R. 442 (Norman Mineta and cosponsors).

1988   On April 20 the U.S. Senate votes 69 to 27 for passage of H.R. 442 in lieu of Senate bill S. 1009 (Alan K. Simpson, Spark Matsunaga, and cosponsors).

On August 10 President Ronald Reagan signs the Civil Liberties Act of 1988; provisions include a formal acknowledgement and apology by the government, a fund to support research and education on the wartime treatment of civilian populations, and a one-time compensatory payment to each of approximately 60,000 survivors of the internment.

1989   President George H. W. Bush signs into law the entitlement program for payments under the redress legislation.

1990   In October the first redress payments are received by the oldest surviving former internees.

1992   On September 22 President Bush signs the Civil Liberties Act Amendments of 1992, allocating supplementary funding for redress.

Manzanar is designated a National Historic Site and the government begins to consider the other sites for designation as National Historic Sites or National Historic Landmarks.

When my father died he was nearly 94. As in the case of the "wonderful one-hoss shay" in the Oliver Wendell Holmes poem, everything seemed to fall apart at once. My mother died of complications from a stroke, the worst of which was inconsolable grief over loss of her ability to communicate. She, who had found her calling in the spoken word and had used language to build a life. The dark shadow of cerebral damage dominated her X-rays, an ugly smudge marking the clumsy, indiscriminate erasure of words and phrases by the thousands, of learning and the memory of learning in English, in Japanese, even some Latin and French. Aphasia. She could only make sounds that lacked meaning in our world, and the only word I thought I could make out was Japanese—*itai,* "it hurts." She could hear and compre-hend enough to know that her losses were permanent, her frustration ongo-ing, her isolation fathomless. She was 84. Robert Frost might have called hers an "immedicable woe," and that diagnosis would have been correct.

Mary Nakadate was the child of an immigrant father who left Japan at the age of 18 in search of work and a better life in America, and found only one of those for sure. She was the child of a picture bride mother who came to America in 1913, as the door on emigration from Japan to the United States was closing. Mary was a female middle child who grew up defined by her siblings' prerogatives and with obligations and expectations to match. But she was smart, inquisitive, and diligent, and everything she did became a part of a constantly growing story.

Like many women before and since, my mother was the family mediator and negotiator. At times she served as emissary from the far kingdom of our father's abrupt, authoritarian ways. She was, necessarily, a translator, recast-ing his dogmatism and making it tolerable to us, and she made our needs have meaning for him: "Dad and I talked it over," she would report, "and now he thinks...." She was a bridge to the public world our father worked in every day and which she knew we would all leave home for eventually, first to seek and then to use the higher education she lacked but was determined would be ours. She was also for us a bridge between two generations and two cultures, reminding us that our story started in Japanese villages long before we were born in Indiana. She read us English nursery rhymes and Mother Goose, and along the way introduced us to Japanese: "*ichi, ni, san,*" she repeated, "one, two, three. And now you see why it is *Issei, Nisei, Sansei.*" She showed us how to reconcile American individualism and the communal devotion of the Japanese; she helped us understand the connection between personal achievement and moving forward as a family, a community, a country. She told us stories of her girlhood in Nihonmachi, and of being a child of "oriental" immigrants in a high school where she and her siblings sat in classrooms with children of the city's elite. But for three decades she held captive her memory of the Minidoka years, finally releasing it when her Yonsei grandchildren began to arrive, when her Sansei children insisted on knowing the whole story so they could pass it on. "It was too painful," she said when she finally freed that gnarled memento of the still-present past, "it was all too painful to talk about."

She was a keeper of memory and teacher of language. While her younger brother grew up reluctantly bilingual (only to become a military translator during World War II), she was an eager and enduring student of language. As a girl she attended Japanese language school—"Chizuko, Tazuko, Fumie, and I were the only ones to attend through grade 12"—and came to know the language and culture inside out. As a young woman she joined both the YWCA and the JACL, finding in both the chance to promote discourse between two communities. She became an articulate code-switcher. And from then on she found herself adeptly mixing and swapping English and Japanese words and phrases in casual conversations with elders and contemporaries, while making volunteer phone calls, interpreting for the Portland-Sapporo Sister City Association, serving as the Japanese Garden's liaison to the Nikkei community. At 57 she acceded to a plea from Portland Community College that she teach a course in conversational Japanese—"just a basic course," on a trial basis. ("I don't have a college degree," she reminded them. "However," they said, "people who do have college degrees keep telling us that you are the one we want.") "I found a good book on the subject," she would later explain, "and learned how to teach it." And so it was for another 26 years. By the time we thought to urge her to finally enroll in college herself she was also teaching classes in Japanese calligraphy and flower arranging, and didn't want to stop.

She was an autodidact, for whom the notion of lifelong learning was intuitive. She read as much as she could every day and set aside the rest, assuming there would be time to take it in later. (Eventually, we hauled several loads of newspapers to the recycling box.) She read news magazines and the *Oregonian, Pacific Citizen,* the Methodist church bulletin, and *Reader's Digest,* just as earlier she had read *Life, Ladies' Home Journal, Parents Magazine,* and books with titles like *Exploring Nature with Your Child.* At one point she tried the Book-of-the-Month Club, but periodicals provided the widest accessible spectrum of language and human interest, information and advice, culture and horror. And after she died we found hundreds of pieces of paper with words and phrases written on them, adding intrigue and flavor to the boxes of bank statements, credit card billings, reminder notes and receipts we sorted through. Words on the backs of envelopes, on corners and margins from newspapers and magazines, on torn-out pages with words circled or underlined, on scraps as small as the fortune in a Chinese cookie.... Verbs, adverbs, and adjectives mostly, the words that give vitality and texture to conversation, to speeches and presentations, to classroom dialogue. A thesaurus worth of words that might enhance her teaching or volunteer work, or that she simply found striking and new and worthy of attention. Or that might be drawn from to make a poem:

> Euphoric shards,
> beguiling
> and repulsive,
> benevolent and
> estranged.

We know she looked them up, because she wore out two dictionaries doing so.

As a young woman in group photographs, she was often the pretty, attractively dressed one, in front-row focus. She grew up sewing most of her own clothes, yet (my daughter once observed) in snapshots and portraits she is never wearing the same dress. But as a wife and mother she survives largely in the margins of the photo albums, having become the designated picture-taker, the attention-getting object her subjects are squinting or smiling at, the foreground shadow in our home movies. In a large-format photograph from the mid-nineties my parents are sitting in their accustomed places in the kitchen of their house in Portland. My father, reading the morning paper, is prominent and in focus, as are the property-line fir trees visible through the window, the birthday cards on the window ledge, the clock pointing at

10:10, the pink walls, the wall calendar, the side desk with its budget-and-scheduling clutter, the refrigerator with family photos stuck to it, the utility closet with the lightweight tool set my mother used for home repairs, the closet door that bears the height-and-date markings of children and grandchildren over four decades. Too close to the camera and out of focus at the front left is my mother, occupied by some morning task. She is visible from behind only as a busy shadow, ineluctably there but on the verge of being an absent presence. Just outside the frame of the picture is the shelf that holds the pocket dictionary she used to look up the words and phrases that demanded her attention because they so clearly nourished the literate world.

THE VIEW FROM 1960

The year before the stroke that robbed her of voice and gesture my mother asked that I drive her to see the house at 1960 SW 16th Street. "I want to show you something," she said. It is a large Craftsman bungalow up in Portland's southwest hills, built in 1911 and now listed in the National Register of Historic Places as the Joseph Gaston House. History says that Joseph Gaston was a post–Civil War speculator and promoter of the Oregon Central Railroad, one of the railroad brotherhood that exploited immigrant laborers like Grandpa Marumoto for half a century. A realtor will tell you that 1960 SW 16th Street is a single-family dwelling with eight bedrooms and six baths, and, at the age of 100 is worth nearly two million dollars. If only for the view.

In the mid-1930s Japanese consul Toyoichi Nakamura and his wife and two children lived there, and with them, my mother, serving as their governess, a young woman with life opening up before her, scanning the horizon.

From 1960 SW 16th you can't see the house on Sunset Boulevard in which my siblings and I grew up and our parents lived for 50 years—it is only a few miles further to the southwest, but on the other side of Council Crest. But from her upstairs window in the Nakamura house Mary Marumoto could see virtually everything of Portland that was to be important in shaping our lives. Uphill to the west was Washington Park, where my parents courted while playing tennis (and above which, eventually, the Portland Japanese Garden would replace the old zoo). Below she could see the Behnke-Walker Business College at 11th and Salmon, where she and her sister took shorthand and bookkeeping once the Depression deprived them of any chance

She Smiled,

but with nothing before or after
to give the smile meaning. A smile
coming from fathomless
internal exile.

That's what it looked like,
her stroke, how she appealed
from an inability to speak,
to make herself known, to be
in the world and of it.

Imprisoned by speechlessness,
our translator and mediator, in
an unreachable oblivion, our
teacher of how to make life make sense,
taking promises, memories, plans,
ambitions, hopes, kind words,
next week's lessons for the classes
she would never again never again never
teach again. Reduced from two languages
to none.
             Is simply being able to talk
too much to ask?

Day after day there in her bed,
always there, inescapably there
for us to visit. A lodestone
to which we were inexorably turned,
as always in the past, but (her true self lost)
now impossible to fix.

Sometimes I came at odd hours,
trying to sneak up and surprise, chastise
my mother for evading us, hoping that
who she was had reappeared. But
there was no surprise, only
that enigmatic smile interrupting

a worried everyday blankness,
and a frightened mask of pain when
a cramp would possess her leg
and make her throat give up
a single, drawn-out
syllable of grief.

Mary Marumoto, high school graduation, 1933.

to seek higher education in Corvallis or Eugene. Below on Park Avenue she could see Lincoln High, where she had excelled at math and chemistry, only blocks away and also in the Goose Hollow neighborhood but (of course) a world away from where her family lived. Off to the northeast were the North Park Blocks, where my father ran free as a little boy, a future Eagle Scout at play in a vista of urban greenness. She could see Union Station and the trains running from it to Seattle and San Francisco and Chicago. Union Station, where only a few years later a train with drawn shades would take her family to Minidoka (and where, 18 years after that I would leave for my first year at Stanford). She could see the Steel Bridge, under which her brother George had fished for carp, and the Broadway Bridge, which was still brand-new itself the year she was born, and the seawall, where steamships from the Pacific docked. And Front Avenue (which a half-century later would be renamed to honor Bill Naito, a postwar civic leader and longtime family friend). She could see Chinatown-Nihonmachi, her home within her hometown. She could see M. Furuya Co. at Second and Davis, where Bun'ichi Nakadate kept the books, having started out as a salesman. She could see the Oregonian Hotel, the "Marumoto Hotel," at NW Third and Couch, her family's modest but tangible (and soon-to-be-lost) piece of the American Dream. And she could see the Quimby Hotel at Third and Burnside, where she was born, and where a close friend of her parents showed them a special way to write her name, not simply the *Mary* she would grow up with but a name that, when spoken, echoed the name of their new country, a name to be written with the characters

米里子
me-ri-ko
Child of America.

BIBLIOGRAPHY

This book is grounded in family stories, including interviews and letters, but I have sought to confirm or clarify certain matters of history, culture, economics, sociology, and law by consulting the work of others. I am particularly grateful for the pioneering contributions of Roger Daniels, Michi Weglyn, and Peter Irons.

Brooks, Charlotte. "In the Twilight Zone between Black and White: Japanese American Resettlement and Community in Chicago, 1942–1945." *Journal of American History* 86 (Mar. 2000): 1655–87.

Broom, Leonard, and John I. Kitsuse. *The Managed Casualty: The Japanese-American Family in World War II.* Berkeley: University of California Press, 1973.

Broom, Leonard, and Ruth Riemer. *Removal and Return: The Socio-Economic Effects of the War on Japanese Americans.* Berkeley: University of California Press, 1949.

Chuman, Frank F. *The Bamboo People: The Law and Japanese Americans.* Del Mar, Calif.: Publisher's Inc., 1976.

Commission on Wartime Relocation and Internment of Civilians. *Personal Justice Denied.* Washington, D.C.: U.S. Government Printing Office, 1982.

Daniels, Roger. *Asian America: Chinese and Japanese in the United States since 1850.* Seattle: University of Washington Press, 1988.

——. *The Politics of Prejudice: The Anti-Japanese Movement in California and the Struggle for Japanese Exclusion.* New York: Atheneum, 1970.

——. "Words Do Matter: A Note on Inappropriate Terminology and the Incarceration of the Japanese Americans." In *Nikkei in the Pacific Northwest,* ed. Fiset and Nomura, 190–214.

Daniels, Roger, Sandra C. Taylor, and Harry H. L. Kitano, eds. *Japanese Americans: From Relocation to Redress,* rev. ed. Seattle: University of Washington Press, 1991.

de Cristoforo, Violet Kazue, comp. and trans. *May Sky—There Is Always Tomorrow: An Anthology of Japanese American Concentration Camp Kaiko Haiku.* Los Angeles: Sun & Moon, 1997.

de Nevers, Klancy Clark. *The Colonel and the Pacifist: Karl Bendetsen, Perry Saito, and the Incarceration of Japanese Americans During World War II.* Salt Lake City: University of Utah Press, 2004.

Fiset, Louis. *Camp Harmony: Seattle's Japanese Americans and the Puyallup Assembly Center.* Urbana: University of Illinois Press, 2009.

Fiset, Louis, and Gail M. Nomura, eds. *Nikkei in the Pacific Northwest: Japanese Americans and Japanese Canadians in the Twentieth Century.* Seattle: Center for the Study of the Pacific Northwest and University of Washington Press, 2005.

Gordon, Linda, and Gary Y. Okihiro, eds. *Impounded: Dorothea Lange and the Censored Images of Japanese American Internment.* New York: Norton, 2006.

Harmon, Rick, Lauren Kessler, and Ruth Webster, eds. *Oregon Historical Quarterly* 94.4 (Winter 1993–94). A special issue devoted to the Japanese in Oregon.

Hatamiya, Leslie T. *Righting a Wrong: Japanese Americans and the Passage of the Civil Liberties Act of 1988.* Stanford, Calif.: Stanford University Press, 1993.

Hirasuna, Delphine. *The Art of Gaman: Arts and Crafts from the Japanese American Internment Camps 1942–1946.* Berkeley, Calif.: Ten Speed, 2005.

Ichioka, Yuji, ed. *Beyond National Boundaries: The Complexity of Japanese-American History. Amerasia Journal:* 23.3 (Winter 1997–98). A special Issue.

———. *The Issei: The World of the First Generation Japanese Immigrants, 1885–1924.* New York: Free Press, 1988.

Irons, Peter. *Justice at War: The Story of the Japanese American Internment Cases.* New York: Oxford University Press, 1983.

Irwin, Catherine. *Twice Orphaned: Voices from the Children's Village of Manzanar.* Fullerton: California State University Center for Oral and Public History, 2008.

Ito, Kazuo. *Issei: A History of Japanese Immigrants in North America.* Seattle: Japanese Community Service, 1973.

James, Thomas. *Exile Within: The Schooling of Japanese Americans 1942–1945.* Cambridge, Mass.: Harvard University Press, 1987.

Kessler, Lauren, ed. "The Japanese in Oregon." *Oregon Historical Quarterly* (Winter 1993–94). A special issue devoted to the Japanese in Oregon.

———. *Stubborn Twig: Three Generations in the Life of a Japanese American Family.* New York: Random, 1993. (Chronicles the Yasui family of Hood River, Oregon.)

Kiyama, Henry (Yoshitaka). *The Four Immigrants Manga: A Japanese Experience in San Francisco, 1904–1924.* Trans. Frederik L. Schodt. Berkeley, Calif.: Stone Bridge, 1999. First published as *Manga Yonin Shosei* in 1931.

Lillquist, Karl. *Imprisoned in the Desert: The Geography of World War II–Era Japanese American Relocation Centers in the Western United States.* Central Washington University, Sept. 2007. Available in PDF through the CWU website: http://www.cwu .edu/geography/sites/cts.cwu.edu.geography/files/covercontentfigs.pdf

Maki, Mitchell T., Harry H. L. Kitano, and S. Megan Berthold. *Achieving the Impossible Dream: How Japanese Americans Obtained Redress.* Urbana: University of Illinois Press, 1999.

Miyamoto, S. Frank. *Social Solidarity among the Japanese in Seattle.* Seattle: University of Washington Press, 1984. First published in 1939.

Muller, Eric L. *Free to Die for Their Country: The Story of the Japanese American Draft Resisters in World War II.* Chicago: University of Chicago Press, 2001.

Nakagawa, Kerry Yo. *Through a Diamond: 100 Years of Japanese American Baseball.* San Francisco: Rudi, 2001.

Nakanishi, Don T., ed. "The Japanese American Internment." *Amerasia Journal* 19.1 (1993). A special issue.

Nisei Baseball Research Project and National Japanese American Historical Society. "Diamonds in the Rough: Japanese Americans in Baseball." 1997. An exhibit. Information may be found under "Traveling Exhibits" on the Exhibits page of www.njahs.org.

Reischauer, Edwin O. *Japan: The Story of a Nation.* New York: McGraw-Hill, 1990.

———. *The United States and Japan.* Cambridge, Mass.: Harvard University Press, 1965 [1950].

Robinson, Greg. *By Order of the President: FDR and the Internment of Japanese Americans.* Cambridge, Mass.: Harvard University Press, 2001.

Shimabukuro, Robert Sadamu. *Born in Seattle: The Campaign for Japanese American Redress.* Seattle: University of Washington Press, 2001.

Shirey, Orville C. *Americans: The Story of the 442nd Combat Team.* Washington, D.C.: Infantry Journal Press, 1946.

Spickard, Paul R. "Injustice Compounded: Amerasians and Non-Japanese Americans in World War II Concentration Camps." *Journal of American Ethnic History* 5.2 (Spring 1986): 5–22.

———. "The Nisei Assume Power: The Japanese Citizens League, 1941–1942." *Pacific Historical Review* 52 (May 1983): 147–74.

Takahashi, Jere. *Nisei/Sansei: Shifting Japanese American Identities and Politics.* Philadelphia: Temple University Press, 1997.

Takezawa, Yasuko I. *Breaking the Silence: Redress and Japanese American Ethnicity.* Ithaca, N.Y.: Cornell University Press, 1995.

tenBroek, Jacobus, Edward N. Barnhart, and Floyd W. Matson. *Prejudice, War, and the Constitution.* Berkeley: University of California Press, 1954.

Thomas, Dorothy S. and Richard Nishimoto. *The Spoilage: Japanese-American Evacuation and Resettlement During World War II.* Berkeley: University of California Press, 1969.

Toll, William. "Permanent Settlement: Japanese Families in Portland in 1920." *Western Historical Quarterly* 28.1 (Spring 1997): 18–43.

Totman, Conrad. *A History of Japan*. Maldon, Mass.: Blackwell, 2000.

Weglyn, Michi. *Years of Infamy: The Untold Story of America's Concentration Camps*. New York: Morrow, 1976.

Wong, Marie Rose. *Sweet Cakes, Long Journey: The Chinatowns of Portland, Oregon*. Seattle: University of Washington Press, 2004.

Yanagisako, Sylvia Junko. *Transforming the Past: Tradition and Kinship Among Japanese Americans*. Stanford, Calif.: Stanford University Press, 1985. Regarding Issei and Nisei in Seattle.

Yasui, Barbara. "The Nikkei in Oregon, 1834–1940." *Oregon Historical Quarterly* 76.3 (Sept. 1975): 225–57.

CREDITS

Some of my own poems in this book have been previously published, some in slightly different form. These earlier printings are acknowledged with appreciation, as follows:

"Home and Away" and "Thank You" first appeared in *Aethlon,* Spring 2001 and Fall 2006/Winter 2007.

"Hoosiers" (as "Hoosiers [2]") first appeared in *And Know This Place: Poetry of Indiana,* ed. Jenny Kander and C. E. Greer (Indianapolis: Indiana Historical Society Press, 2011).

"Chief Joseph Slept Here" first appeared in *Cottonwood,* Spring 2007.

"Aboard the Amtrak Cascade: Portland to Seattle, via Vancouver, Kelso-Longview, Centralia, Olympia-Lacey, Tacoma (March 1999)," "Minidoka, Idaho 1944–45," and "Go for Broke" first appeared in *Flyway,* Fall 2000 and Spring 2002.

NEIL NAKADATE is Professor Emeritus, having taught American literature at the University of Texas and then at Iowa State University, where he received the Iowa State University Foundation Award for Career Achievement in Teaching. He has written a critical study on Jane Smiley, co-authored and co-edited books on rhetoric and writing, and edited books on Robert Penn Warren. He is a graduate of Stanford University and earned his M.A. and Ph.D. at Indiana University in Bloomington.

⌘

CPSIA information can be obtained at www.ICGtesting.com
Printed in the USA
LVOW12s0119030913

350645LV00005B/13/P

9 780253 011022